A SENSE OF THE FUTURE

A SENSE OF THE FUTURE
Essays in Natural Philosophy

J. Bronowski

Selected and edited by Piero E. Ariotti
in collaboration with Rita Bronowski

The MIT Press
Cambridge, Massachusetts, and London, England

This book was set in V-I-P Palatino by The MIT Press Media Department Computer Composition Group and printed and bound by The Murray Printing Company in the United States of America

Second printing, November 1977
Third printing, January 1978
Fourth printing, March 1978

Library of Congress Cataloging in Publication Data

Bronowski, Jacob, 1908–1974.
A sense of the future.

Includes bibliographical references and index.
1. Science—Philosophy—Addresses, essays, lectures. 2. Time perspective—Addresses, essays, lectures. I. Title.
B67.B7 1977 192 77–9292
ISBN 0–262–02128–5

ACKNOWLEDGMENTS

The editor and Mrs. Rita Bronowski gratefully acknowledge permission from the copyright holders to republish the essays of this collection: The Scientific American, Inc. for "The Creative Process" in *Scientific American*, September 1958; The University of Texas for "On Art and Science" in *The Creative Mind and Method*, 1960; the American Academy and Institute of Arts and Letters for "The Reach of Imagination" given on 25 May 1966, as the Blashfield Address; *The Political Quarterly* for "The Logic of Nature," copyright 1955; the British Association for the Advancement of Science for "The Logic of Experiment" in *The Advancement of Science*, 1952; the Scientific Research Society of North America for "The Logic of the Mind" in the *American Scientist*, journal of Sigma Xi, March 1966; The Open Court Publishing Company, La Salle, Illinois, for "Humanism and the Growth of Knowledge" in *The Philosophy of Karl P. Popper*, copyright 1974 by The Library of Living Philosophers, Inc.; Mouton & Co., The Hague, for "Human and Animal Languages" in *To Honor Roman Jakobson*, 1967, and "Language in a Biological Frame" in *Current Trends in Linguistics*, 1974; Nyrev, Inc. for "Where do we go From Here" in *The New York Review of Books*, copyright 1965; the Institute of General Semantics for "Towards a Philosophy of Biology" in *General Semantics Bulletin*, 1968, as the Alfred Korzybski Memorial Lecture, 1967; the Curtis Publishing Co. for "A Moral for an Age of Plenty" in *The Saturday Evening Post*, copyright 1960; The Rationalist Press Association, London, for "The Human Values" in *The New Humanist*, November 1955, and for "The Values of Science" in *The Rationalist Annual*, 1960; the Honorary Editor of the Royal Society of Canada for "The Principle of Tolerance" in *Transactions of the Royal Society of Canada Mémoires de la Société Royale du Canada*, 1974; *Encounter* for "Disestablishing Science," 1971; Southplace Ethical Society, London, for "The Fulfillment of Man" in the *Monthly Record*, 1954.

The title essay, "A Sense of the Future," was first published by *The Listener*, London, and broadcast on the BBC Home-Service in 1948. The essay "New Concepts in the Evolution of Complexity: Stratified Stability and Unbounded Plans" first appeared in *Zygon*, in March 1970.

CONTENTS

INTRODUCTION

Poet, mathematician, physicist, administrator, playwright, philosopher, and interpreter of science, culture, and man, critic of poetry, literature, and art, student of biology, language, and society, teacher, Jacob Bronowski found interest and excitement in many and varied fields. But through the diversity and extent of his interests he pursued one unifying thread. That thread is best represented in his own words:

> My ambition has been to create a philosophy for the twentieth century which shall be all of one piece. There cannot be a decent philosophy, there cannot even be a decent science, without humanity. For me, the understanding of nature has as its goal the understanding of human nature, and of the human condition within nature.

Such was his lifelong intent—an intent already in evidence during his undergraduate days at Cambridge, England. There, although pursuing the study of mathematics, he founded, contributed to, and edited a poetry magazine significantly called *Experiment*. Science, the arts, and the humanities were then for him and were to remain facets of the same human capacity for imagination and understanding. They were not, he was to insist throughout his life, distinct and separate entities. Max Born once said that physics is philosophy. Bronowski went further, insisting that all science is philosophy. Adopting a term no longer current, he called that body of inquiry and of understanding "natural philosophy."

The civil war in Spain, the greater conflict that followed it with its almost universal suffering, the horrors of the extermination camps, and, finally, the obliteration of the two Japanese cities—which he visited soon after the end of the war as deputy chief of the British Mission in Japan—reinforced his belief that science and philosophy had to be not only human, which they undoubtedly were, but humane also.

Bronowski sought and found in science a man-made wellspring of values which not only confirmed undogmatically the values of the Old and New Testaments but could replace the bankrupt principles of state supremacy, authoritarianism, nationalism, and religious, political, and racial dogma that had lain behind the conflicts and human misery he had witnessed. Some of the results of his lifelong search and study he delineated in various books. Others he left in a considerable body of published and unpublished shorter works. These comprise lectures delivered to various learned bodies and institutions, essays of various lengths and degrees of complexity, studies, reviews, and reports. The present selection is drawn from these previously uncollected sources.

Bronowski's wide interests mean that like his books his shorter works are concerned with a multiplicity of subjects and topics ranging from science and philosophy to history, poetry, literature, the arts and humanities, and to questions of social concern. A selection that embraced all those concerns would have required a volume addressed to all at large and to no one in particular. What would have been gained in generalized appeal would have been lost in the resulting incompleteness of treatment of each topic. The present volume has therefore been given a focus: science as natural philosophy; its scope, nature, limitations, implications, and responsibilities. Another volume will be concerned with his aesthetics and philosophy of poetry, literature, and the arts.

The editor of posthumously published short works faces a grave danger—that of even unwittingly coloring the meaning and significance of the thoughts of his author through his own views. To some extent such intrusion is unavoidable. It is, and has to be, the editor who selects and orders the parts which are to be gathered between the covers of the printed volume. But to a greater extent the editor can avoid this danger if he refrains from intruding into the words of his author with abstracts, introductory pieces, descriptions, or summaries. In this volume Bronowski will speak by himself, for himself, and as he himself did without commentaries, exegeses, or critiques. He will speak in his own words, without additions or deletions. He is quite capable of doing so.

Piero E. Ariotti
Del Mar, California
April 1977

A SENSE OF THE FUTURE

1
A SENSE OF THE FUTURE

One hundred years ago, if you had walked on a summer evening into the country just beyond Bromley in Kent, you might have come on a remarkable sight. In the greenhouse of one of the larger and uglier houses of the neighborhood, a tall man in his sixties was stooping over potted plants. Beside him sat a younger man, just as absorbed; and the younger man was playing the bassoon. This earnest pair was Charles Darwin and his son Frank; and they were making a scientific experiment. Darwin wanted to know exactly what tells an insect-eating plant like the common sundew to close its leaves when a fly settles on it. So he was going through the possible causes methodically one by one. Noise was not a likely cause; but it might just have worked; and Darwin was not the man to rule out anything. He had tried sand and water and bits of hard-boiled egg, and now he was trying Frank's bassoon. Darwin never did get to the bottom of what makes the sundew close. But he almost did, and the next generation finished his work. He was well content with that. Darwin at sixty was a famous scientist who had changed our whole understanding of nature; yet he remained content to do tidy experiments that would bear fruit somewhere, sometime in the future.

This is the sense of the future I want to talk about, at first hand, as a scientist. I am distressed to see how many people today are afraid of the future and of science together. I believe that these fears are mistaken. They seem to me to misunderstand the methods of science and spring from a gloom about what it has done, which has simply forgotten the facts. We sit under the shadow of the nine o'clock news, nursing our sense of doom, and we think ourselves worse off than our forefathers a hundred and seventy years ago, who were at war with Napoleon for a generation. But a hundred and seventy years ago, the working week was eighty hours for children. Cholera was more common in England than flu. The country could barely support ten million people, and not a million of them could read. You know how all this has been changed; and don't let anyone tell you that nothing has been gained but comfort. Think of the gain in life and health alone: a population which has topped fifty millions, the infant death rate cut by 80 or 90 percent, and the span of life enlarged by at least twenty-five years. The sewer and the fertilizer have done that, and the linotype and the X-ray tube and the statistician puzzling over inheritance. They have been real liberators. Every machine has been a liberator. They have freed us from drudgery and disease and ignorance and from the misery Hogarth painted that could forget itself only in the stupor of drink.

We owe that miracle to science; and it is a miracle. But the scientists who have worked it have been neither gods nor witch doctors. They have been men: men who had faith in the future; and they have used no magic. What they have used is at bottom only Darwin's method, because that method is science. Science is experiment; science is trying things. It is trying each possible alternative in turn, intelligently and systematically; and throwing away what won't work, and accepting what will, no matter how it goes against our prejudices. And what works adds one more piece to the slow, laborious, but triumphant understanding of our world.

This is not a secret or a mysterious progress. If it sometimes seems so, that is just because the day-to-day work of science is so unspectacular. You hear nothing from the research worker for years, and then, suddenly, there is the result in the headlines: penicillin or the jet engine or nuclear fission. No one tells the layman about the years of experiment and failure. How is he to know what has not been done, or to guess the labor of what has? What is he to think but to marvel at the skill of science, and to fear its power?

I believe that both these feelings do equal harm: the feeling of marvel as much as the fear. Because they have this in common, that they both want to persuade the layman that there is nothing he can do for himself. Science is the new magic, they whisper; it is out of your hands; for good or ill, your salvation or your doom is the business of others.

That is why I have attacked the magic before the fear: because the marvel lies below the fear. In the minds of most people today, the fear is plainly uppermost. They are afraid of the future; and if you ask them why, they conveniently blame the atomic bomb. But the atomic bomb is only the scapegoat for our fears. We are not afraid of the future because of a bomb. We are afraid of bombs because we have no faith in the future. We no longer have faith in our ability, as individuals or as nations, to control our own future. That loss of confidence has not sprung overnight from the invention of a weapon. The atomic bomb has merely brought home to us, harshly, as a matter of life and death, what has long been growing: our failure to face, our refusal to face, as individuals and as nations, the place of science in our world.

There is the taproot of our fears. In our hearts, of course, we know that the future belongs to science; we do not deceive ourselves about that. But we do not want to have to think like scientists. We want to cling to the doctrines and prejudices which we imagine, quite wrongly, made the world snug seventy years ago. We do not care about the future; we just want that world to last our time. Because we do not feel equal to the new ideas; we have been told that science is mysterious and difficult. And so we let the exciting new knowledge slip from us, a little further every day, and our confidence with it; and then, face to face with the sense of our helplessness, we pretend that it is all a conspiracy among nuclear physicists.

It is in our power to change that in our own generation. As nations, we can apply to affairs of state the realism of science: holding to what works and discarding what does not. As individuals, we can grasp the commonsense ideas of science. And there is the most important lesson we must learn: it is the *ideas* of science that are remaking the world, not its mechanical achievements. When we have learned that, we will see the achievements too in their proper place. The atomic bomb is not a great achievement of science. But science has made a great discovery: the fundamental discovery that we can tap atomic energy. That is an achievement not of bickering nations but of man. And we have the whole history of science to tell us that every fundamental discovery has in the end brought men more good than harm. I said "has in the end" almost by habit: has, if we are willing to look forward. Every scientist looks forward; what else is research but to begin what others will finish and enjoy? And what other incentive can satisfy any of us but that sense of the future?

Disaster threatens us only if we perpetuate the division between science and our own everyday living and thinking. Let no one tell you again that science is only for specialists; it is not. It is no different from history or good talk or reading a novel; some people do it better and some worse; some make a life's work of it; but it is within the reach of everybody.

Science is as human as Darwin and his bassoon, and no harder to understand. Its values are the human values: honesty, tolerance, independence, commonsense, and singleness of mind. Its achievements are among the great achievements of man: the Greeks ranked Pythagoras with Homer. And it has made its way not secretly but by sticking to the plain facts and only the facts—never mind who discovered them or who challenges them. Science listened equally to Newton and his friend Christopher Wren, to Darwin and his critic Samuel Butler: and listens today to every bright lad with an idea as patiently as to the professors.

If you want to know what happens to science when it allows itself to be dominated by authority, political or scientific, let me take you to a field of which I have some special knowledge: German research during the war. We went into the war very much afraid of German science: it had once had a great reputation. Yet the Germans all through the war never took a fundamental step, whether in U-boat research, in radar bombing, or in nuclear physics. Why were they, the professional warmakers, outclassed by us? One example will tell you. About the time that we had our first atomic pile working, Himmler's director of war research was sending an investigator to Denmark to discover—believe it or not—how the Vikings knitted. By one of those exquisite strokes of irony which dogged the Nazis, the name of his investigator—believe it or not—was Miss Piffl.

To listen to everyone; to silence no one; to honor and promote those who are right—these have given science its power in our world, and its humanity. Don't be deceived by those who say that science is narrow; a narrow, bigoted power is as brittle as Himmler's. Have you been told that science is dogmatic? There is not a field of science which has not been made over from top to bottom in the last fifty years. Science has filled our world because it has been tolerant and flexible and endlessly open to new ideas. In the best sense of that difficult word, science is a democratic method. That has been its strength: that and its confidence that nothing can be more important than what is true.

Does that seem to you after all a very ordinary tradition? Of course it is. It is the tradition for which Europe has hankered ever since the Renaissance: free inquiry and personal action. It is the climate of the arts as much as of science. England led the world in both, because from Elizabethan times she made that tradition of independence her actual way of living. That is why the Authorized Version of the Bible, the first table of logarithms, and Shakespeare's First Folio all came out in England within twelve years. It is our inheritance of freedom, which has liberated the mind with the body. The sense of the future and that tradition are one, if we are willing to unite them. The ideas of science are not special ideas; we can all get at the heart of them—that is, all of us who are willing to find Darwin's sundew more stirring than the Vikings. What we need is to stop shutting our minds to these ideas; to stop being afraid of them. We stand on the threshold of a great age of science; we are already over the threshold; it is for us to make that future our own.

2
THE CREATIVE PROCESS

The most remarkable discovery made by scientists is science itself. The discovery must be compared in importance with the invention of cave-painting and of writing. Like these earlier human creations, science is an attempt to control our surroundings by entering into them and understanding them from inside. And like them, science has surely made a critical step in human development which cannot be reversed. We cannot conceive a future society without science.

I have used three words to describe these far-reaching changes: discovery, invention, and creation. There are contexts in which one of these words is more appropriate than the others. Christopher Columbus discovered the West Indies, and Alexander Graham Bell invented the telephone. We do not call their achievements creations because they are not personal enough. The West Indies were there all the time; and as for the telephone, we feel that Bell's ingenious thought was somehow not fundamental. The groundwork was there, and if not Bell then someone else would have stumbled on the telephone as casually as on the West Indies.

By contrast, we feel that *Othello* is genuinely a creation. This is not because *Othello* came out of a clear sky; it did not. There were Elizabethan dramatists before Shakespeare, and without them he could not have written as he did. Yet within their tradition *Othello* remains profoundly personal; and though every element in the play has been a theme of other poets, we know that the amalgam of these elements is Shakespeare's; we feel the presence of his single mind. The Elizabethan drama would have gone on without Shakespeare, but no one else would have written *Othello*.

There are discoveries in science like Columbus's, of something which was always there: the discovery of sex in plants, for example. There are tidy inventions like Bell's, which combine a set of known principles: the use of a beam of electrons as a microscope, for example. Now we have to ask the question: Is there anything more? Does a scientific theory, however deep, ever reach the roundness, the expression of a whole personality that we get from *Othello*?

7
The Creative Process

A fact is discovered, a theory is invented. Is any theory ever deep enough for it to be truly called a creation? Most nonscientists would answer: No! Science, they would say, engages only part of the mind—the rational intellect—but creation must engage the whole mind. Science demands none of the groundswell of emotion, none of that rich bottom of personality, which fills out the work of art.

This picture by the nonscientist of how a scientist works is of course mistaken. A gifted man cannot handle bacteria or equations without taking fire from what he does and having his emotions engaged. It may happen that his emotions are immature, but then so equally are the intellects of many poets. When Ella Wheeler Wilcox died, having published poems from the age of seven, *The Times* of London wrote that she was "the most popular poet of either sex and of any age, read by thousands who never open Shakespeare." A scientist who is emotionally immature is like a poet who is intellectually backward: both produce work which appeals to others like them, but which is second-rate.

I am not discussing the second-rate, and neither am I discussing all that useful but commonplace work which fills most of our lives, whether we are chemists or architects. There were in my laboratory of the British National Coal Board about two hundred industrial scientists—pleasant, intelligent, sprightly people who thoroughly earned their pay. It is ridiculous to ask whether they were creators who produced works that could be compared with *Othello*. They were men with the same ambitions as other university graduates, and their work was most like the work of a college department of Greek or of English. When the Greek departments produce a Sophocles, or the English departments produce a Shakespeare, then I shall begin to look in my laboratory for a Newton.

Literature ranges from Shakespeare to Ella Wheeler Wilcox, and science ranges from relativity to market research. A comparison must be of the best with the best. We must look for what is created in the deep scientific theories: in Copernicus and Darwin, in Thomas Young's theory of light and in William Rowan Hamilton's equations, in the pioneering concepts of Freud, of Bohr, and of Pavlov.

The most remarkable discovery made by scientists, I have said, is science itself. It is therefore worth considering the history of this discovery, which was not made all at once but in two periods. The first period falls in the great age of Greece, between 600 B.C. and 300 B.C. The second period begins roughly with the Renaissance, and is given impetus at several points by the rediscovery of Greek mathematics and philosophy.

When one looks at these two periods of history, it leaps to the eye that they were not specifically scientific. On the contrary, Greece between Pythagoras and Aristotle is still, in the minds of most scholars, a shining sequence of classical texts. The Renaissance is still thought of as a rebirth of art, and only specialists are uncouth enough to link it also with what is at last being called, reluctantly, the Scientific Revolution. The accepted view of Greece and of the Renaissance is that they were the great creative periods of literature and art. Now that we recognize in them also the two periods in which science was born, we must surely ask whether this conjunction is accidental. Is it a coincidence that Phidias and the Greek dramatists lived in the time of Socrates? Is it a coincidence that Galileo shared the patronage of the Venetian republic with sculptors and painters? Is it a coincidence that, when Galileo was at the height of his intellectual power, there were published in England in the span of twelve years these three works: the Authorized Version of the Bible, the First Folio of Shakespeare, and the first table of logarithms?

The sciences and the arts have flourished together. And they have been fixed together as sharply in place as in time. In some way both spring from one civilization: the civilization of the Mediterranean, which expresses itself in action. There are civilizations which have a different outlook; they express themselves in contemplation, and in them neither science nor art is practiced as such. For a civilization which expresses itself in contemplation values no creative activity. What it values is a mystic immersion in nature, the union with what already exists.

The contemplative civilization we know best is that of the Middle Ages. It has left its own monuments, from the Bayeux tapestry to the cathedrals; and characteristically they are anonymous. The Middle Ages did not value the cathedrals, but only the act of worship which they served. It seems to me that the works of Asia Minor and of India (if I understand them) have the same anonymous quality of contemplation and, like the cathedrals, were made by craftsmen rather than by artists. For the artist as a creator is personal; he cannot drop his work and have it taken up by another without doing it violence. It may be odd to claim the same personal engagement for the scientist; yet in this the scientist stands to the technician much as the artist stands to the craftsman. It is at least remarkable that science has not flourished either in an anonymous age, such as the age of medieval crafts, or in an anonymous place, such as the craftsmanlike countries of the East.

The change from an outlook of contemplation to one of action is striking in the long transition of the Renaissance and the Scientific Revolution. The new men, even when they are churchmen, have ideals which are flatly opposed to the monastic and withdrawn ideals of the Middle Ages. Their outlook is active, whether they are artists, humanist scholars, or scientists.

The new man is represented by Leonardo da Vinci, whose achievement has never, I think, been rightly understood. There is an obvious difference between Leonardo's painting and that of his elders—between, for example, an angel painted by him and one by Verrocchio. It is usual to say that Leonardo's angel is more human and more tender; and this is true, but it misses the point. Leonardo's pictures of children and of women are human and tender; yet the evidence is powerful that Leonardo liked neither children nor women. Why then did he paint them as if he were entering their lives? Not because he saw them as people, but because he saw them as expressive parts of nature. We do not understand the luminous and transparent affection with which Leonardo lingers on a head or a hand until we look at the equal affection with which he paints the grass and the flowers in the same picture.

To call Leonardo either a human or a naturalist painter does not go to the root of his mind. He is a painter to whom the detail of nature speaks aloud; for him, nature expresses herself in the detail. This is a view which other Renaissance artists had; they lavished care on perspective and on flesh tones because these seemed to them (as they had not seemed to the weavers of the Bayeux tapestry) to carry the message of nature. But Leonardo went further; he took this artist's vision into science. He understood that science as much as painting has to find the design of nature in her detail.

When Leonardo was born in 1452, science was still Aristotle's structure of cosmic theories, and the criticism of Aristotle in Paris and Padua was equally grandiose. Leonardo distrusted all large theories, and this is one reason why his experiments and machines have been forgotten. Yet he gave science what it most needed, the artist's sense that the detail of nature is significant. Until science had this sense, no one could care—or could think that it mattered—how fast two unequal masses fall, and whether the orbits of the planets are accurately circles or ellipses.

The power which the scientific method has developed has grown from a procedure which the Greeks did not discover, for which I will retain the old-fashioned name of induction. This procedure is useless unless it is followed into the detail of nature; its discovery therefore flows from Leonardo's vision.

Francis Bacon in 1620 and Christian Huygens in 1690 set down the first intellectual bases of induction. They saw that it is not possible to reach an explanation of what happens in nature by deductive steps. Every explanation goes beyond our experience and thereby becomes a speculation. Huygens says, and philosophers have sheepishly followed him in this, that an explanation should therefore be called probable. He means that no induction is unique; there is always a set—an infinite set—of alternative hypothetical theories between which we must choose.

The man who proposes a theory makes a choice—an imaginative choice which outstrips the facts. The creative activity of science lies here, in the process of induction understood as the making of hypothetical theories. For induction imagines more than there is ground for, and creates relations which at bottom can never be verified. Every induction is a speculation, and it guesses at a unity which the facts present but do not strictly imply. The most compelling example is the periodic table of Mendeleev and the whole theory of atomic structure which was ultimately created to explain it.

To put the matter more formally: a scientific theory cannot be constructed from the facts by any procedure which can be laid down in advance, as if for a machine. To the man who makes the theory, it may seem as inevitable as the ending of *Othello* must have seemed to Shakespeare. But the theory is inevitable only to him; it is his choice, as a mind and as a person, among the alternatives which are open to everyone.

There are scientists who deny what I have said—that we are free to choose between alternative theories. They grant that there are alternative theories, but they hold that the choice between them is made mechanically. The principle of choice, in their view, is Occam's razor: we choose, among the theories which fit the facts we know now, that one which is simplest. On this view, Newton's laws were the simplest theory which covered the facts of gravitation as they were then known; and general relativity is not a new conception but is the simplest theory which fits the additional facts.

This would be a plausible view if it had a meaning. Alas, it turns out to be a verbal deception, for we cannot define simplicity; we cannot even say what we mean by the simpler of two inductions. The tests which have been proposed are hopelessly artificial and, for example, can compare theories only if they can be expressed in differential equations of the same kind. Simplicity itself turns out to be a principle of choice which cannot be mechanized.

Of course every innovator has thought that his way of arranging the facts is particularly simple, but this is a delusion. Copernicus's theory in his day was not simple to others, because it demanded two rotations of the earth—a daily one and a yearly one—in place of one rotation of the sun. What made his theory seem simple to Copernicus was something else: an aesthetic sense of unity. The motion of all the planets around the sun was both simple and beautiful to him, because it expressed the unity of God's design. The same thought has moved scientists ever since: that nature has a unity, and that this unity makes her laws seem beautiful in simplicity.

The scientist's demand that nature shall be lawful is a demand for unity. When he frames a new law, he links and organizes phenomena which were thought different in kind; for example, general relativity links light with gravitation. In such a law we feel that the disorder of nature has been made to reveal a pattern, and that under the colored chaos there rules a more profound unity.

A man becomes creative, whether he is an artist or a scientist, when he finds a new unity in the variety of nature. He does so by finding a likeness between things which were not thought alike before, and this gives him a sense at the same time of richness and of understanding. The creative mind is a mind that looks for unexpected likenesses. This is not a mechanical procedure, and I believe that it engages the whole personality in science as in the arts. Certainly I cannot separate the abounding mind of Thomas Young (which all but read the Rosetta stone) from his recovery of the wave theory of light, or the awkardness of J. J. Thomson in experiment from his discovery of the electron. To me, William Rowan Hamilton drinking himself to death is as much part of his prodigal work as is any drunken young poet; and the childlike vision of Einstein has a poet's innocence.

When Max Planck proposed that the radiation of heat is discontinuous, he seems to us now to have been driven by nothing but the facts of experiment. But we are deceived; the facts did not go so far as this. The facts showed that the radiation is not continuous; they did not show that the only alternative is Planck's hail of quanta. This is an analogy which imagination and history brought into Planck's mind. So the later conflict in quantum physics between the behavior of matter as a wave and as a particle is a conflict between analogies, between poetic metaphors; and each metaphor enriches our understanding of the world without completing it.

In *Auguries of Innocence* William Blake wrote:

A dog starv'd at his Master's gate
Predicts the ruin of the State.

This seems to me to have the same imaginative incisiveness, the same understanding crowded into metaphor, that Planck had. And the imagery is as factual, as exact in observation, as that on which Planck built; the poetry would be meaningless if Blake used the words "dog," "master," and "State" less robustly than he does. Why does Blake say dog and not cat? Why does he say master and not mistress? Because the picture he is creating depends on our factual grasp of the relation between dog and master. Blake is saying that when the master's conscience no longer urges him to respect his dog, the whole society is in decay (is, in fact, going to the dogs). This profound thought came to Blake again and again: that a morality expresses itself in what he called its Minute Particulars—that the moral detail is significant of a society. As for the emotional power of the couplet, it comes, I think, from the change of scale between the metaphor and its application: between the dog at the gate and the ruined State. This is why Blake, in writing it, seems to me to transmit the same excitement that Planck felt when he discovered—no, when he created—the quantum.

One of the values which science has made natural to us is originality; as I said earlier, in spite of appearances science is not anonymous. The growing tradition of science has now influenced the appreciation of works of art, so that we expect both to be original in the same way. We expect artists as well as scientists to be forward-looking, to fly in the face of what is established, and to create not what is acceptable but what will become accepted. One result of this prizing or originality is that the artist now shares the unpopularity of the scientist: the large public dislikes and fears the way that both of them look at the world.

As a more important result, the way in which the artist looks at the world has come close to the scientist's. For example, in what I have written science is pictured as preoccupied less with facts than with relations, less with numbers than with arrangement. This new vision, the search for structure, is also marked in modern art.

I underline this common vision because I believe that history will look back on it as characteristic of our age. A hundred years ago the way to advance physics and chemistry seemed to be by making more and more exact measurements. Science then was a quantitative affair, and this nineteenth-century picture of the scientist preoccupied with numbers—the picture of Phineas Fogg at the beginning of Jules Verne's *Around the World in Eighty Days*—is still large in the popular mind.

But in fact the concern of science in our age is different: it is with relation, with structure, and with shape. Today we hardly ask how large space is, but whether it is open or closed on itself. We say that rubber stretches because its atoms are strung out in chains, and a diamond does not because the atoms are locked in a closed pattern of rings. When we ask why bacteria absorb the sulfa drug on which they cannot grow, we are answered that the drug deceives them: its molecules have the same shape as the body chemical that the bacteria need. And the most arresting discovery of the 1950s was the elucidation of the geometrical arrangement by which the nucleic acid in a living cell makes copies of itself when the cell divides.

Ours is not the first age whose science is preoccupied with pattern and arrangement; Greek thought was occupied in the same way, so that Plutarch quotes it as Plato's opinion that God is a geometer. And just as Greek thought looked for the shape of things in art and in mathematics together, so our age looks for the shaping skeleton below the appearances in art as well as in science. To us the form is meaningful when it expresses the logical structure; and even in everyday things—in buildings or in airplanes—we now think those shapes beautiful that, spare and direct, are dictated by their function. Certainly in works of art, what drives the best painters and sculptors today is the search for the underlying organization of nature. Unlike the Impressionists, modern painters are looking for the order below the surface, the skull beneath the skin. And abstract sculpture often looks like an exercise in topology, exactly because the sculptor shares the vision of the topologist.

3
ON ART AND SCIENCE

I would say that there is a physiological need, in living matter, to create. The laws of nature are such that nature is running down all the time, things are becoming disorderly all the time, and living matter is constantly opposed to this. It is constantly trying to create order. The word "creation" means "the creation of order," the finding in nature of links, of likenesses, of hidden patterns which the living thing—the plant, the animal, the human mind—picks out and arranges.

To my mind, it is a mistake to think of creative activity as something unusual. I hold that the creative activity is normal to all living things. Creation is the finding of order in what was disorderly, and this is a characteristically human activity.

So I would say that the ability to work creatively in more fields than one is a historical accident, which pertains to some people who have had, by chance or by the nature of their environment, the skill needed in several fields. No more than that.

I can speak about my own case with some confidence, and I would like to tell you a simple story about this. Just after World War II, I became interested in a conflict between the social and the personal activity of many people that I knew. At this time I began to work with people who had rather rebellious attitudes toward the societies in which they were living and who often complained that they were not allowed to be the people that they wanted to be. This made me very interested in the protesting personality, the person who feels that society is thwarting him and that he could express himself better outside society. Yet this person knows perfectly well that human beings can only live and express themselves inside society; and this conflict exists in all of us all the time. I began reading a great deal about this; I read a good deal of anthropology, and of psychology, and the history of revolutionary movements. I had it in mind to write a book on this subject. And then quite suddenly, almost overnight, I realized that this was not at all the way to express what I wanted to say. The way to express what I wanted to say was in a perfectly simple drama about what happened to a man in a concentration camp during the war. So I wrote a play called *The Face of Violence*.

I had been three or four years collecting this material, none of which was relevant to what I wrote. I wrote the actual play in a little over a week, during which I worked for twenty-four hours a day. I never stopped at all; and I never changed anything. When the play was finished, it said all the things that I had wanted to say about the protesting personality. Without ever mentioning them specifically the play comments on the Roman Saturnalia, the Crucifixion, Frazer's *Golden Bough*, and revolutionaries and people who had been executed in China. Somehow this all expresses itself. That seems to me to be a characteristic example of how the mind spends a long time digesting the available material, and then the act of creation is an act of finding the right order to express the whole complexity.

I have made some scientific discoveries which seemed to me to have occurred in just the same way. And of course some very great scientists and mathematicians have said that they had to let the material whirl around, mill about, lie fallow in their minds; then, quite suddenly, it seemed to organize itself for them. And what you say, whether in the sciences or in the arts, never exists until it has been said.

I stated earlier that creation exists in finding unity, finding likenesses, finding pattern. You will recall that Coleridge in his many stumblings attempts (all of them brilliant and all of them inconclusive) to find the definition of beauty, always came back to the same definition that beauty is "unity in variety." Now this to me is the creative process. Nature is chaos. It is full of infinite variety, and whether you are Leonardo da Vinci or whether you are Isaac Newton or whether you are modestly sitting down thinking about acts of revolt, there comes a moment when many different aspects suddenly crystallize in a single unity. You have found the key; you have found the clue; you have found the path which organizes the material. You have found what Coleridge called "unity in variety." That is the moment of creation.

Now in my view the appreciation of art or mathematics or any creative act is an act of re-creation; when the man makes *you* see the unexpected likeness, makes *you* feel it to be natural that this likeness exists, then you in your modest way are recreating. You relive the act of creation, and that is why in my opinion appreciation is not passive. It is an activity of the same kind. And if that is true, it is an activity in which one can be trained. I think you can be trained to be a better appreciator than you were and possibly even an original creator. At any rate you can make the most of your native creative gifts.

It is possible to regard creation as a rather special process which could express itself either in making things or in destroying them. I do not share this view. I say that the opposite of creation is not destruction but simply disorder. The opposite of the created work is simply chaos. And therefore, I do not agree that there is a personality which has the creative impulse in reverse, which wants to destroy for this reason.

The act of creation is, I am sure, the same in science as in art. It is a natural, human, living act. Yet, of course, a poem is obviously not like a theorem. How does it differ? It has nothing to do with how it is composed; it differs because it matches human experience in a different way. Take a theorem like the Pythagorean theorem; this is a theorem every child rediscovers. They always rediscover it in the same form; their experience is intellectual and can be exactly matched. In the arts this does not happen. Many people are going to paint pictures with a human being and an animal, but nobody is going to paint *The Lady with the Stoat* again exactly as Leonardo did. Many people are going to write plays, not exactly like *Oedipus Rex*, but on a similar theme. In the arts, it is not possible for the experience of one individual to match that of another, as if it were a blueprint. You do not read a work of art for this purpose; you re-create it, but you do not re-create the blueprint. You explore your own experience; you learn; you live; you expand inside. Now this, I think, is the difference between the arts and the sciences, and it lies not in the process of creation but in the nature of the match between the created work and your own act of re-creation in appreciating it.

There have been many great discoveries, both in science and in art, in which the critical link has been met by chance. There are famous discoveries, like the discovery of a workable process for manufacturing synthetic indigo, which occurred because a laboratory boy broke a thermometer when he was stirring the mixture, and it turned out that mercury was the one catalyst that was needed. In the arts, Dryden said that he preferred to write in verse which is rhymed rather than in verse which is unrhymed because, he says quite frankly, "I have often had a very happy thought as a result of looking for a rhyme." There is a well-known example of a composer, I think it was Gounod, who made quite a considerable change in a famous passage by an accident in which he spilled some medicine on the page instead of writing with ink. And there are many such examples.

Why does chance enter in this way? The answer is simply that the mind is roving in a highly charged, active way and is looking for connections, for unseen likenesses in these circumstances. It is the highly inquiring mind which at that moment seizes the chance and turns what was an accident into something providential. The world is full of people who are always claiming that they really made the discovery, only they missed it. There were many people whose photographic plates had been fogged before Röntgen in fact asked himself, "Why is the plate fogged?" In a funny way, asking the question, being inquisitive enough not to throw the plates away, is the nature of the inquiring mind. It was chance; but it was chance offered to the highly active and inquiring mind in this creative state when it was looking for hidden likenesses.

Now the man who makes the discovery, whether he is a scientist or an artist, must make the discovery even if his creation produces works which are rather ambivalent and can be used for one purpose or another. Society has to make some judgment about this, but I do not think the creator has to make this judgment. I do not think either the scientist or the artist should be a censor on behalf of society. Any man who discovered the destructive effects of atomic energy (or before that of nitroglycerine, or the radiation effects of long-lived cobalt or long-lived strontium isotopes) and who withheld this discovery from mankind in my opinion is a maniac. And I use this word quite deliberately; he is a maniac because he has no notion of what can be made of these forces that he has discovered. Now if society wants to judge what is right or wrong for it, that is society's business, but when a scientist says, "I know what is good for you," he behaves like Klaus Fuchs did by handing out other people's secrets. For you to ask the scientist to keep a secret is just as bad as for him to go and give it to a foreign embassy. What business has he to decide what the nation wants to do with the knowledge which it possesses? This is not a subject for an individual's decision at all. He has no special competence in this. And I hold this to be equally true of the artist and the scientist.

Having said that the creative activity is normal, that its expression is different in the arts and the sciences, but that it is a natural thing in both, we come to the question of how we can canalize the very high prestige which the scientist enjoys today so as to make him not just a technician but a creator. Now I do not think that scientists have yet created anything which could be called a system of values. The physical sciences do not try to, and the social sciences are still in a state of exploration. But a scientist, in order to be a good creator, has to work out for himself a set of values by which he is going to live. He has to be very independent in thought. He has to take a very questioning attitude to whatever he sees and whatever anybody else sees. He has to make a special fetish of originality and of contradiction, of dissent in general. Without this he is not going to create anything new at all. If you can live in such a world, you have to be extremely tolerant of the dissent of others. You have both to recognize the fallibility of their achievement and yet do them honor because it is their achievement. I hold that you cannot carry out the activity of science if you do not have a society organized in this way: a society rich in dissent and yet rich in tolerance and rich in honor. I think that in this are the beginnings of principles which the scientist can teach to the world at large.

Some may say that in general human beings are inspired by a myth, a symbol, something which transcends a set of values. What can science put up? Let us think of this historically for a moment: the myth of Genesis was not destroyed by my generation of scientists; it was destroyed over a hundred years ago, in 1858 and 1859 when Darwin wrote and then published *The Origin of Species*. This really destroyed the belief of people in the literal account of the Creation. What did they learn in its place? I trust they learned an enormous revulsion. Bishop Wilberforce asked whether Huxley claimed to have been descended from an ape through his father or his mother; there was a general feeling that it was somehow terrible to be as one with the animals. Now time has cured that. We feel instead that we have something to be very proud of in having transcended the animal stock so as to become people who possess and use certain gifts that animals cannot. The chief of these is the use of language; that is, the use of concepts. I would also say, the making of patterns—animals only have habits, they have no conceptual patterns. Human beings are to us now the creators in a way they were not when Darwin wrote. And we could now say that what has really happened is that for the myth of creation, scientists have substituted the myth of creativity. And this gives us the sense that it is human beings who are peculiarly the creators. Of course I do not think this is a myth; but it is the nature of myth that those who hold it do not believe it to be a myth. Certainly science has enabled us to see human life and the place of humanity in rather special ways. Human beings are seen to have within themselves the ability each to fulfill himself, each to fulfill the essentially human part of the creative potential. If we have to call something a myth, I am proud to call that a myth.

4
THE REACH OF IMAGINATION

Before me floats an image, man or shade,
Shade more than man, more image than a shade.
W. B. Yeats, *Byzantium* (1930)

For three thousand years, poets have been enchanted and moved and perplexed by the power of their own imagination. In a short and summary essay I can hope at most to lift one small corner of that mystery; and yet it is a critical corner. I shall ask, What goes on in the mind when we imagine? You will hear from me that one answer to this question is fairly specific: which is to say, that we can describe the working of the imagination. And when we describe it as I shall do, it becomes plain that imagination is a specifically *human* gift. To imagine is the characteristic act, not of the poet's mind, or the painter's, or the scientist's, but of the mind of man.

My stress here on the word "human" implies that there is a clear difference in this between the actions of men and those of other animals. Let me then start with a classical experiment with animals and children which Walter Hunter thought out in Chicago about 1910. That was the time when scientists were agog with the success of Ivan Pavlov in forming and changing the reflex actions of dogs, which Pavlov had first announced in 1903. Pavlov had been given a Nobel prize the next year, in 1904, although in fairness I should say that the award did not cite his work on the conditioned reflex, but on the digestive glands.

Hunter duly trained some dogs and other animals on Pavlov's lines. They were taught that when a light came on over one of three tunnels out of their cage, that tunnel would be open; they could escape down it, and were rewarded with food if they did. But once he had fixed that conditioned reflex, Hunter added to it a deeper idea: he gave the mechanical experiment a new dimension, literally—the dimension of time. Now he no longer let the dog go to the lighted tunnel at once; instead, he put out the light, and then kept the dog waiting a little while before he let him go. In this way Hunter timed how long an animal can remember where it has last seen the signal light to its escape route.

The results were and are staggering. A dog or a rat forgets which one of three tunnels has been lit up within a matter of seconds—in Hunter's experiment, ten seconds at most. If you want such an animal to do much better than this, you must make the task much simpler: you must face it with only two tunnels to choose from. Even so, the best that Hunter could do was to have a dog remember for five minutes which one of two tunnels had been lit up.

I am not quoting these times as if they were exact and universal: they surely are not. Hunter's experiment, more than fifty years old now, had many faults of detail. For example, there were too few animals, they were oddly picked, and they did not all behave consistently. It may be unfair to test a dog for what it *saw*, when it commonly follows its nose rather than its eyes. It may be unfair to test any animal in the unnatural setting of a laboratory cage. And there are higher animals, such as chimpanzees and other primates, which certainly have longer memories than the animals that Hunter tried.

Yet when all these provisos have been made (and met, by more modern experiments), the facts are still startling and characteristic. An animal cannot recall a signal from the past for even a short fraction of the time that a man can—for even a short fraction of the time that a child can. Hunter made comparable tests with six-year-old children, and found, of course, that they were incomparably better than the best of his animals. There is a striking and basic difference between a man's ability to imagine something that he saw or experienced, and an animal's failure.

Animals make up for this by other and extraordinary gifts. The salmon and the carrier pigeon can find their way home as we cannot; they have, as it were, a practical memory that man cannot match. But their actions always depend on some form of habit: on instinct or on learning, which reproduce by rote a train of known responses. They do not depend, as human memory does, on the recollection of absent things.

Where is it that the animal falls short? We get a clue to the answer, I think, when Hunter tells us how the animals in his experiment tried to fix their recollection. They most often pointed themselves at the light before it went out, as some gundogs point rigidly at the game they scent—and get the name "pointer" from the posture. The animal makes ready to act by building the signal into its action. There is a primitive imagery in its stance, it seems to me; it is as if the animal were trying to fix the light in its mind by fixing it in its body. And indeed, how else can a dog mark and (as it were) name one of three tunnels, when it has no such words as "left" and "right" and no such numbers as "one," "two," "three"? The directed gesture of attention and readiness is perhaps the only symbolic device that the dog commands to hold on to the past, and thereby to guide itself into the future.

I used the verb "to imagine" a moment ago, and now I have some ground for giving it a meaning. "To imagine" means to make images and to move them about inside one's head in new arrangements. When you and I recall the past, we imagine it in this direct and homely sense. The tool that puts the human mind ahead of the animal is imagery. For us, memory does not demand the preoccupation that it demands in animals, and it lasts immensely longer, because we fix it in images or other substitute symbols. With the same symbolic vocabulary we spell out the future—not one but many futures, which we weigh one against another.

I am using the word "image" in a wide meaning, which does not restrict it to the mind's eye as a visual organ. An image in my usage is what Charles Peirce called a "sign," without regard for its sensory quality. Peirce distinguished between different forms of signs, but there is no reason to make his distinction here, for the imagination works equally with them all, and that is why I call them all images.

Indeed, the most important images for human beings are simply words, which are abstract symbols. Animals do not have words, in our sense: there is no specific center for language in the brain of any animal, as there is in the human brain. In this respect at least, we know that the human imagination depends on a configuration in the brain that has only evolved in the last one or two million years. In the same period, evolution has greatly enlarged the front lobes in the human brain, which govern the sense of the past and the future; and it is a fair guess that they are probably the seat of our other images. (Part of the evidence for this guess is that damage to the front lobes in primates reduces them to the state of Hunter's animals.) If the guess turns out to be right, we shall know why man has come to look like a highbrow or an egghead: because otherwise there would not be room in his head for his imagination.

The images play out for us events which are not present to our senses, and thereby guard the past and create the future—a future that does not yet exist, and may never come to exist in that form. By contrast, the lack of symbolic ideas, or their rudimentary poverty, cuts off an animal from the past and the future alike, and imprisons it in the present. Of all the distinctions between man and animal, the characteristic gift which makes us human is the power to work with symbolic images: the gift of imagination.

This is really a remarkable finding. When Philip Sidney in 1580 defended poets (and all unconventional thinkers) from the Puritan charge that they were liars, he said that a maker must imagine things that are not. Halfway between Sidney and us, William Blake said, "What is now proved was once only imagin'd." About the same time, in 1796, Samuel Taylor Coleridge for the first time distinguished between the passive fancy and the active imagination, "the living Power and prime Agent of all human Perception." Now we see that they were right, and precisely right: the human gift is the gift of imagination—and that is not just a literary phrase.

Nor is it just a literary gift; it is, I repeat, characteristically human. Almost everything that we do that is worth doing is done in the first place in the mind's eye. The richness of human life is that we have many lives; we live the events that do not happen (and some that cannot) as vividly as those that do; and if thereby we die a thousand deaths, that is the price we pay for living a thousand lives. (A cat, of course, has only nine.) Literature is alive to us because we live its images, but so is any play of the mind—so is chess: the lines of play that we foresee and try in our heads and dismiss are as much a part of the game as the moves that we make. John Keats said that the unheard melodies are sweeter, and all chess players sadly recall that the combinations that they planned and which never came to be played were the best.

I make this point to remind you, insistently, that imagination is the manipulation of images in one's head; and that the rational manipulation belongs to that, as well as the literary and artistic manipulation. When a child begins to play games with things that stand for other things, with chairs or chessmen, he enters the gateway to reason and imagination together. For the human reason discovers new relations between things not by deduction, but by that unpredictable blend of speculation and insight that scientists call induction, which—like other forms of imagination—cannot be formalized. We see it at work when Walter Hunter inquires into a child's memory, as much as when Blake and Coleridge do. Only a restless and original mind would have asked Hunter's questions and could have conceived his experiments, in a science that was dominated by Pavlov's reflex arcs and was heading toward the behaviorism of John Watson.

Let me find a spectacular example for you from history. What is the most famous experiment that you had described to you as a child? I will hazard that it is the experiment that Galileo is said to have made in Sidney's age, in Pisa about 1590, by dropping two unequal balls from the Leaning Tower. There, we say, is a man in the modern mold, a man after our own hearts: he insisted on questioning the authority of Aristotle and St. Thomas Aquinas, and seeing with his own eyes whether (as they said) the heavy ball would reach the ground before the light one. Seeing is believing.

Yet seeing is also imagining. Galileo did challenge the authority of Aristotle, and he did look hard at his mechanics. But the eye that Galileo used was the mind's eye. He did not drop balls from the Leaning Tower of Pisa—and if he had, he would have got a very doubtful answer.[1] Instead, Galileo made an imaginary

[1]So Vincenzo Renieri wrote to Galileo from Pisa as late as 1641, reporting on a recent test between a cannonball and a musketball. Galileo had made one of the characters in the *Discorsi* say that this test works well enough "provided both are dropped from a height of 200 cubits." This is twice as high as the Leaning Tower's 185 feet (1 cubit = 60 cm).

experiment (or, as the Germans say, "thought experiment") in his head, which I will describe as he did years later in the book he wrote after the Holy Office silenced him, the *Discorsi . . . intorno a due nuove scienze*, which was smuggled out to be printed in The Netherlands in 1638.

Suppose, said Galileo, that you drop two unequal balls from the tower at the same time. And suppose that Aristotle is right—suppose that the heavy ball falls faster, so that it steadily gains on the light ball and hits the ground first. Very well. Now imagine the same experiment done again, with only one difference: this time the two unequal balls are joined by a string between them. The heavy ball will again move ahead, but now the light ball holds it back and acts as a drag or brake. So the light ball will be speeded up and the heavy ball will be slowed down; they must reach the ground together because they are tied together, but they cannot reach the ground as quickly as the heavy ball alone. Yet the string between them has turned the two balls into a single mass which is heavier than either ball—and surely (according to Aristotle) this mass should therefore move faster than either ball? Galileo's imaginary experiment has uncovered a contradiction; he says trenchantly, "You see how, from your assumption that a heavier body falls more rapidly than a lighter one, I infer that a (still) heavier body falls more slowly." There is only one way out of the contradiction: the heavy ball and the light ball must fall at the same rate, so that they go on falling at the same rate when they are tied together.

This argument is not conclusive, for nature might be more subtle (when the two balls are joined) than Galileo has allowed. And yet it is something more important: it is suggestive, it is stimulating, it opens a new view—in a word, it is imaginative. It cannot be settled without an actual experiment, because nothing that we imagine can become knowledge until we have translated it into, and backed it by, real experience. The test of imagination is experience. But then, that is as true of literature and the arts as it is of science. In science, the imaginary experiment is tested by confronting it with physical experience; and in literature, the imaginative conception is tested by confronting it with human experience. The superficial speculation in science is dismissed because it is found to falsify nature; and the shallow work of art is discarded because it is found to be untrue to our own nature. So when Ella Wheeler Wilcox died in 1919, more people were reading her verses than Shakespeare's; yet in a few years her work was dead. It had been buried by its poverty of emotion and its trivialness of thought: which is to say that it had been proved to be as false to the nature of man as, say, Jean Baptiste Lamarck and Trofim Lysenko were false to the nature of inheritance. The strength of the imagination, its enriching power and excitement, lies in its interplay with reality—physical and emotional.

I doubt if there is much to choose here between science and the arts: the imagination is not much more free, and not much less free, in one than in the other. All great scientists have used their imagination freely, and let it ride them to outrageous conclusions without crying "Halt!" Albert Einstein fiddled with imaginary experiments from boyhood, and was wonderfully ignorant of the facts that they were supposed to bear on. When he wrote the first of his beautiful papers on the random movement of atoms, he did not know that the Brownian motion which it predicted could be seen in any laboratory. He was sixteen when he invented the paradox that he resolved ten years later, in 1905, in the theory of relativity, and it bulked much larger in his mind than the experiment of Albert Michelson and Edward Morley which had upset every other physicist since 1881. All his life Einstein loved to make up teasing puzzles like Galileo's, about falling lifts and the detection of gravity; and they carry the nub of the problems of general relativity on which he was working.

Indeed, it could not be otherwise. The power that man has over nature and himself, and that a dog lacks, lies in his command of imaginary experience. He alone has the symbols which fix the past and play with the future, possible and impossible. In the Renaissance, the symbolism of memory was thought to be mystical, and devices that were invented as mnemonics (by Giordano Bruno, for example, and by Robert Fludd) were interpreted as magic signs. The symbol is the tool which gives man his power, and it is the same tool whether the symbols are images or words, mathematical signs or mesons. And the symbols have a reach and a roundness that goes beyond their literal and practical meaning. They are the rich concepts under which the mind gathers many particulars into one name, and many instances into one general induction. When a man says "left" and "right," he is outdistancing the dog not only in looking for a light; he is setting in train all the shifts of meaning, the overtones and the ambiguities, between "gauche" and "adroit" and "dexterous," between "sinister" and the sense of right. When a man counts "one, two, three," he is not only doing mathematics; he is on the path to the mysticism of numbers in Pythagoras and Vitruvius and Kepler, to the Trinity and the signs of the zodiac.

I have described imagination as the ability to make images and to move them about inside one's head in new arrangements. This is the faculty that is specifically human, and it is the common root from which science and literature both spring and grow and flourish together. For they do flourish (and languish) together; the great ages of science are the great ages of all the arts, because in them powerful minds have taken fire from one another, breathless and higgledy-piggledy, without asking too nicely whether they ought to tie their imagination to falling balls or a haunted island. Galileo and Shakespeare, who were born in the same year, grew into greatness in the same age; when Galileo was looking through his telescope at the moon, Shakespeare was writing *The Tempest*; and all Europe was in ferment, from Johannes Kepler to Peter Paul Rubens, and from the first table of logarithms by John Napier to the Authorized Version of the Bible.

Let me end with a last and spirited example of the common inspiration of literature and science, because it is as much alive today as it was three hundred years ago. What I have in mind is man's ageless fantasy, to fly to the moon. I do not display this to you as a high scientific enterprise; on the contrary, I think we have more important discoveries to make here on earth than wait for us, beckoning, at the horned surface of the moon. Yet I cannot belittle the fascination which that ice-blue journey has had for the imagination of men, long before it drew us to our television screens to watch the tumbling of astronauts. Plutarch and Lucian, Ariosto and Ben Jonson wrote about it, before the days of

Jules Verne and H. G. Wells and science fiction. The seventeenth century was heady with new dreams and fables about voyages to the moon. Kepler wrote one full of deep scientific ideas, which (alas) simply got his mother accused of witchcraft. In England, Francis Godwin wrote a wild and splendid work, *The Man in the Moone*, and the astronomer John Wilkins wrote a wild and learned one, *The Discovery of a New World*. They did not draw a line between science and fancy; for example, they all tried to guess just where in the journey the earth's gravity would stop. Only Kepler understood that gravity has no boundary, and put a law to it—which happened to be the wrong law.[2]

All this was a few years before Isaac Newton was born, and it was all in his head that day in 1666 when he sat in his mother's garden, a young man of twenty-three, and thought about the reach of gravity. This was how he came to conceive his brilliant image, that the moon is like a ball which has been thrown so hard that it falls exactly as fast as the horizon, all the way round the earth. The image will do for any satellite, and Newton modestly calculated how long therefore an astronaut would take to fall round the earth once. He made it ninety minutes, and we have all seen now that he was right; but Newton had no way to check that. Instead he went on to calculate how long in that case the distant moon would take to round the earth, if indeed it behaved like a thrown ball that falls in the earth's gravity, and if gravity obeyed a law of inverse squares. He found that the answer would be twenty-eight days.

In that telling figure, the imagination that day chimed with nature, and made a harmony. We shall hear an echo of that harmony on the day when we land on the moon, because it will be not a technical but an imaginative triumph, that reaches back to the beginning of modern science and literature both. All great

[2]Kepler may have got the idea of a universal gravity from the neoplatonic thought that all things in nature must attract one another because they are infused with a share of God's universal love. If this is so, then this farfetched path of the imagination runs back through Nicholas of Cusa to the fifth-century imposter who called himself Dionysius the Areopagite. See Pierre Duhem, *Le Système du Monde*, IV-58, p. 364.

acts of imagination are like this, in the arts and in science, and convince us because they fill out reality with a deeper sense of rightness. We start with the simplest vocabulary of images, with "left" and "right" and "one, two, three," and before we know how it happened the words and the numbers have conspired to make a match with nature: we catch in them the pattern of mind and matter as one.

5
THE LOGIC OF NATURE

A scientific revolution began with the discovery, in the last years of the century, of radioactivity and of the electron. Since then new phenomena have been unfolded, and new concepts have been formed to connect and to elucidate them, at a pace which makes ours one of the great creative ages in human history. Historians are only just learning to speak easily of the first scientific revolution in the sixteenth and seventeenth centuries, and to recognize it as an event which, in Professor Butterfield's phrase, "outshines everything since the rise of Christianity and reduces the Renaissance and Reformation to the rank of mere episodes." While they are busy at learning this, the second scientific revolution is already long on the move, and is making over both our lives and our thoughts as powerfully as did the first.

It is therefore puzzling that, in this surge of discovery, the public has grown less confident of the heroic mission of science than it was at the turn of the century. There is now a mutinous undertone in the respect which is paid to the scientist; his leadership is no longer taken for granted, even by the progressive and the young; and indeed, he himself has been infected by the doubts of others. First his moral and now his intellectual status has been questioned until, by an artful inversion, the crusade for truth as an end which T. H. Huxley once led, and the rejection of all expedient means, have been made to look like stuffy Victorian prejudices.

This muttering of thunder against science has grown louder since the first atomic bomb was dropped in 1945. It has formed the climate in which the military men who dropped the bomb were able, by the same ironic trick of inversion, to disgrace Robert Oppenheimer, the scientist who made it. But the dilemma of the modern scientist is older than the atomic bomb, older even than the slow erosion since 1918 of the dignity of nations by hooligan leaders of private armies and undeclared wars, which at last made the use of the bomb seem both necessary and natural.

The dilemma rises at the confrontation of personal discovery and public use; and it troubles every scientist, whether he calls his work pure or applied research, in a time of revolution when his most remote finding may change the world.

The public sign of this dilemma, I have said, is that the scientist is not only disliked (as any don is) but distrusted. The state treats him as indispensable but unreliable, a hangdog hangman who has the bad manners to be good at war work and the impertinence to find it distasteful. The public thinks that he has no conscience, and his security officer fears that he has two consciences. And in fact, the private sign of the scientist's dilemma now is an ambivalence of conscience. He is unhappy between his scientific creed and his social loyalty: between, that is, the long and triumphant tradition of open publication, and a society which still hopes to survive by the peasant adage "least said, soonest mended."

All these divisions, I believe, derive from one gap at the center: the distance between the new view of the world which science has been forming, and the view ossified in vernacular speech and thought. Between the personal discovery and the public use of a mechanism, a principle, or a concept, there must be a translation of thought; and the years since 1900 have opened a gap across which, at present, translation is almost impossible. The laboratory language and the everyday have, for the time being, no bridging metaphors in common. The public still pictures nature as the first scientific revolution did, as an engine; and there is no way of putting into this picture the algebra of nature which the laboratory now conceives. The translation is as false, at bottom, as one of Shakespeare's *Sonnets* into Chinese ideographs: the two languages do not have the same structure, nor an imagery to flash and fire a spark from one into the other. Today the scientist's language shares no imagery with the vernacular, and is as private and imprisoned as the modern poet's or the modern painter's. The public is at a loss, and afraid of them all. It puts its fear of the scientist into robust terms: he is going to blow man off the earth, or (in alternate weeks) he is going to overpopulate it. But the fear remains an intellectual fear of change; men are aware that their control of the world will slip away to those with a different way of thinking; and they do not like what is different—least of all in thinking.

How does the layman think of a law of nature? He thinks of it as something which dictates the sequence of events, so that the end follows rigidly from the beginning. The pioneers of the seventeenth century, Thomas Hobbes and Isaac Newton, took over this form from mathematics, and particularly (as Hobbes tells) from Euclid's geometry. In Euclid, each proposition flows from those which precede it by logical necessity; and so in physics, they argued, each happening must flow from those which precede it by natural necessity. Cause must lead unalterably to effect. The laws of nature are to be like the laws of deductive reasoning: by these steps we are to go from first to last, from first cause to the last effect, along a path which is unique, certain, and (in principle) predictable in every detail.

And the detail, on this traditional view, is important. We may not be able to formulate an exact law between one large event and another, between a thundercloud and where the lightning strikes, or between a war and the male birthrate. But we are to believe that we suffer these uncertainties only because we lack the detail. To grow more assured, we need only (we are assured) divide the phenomena more finely: to map every electric charge, or to trace the love life of every soldier. On this view (which is explicit in Hobbes's theory of sensation, and implicit in Newton's infinitesimal calculus) nature is continuous, and her parts and processes can be divided indefinitely. We shall find her mechanism if we go on looking for smaller and smaller hairsprings.

The concepts which science evolved from the seventeenth to the nineteenth centuries were formed, and sometimes were challenged, on these bases. The first of them, Newton's concept of gravitational force, worked by cause and effect; yet it outraged philosophers, because it laid down no machinery by which the force might cannon from point to neighboring point. Direct action at a distance was unimaginable. Space must be a ready-made box which can be divided infinitely; so must time; and mass and energy and the electric field must be tangible gears which mesh and drive in these boxes, to make a universal clockwork.

In the nineteenth century, this view of nature had become ingrained in language and thought; and rightly so. For it had been consistently and enormously successful, all the way from astronomy to chemistry, and from the structure of plants to the theory of evolution. And the business of science is to succeed; it is an empirical, not a metaphysical study. The test of the explanations which science offers is that they shall so connect one event with another that we can coherently predict the results of our actions. By this test, its classical methods had toward the end of the last century had two hundred and fifty years without a failure.

But by the same test, at the end of the last century classical science failed. This needs to be said roundly, for many people still speak as if the choice between the old and the new picture of nature were a matter of philosophical taste. It is not: it is matter of fact.

Facts began to accumulate around 1900 which did not fulfill the classical predictions. The speed of light did not behave like other speeds. The orbit of the planet Mercury did not keep time. The mass of the newly discovered electrons changed with their speed. The flow of energy from a radiant body did not fit a continuous pattern. Neither, in biology, did inheritance behave continuously. Radioactivity showed that matter was subject to unpredictable eruptions of instability.

In some of these examples, the error of the classical model was small; and this prompted men then, and does so even now, to hope that it might yet be corrected by some minor compromise—a refinement of calculation or hypothesis. Such hopes miss the substance of the problem. Of course the errors in the relative speed of light and in the orbit of Mercury are small; if they had been large, the Newtonian system would have been wildly out of step long ago. The errors are not large—they are critical. For they will not let these findings fit into the classical frame. And that rigid, causal frame allows no uncertainty, no tolerance of fit. If the findings are accurate, then Newton's mechanics are at fault: only minutely at fault, and yet fundamentally faulty.

The second scientific revolution is (like the first) a revolution of concepts; and like the first, it was forced upon its makers by the obstinacy of the facts. The flow of radiant energy is as modest and as practical a study as the fall of weights. And when that flow was shown by Max Planck in 1900 to have a discontinuous pattern, the act was as decisive as when, about 1590, Galileo is said to have dropped (so his first biographer claims) two unlike weights from the Leaning Tower of Pisa and seen them fall side by side.

Nineteenth-century chemists and others had of course long proved what the Greeks had guessed, that matter is put together from atoms. And there are difficulties in squaring a world of atoms with a belief in continuity of action; they had made Newton noncommittal. The difficulties at once became insuperable when Planck showed that energy too is atomic: it comes in indivisible pieces. No longer could nature be imagined to glide from one state to another by infinite degrees. The parts of nature leap, and her states are as separate as the frames in a film.

This picture has slowly made over all our concepts. For example, think of an atom radiating one of its characteristic colors—a yellow line of sodium, say. It gets the precise energy for this when one of its electrons makes the precise leap from one of its characteristic orbits to another. This leap takes no time and does not pass through the space between: the electron disappears from one orbit and instantly appears in another. It does not make much sense to call something with this behavior a particle; it does not even make sense to ask whether what appears in the two orbits is "the same" electron. Neither does it make sense to give the electron one place at one time in its orbit; its possible positions are spread round the orbit like a wave. The electron, in short, is an electron and nothing else, with its own unusual but definite laws; and words like "particle" and "wave" are mere metaphors, each of which describes an aspect and no more of the whole algebra of its behavior.

Or picture the light from a sodium lamp beamed through two holes in a screen. The light ripples from the two holes in waves, which overlap to form a pattern of dark and bright. These waves are made up of single photons of light, sent out by the leaps of single electrons. Through which hole does any one photon go, to take its place in the pattern of dark and bright? We cannot tell, for the question does not make sense. The single photon, the piece of energy, is sent off on its journey and it appears at the end, in one of several possible places. This is all that we can say of it; it is useless to ask for more.

Useless, that is, so long as we insist on following single photons one by one. For the units of energy and of matter obstinately contradict the dogma of classical mechanics, that the processes of nature must be infinitely divisible and infinitely predictable.

What is predictable is the statistics of collections: that half the light goes through each hole, and the pattern it makes of dark and bright.

This statistical outlook had already been developed in biology. There its origins were different: it had been forced on biologists by the practical difficulties of their work.

The physical sciences have evolved a method of experiment which studies phenomena one factor at a time. When you want to learn how pressure changes the volume of a gas, you keep its temperature constant. The experiment is limited, and isolated from its environment.

Such a separation is seldom possible in work with living things. The experimenter who studies tall families or the efficacy of a drug has to put up with a motley and shifting background of other factors. He cannot shut them out, yet their variations threaten to mask the clear effect he wants to uncover.

Biologists had therefore taken up statistical techniques, and from them were thinking out a new grammar of science. (The phrase was used by Karl Pearson in 1900.) They learned to work with the evidence as it stood, and to measure an effect as it were by its contrast against the background of variation. They no longer tried to idealize experiment, and instead they accepted the reality—that, however delicately we work, the random still clings about the systematic, the fluctuations still blur the trend.

We can have no vision of nature except as an assembly of such downright and fallible evidence.

On this view, once again, our description of nature is not a mechanism but an algebra. And once again, prediction is limited because description itself must keep to the states that we observe. But prediction does not thereby become guesswork: it becomes factual. The future is not already determined, but neither is it arbitrary. We know its possible states, and what weight to give to each; it has a defined area of uncertainty which we can calculate and within which we can expect it with confidence.

The statistical thought set going by the biologists has much in common, then, with the new thought in small-scale physics. Moreover, the work of Gregor Mendel, rediscovered in 1900, showed that the biological units of inheritance are discontinuous, so that a species moves by leaps as a physical system does.

Yet these likenesses are, to me, less interesting than another strand in statistics. It is an active science. It does not picture the world as given and the scientist as a neutral observer outside it. Science here is an activity within the world it pictures, and the activity cannot be taken out of the picture; it limits and shapes it, together. The model of nature is not made of what scientists see but of what they do.

This strand runs from statistics to another scale of physics: the large scale of relativity.

The large question in physics at the turn of the century was, why light looked to go equally fast, however you yourself moved in relation to it. To the young Albert Einstein, this question took a deeper form: What do you take for granted when you measure the speed of light or of anything else? You take for granted that space is already measured out, and that the time at different points of it is known. But how do you compare the time at two points in space? You send a signal from one to the other: a light wave or some other wave of the same kind. As soon as this has been said, it is clear that the light signal is inextricably raveled up in the measurement of its own speed.

For two hundred years and more, physics had been seen as a flat record of events, which are unrolled in a universal space and time. Einstein now asked of this view, not whether it is tenable in some abstract sense, but whether it is practical. Do physicists record events? Do they know independently when and where they happen? Once these bland, searching questions are asked, the answers are plain, and they are: No! Physics does not record events but observations. And event, signal, and observation are linked in a way which cannot be taken apart. We cannot abstract the event, we can only study the relation between observations. Relativity is the understanding of the world not as events but as relations.

Once again science here is an activity, and a realistic activity, which builds its concepts from the operations which scientists must actually carry out. And once again, this strict outlook is more than a philosophical puritanism. Einstein in 1905 put it into equations, and at once it explained the constant speed of light, and linked space with time, and mass with energy. Ten years later, when he extended it to a deeper understanding of mass, it explained the erratic behavior of Mercury, and foresaw the bending of light toward the sun.

So the second scientific revolution has abandoned the hidden tenets of the first. Its model of nature no longer assumes that she must be causal, continuous, and independent. These assumptions were idealized from everyday experience, and they were right, and splendidly successful, during two centuries when physics worked and measured on the everyday scale. They have turned out to be false on the small scale of the atom and on the large scale of the nebulas, and at least inappropriate to studies of the living.

I have said that the long success of the rigid model of nature has made it part of the vernacular. We think by habit of nature as a causal, continuous, and independent mechanism, which thumps along inexorably while we peck or goggle at it.

This is no longer the scientist's picture; but it has now become, by an ironic transfer, the popular picture of a scientist. It lends itself to the basic totalitarian tricks which exploit the insecurity of the ignorant: an awe of the specialist, a hidden hatred of him, and a cleft between his way of thinking and theirs.

These tricks have been worked against scientists and others, first in Germany, and since then both in the East and in the West. They can be used so long as ignorance of the roots of modern science and a secrecy which stems from ignorance threaten our values and through them our civilization.

But the counterattack on science also has subtler spokesmen. They shake their heads over modern thought, more in sorrow than in anger. Alas, they say, we should have liked to believe in a logical world. We were on the very point of giving up divine intervention, exorcism, seances, organic compost, Himmler's *Welteislehre*, and blood and soil. And now, when we were standing stripped for total immersion in the waters of rationalism, what does science do but tip them away. Science has admitted that the electron is not a billiard ball, and we must therefore return naked to a belief in papal infallibility, astrology, and the unfitness of the lower orders.

If this misunderstanding of the scientific method were not deliberate, it would be laughable. For the foundations of science are not metaphysical; they are empirical, an analysis of what we actually do to make predictions which we actually test. As metaphysics, Leibniz had pointed out long ago that space and time are not things but relations. David Hume had shown that we can believe in causality only by habit, and not by logic. Their speculations had no influence (until Einstein read them), because when they were made they had no application.

The new thought in science is based on new facts. These critical facts will not fit a framework which insists that natural laws must be causal, continuous, and independent of us. And it is useless to insist on habit and metaphysic in the face of the facts. We must learn a more delicate conception of the laws of nature. A law does not become less real because it is statistical, and because we cannot picture a mechanism to express its algebra. Nature does not become less logical because her logic is not Euclid's. Science is not the imposition of our logic on nature, but the arduous understanding of her own.

And of course the new science is not lawless. On the contrary, its predictions are of a formidable accuracy, as Hiroshima and Calder Hall testify. But they do not claim a greater accuracy than they can have. We recognize now that the world is not made on a pattern which can be described by specifying its separate points. Because such descriptions are limited, so are the predictions made from them. But the predictions are not lawless; each has a calculated uncertainty, within which we work confidently and methodically.

For it is the method, the activity of science which expresses its profound rationalism. The neat debaters who seek in the new science an apology for religious and social obscurantism want desperately to keep at bay the method of science itself. Science is as irrational as we are, they cry, because it no longer imposes on nature the logic of the nineteenth century. But science is not an exercise in textbook logic. Science is rational because it is the unprejudiced discovery of the logic of nature.

6
THE LOGIC OF EXPERIMENT

The use of mathematics to describe the whereabouts of moving bodies, in astronomy and mechanics, has an ancient history; it was thought natural long before Copernicus and Galileo. But the notion that mathematics is central to all science is younger. If we want to fix its birth in a single dramatic date, we may choose the night of November 10, 1619. That night the young Descartes (he was twenty-three) had a mystical experience in which it was shown to him that the key to the universe is its mathematical order. He spoke of that moment with awe, not as a discovery but as a revelation, to the end of his life.

Since Descartes had in mind a mathematics of order, he was looking for a kind of geometry. He wanted to find in the world what he had found in Euclid. Yet mechanics then, as now, more often described events by numbers than by their configuration. It was therefore appropriate that Descartes became a pioneer in the use of graphical methods to link geometry with arithmetic. The notion of imposing a gigantic coordinate system on the universe was certainly, in Descartes's mind, one step in giving it a logical order.

Within a few years of Descartes's vision, something very like it changed the life of Thomas Hobbes. It was, of course, a more sober affair; Hobbes picked up the first book of Euclid, perhaps in the library of his patrons the Cavendishes, and actually read it. He was by then a man of middle age, but he had had a classical education, and he seems to have been unprepared for the heady pleasure of reading a book in which the assertions actually form an argument. In the phrase of his friend Aubrey, "This made him in love with geometry."

It was plain to Hobbes that the world could be as rational as Euclid, if he could find in its progression some analogue to logical entailment. He found this analogue in the principle of cause and effect. Hobbes held that a cause entails its effect as rigorously as Euclid's axioms entail the pons asinorum. In fact, we use the verb "to follow" to describe both kinds of consequence, as a matter of course.

The triumphant work of the great generation which followed (I use the word advisedly), with Newton at its head, grew from the conception of Hobbes and Descartes. That generation abandoned once for all the attempt to deduce the laws of nature from her facts, by any process of forward reasoning. Instead, the new scientists invented a more tentative method. They singled out a set of principles or axioms, such as Newton's laws of motion and the law of inverse squares; they worked out what kind of a world would follow from these; and they judged the axioms right or wrong by checking their fictitious world against the real world. Huygens puts this clearly in his *Treatise on Light*, where he says "Here principles are tested by the consequences derived from them." In my view, this is the essence of the inductive mind.

Huygens also saw that this inductive method can never establish its axioms conclusively, because there may (and indeed will) exist other sets of axioms with the same physical consequences. It was on this ground, and this alone, that Huygens thought natural science less certain than geometry because he thought the axioms of geometry to be self-evident.

The classical criticism of scientific inference was made fifty years after Huygens wrote this, by David Hume in 1739. Hume says bluntly:

> All reasonings concerning cause and effect are founded on experience, and all reasonings from experience are founded on the supposition, that the course of nature will continue uniformly the same.
>
> We are determined by CUSTOM alone to suppose the future conformable to the past. When I see a billiard-ball moving towards another, my mind is immediately carry'd by habit to the usual effect, and anticipates my sight by conceiving the second ball in motion. There is nothing in these objects, abstractly considered, and independent of experience, which leads me to form any such conclusion: and even after I have had experience of many repeated effects of this kind, there is no argument which determines me to suppose, that the effect will be conformable to past experience.

Hume has here seized an important point. The events of nature take place in time, which is a dimension that we cannot explore at will. In this they differ from the theorems of geometry as Hume conceived them, embedded in space in which he was free to move to and fro as he pleased. In an odd way, Hume's generation had suddenly grown aware of the frightening uncertainty of time. It was in his lifetime that crowds marched through London shouting "Give us back our eleven days," not much more than two hundred years ago.

Yet if we look at Hume's objections carefully, we see that they confuse two distinct ways in which time enters into scientific inference. When I say that the dog has evolved from a wolf, I state one kind of theorem which relates to time. And when I say that my dog will have puppies next month, I state another kind of theorem about time. The evidence for both theorems lies in our experience, without which we cannot hope to know the world as it is. Both theorems may therefore be wrong because I have misunderstood experience. And this is the only way in which the first theorem can be wrong: because I have misread the past. But this has nothing to do with Hume's criticism, that the future may at any moment decide to break with the past. A future change in the laws of nature can only affect theorems of the second kind; it can only stop my dog from having puppies. But it comes too late to falsify the theory of evolution.

It was Hume's point that the laws of nature may turn topsy-turvy at any moment. At midnight we may step into a hole in time and pitch on our heads. As an objection to prediction, this is of course unanswerable: as unanswerable as solipsism, and as pointless. For it simply asserts that there can exist no sanction, within our experience, which allows us to step from the territory of our experience into what lies outside it. Mathematicians are taught this in childhood when they are warned that it is unwise to extrapolate. And in my view this objection holds for space as for time. We might equally stumble on a hole in space across which the laws of nature change abruptly. In this vein it is open to anyone to believe that the light which reaches us from distant nebulas is not reddened by the Doppler shift, but by crossing a discontinuity in the laws of physics which cuts off our galaxy like a picture frame. Believe it, and welcome; but what help is it? None.

The purpose of science is indeed prediction beyond our experience. But its practice stands apart from these speculations, because they offer no guide alternative to experience. When we ask "How is a scientific theory made?" we always have in mind a way of arranging the facts of experience. We may have to wait to prove a theory incomplete or plain wrong. But after that, what we use is always a set of facts *in the past*. The future in the sense of Hume, a time that may have a hole in it, does not exist in science. At any instant, the scientist has only a record of the past—and he must assume that when he plays the record, he experiences the past truly. He is now asked to give order to these experiences. This order is his theory.

How the scientist teases out such a theory from the facts or processes which he has recorded is the crucial question of the later part of this essay. But the form of the theory I have already implied; it was stated by Huygens. The scientist postulates a set of entities which he supposes, as it were, to lie under the recorded events: atoms or quanta or cells or genes or reflexes. He formulates axioms which these entities are to obey, and allowable operations on them. Of course many of his axioms are not stated explicitly; but the history of Euclid, from the time of John Playfair to our own day, shows that this happens to the most scrupulous geometer. To this apparatus the scientist adds a dictionary to say what conjunctions of his entities can be observed, and what these observable appearances are. And thereupon he sets his model going.

I say "sets his model going," and the metaphor is meant to underline the importance of time in this system. For let there be no mistake about this: our theory at any moment describes only the past, but this by no means removes time from it. To suppose that all statements about time must refer to future time is precisely the confusion which I criticize in Hume.

A scientific theory describes the behavior of things in time. Its axioms must include some which say how the postulated entities move or change in time. Axioms of this kind are essentially rules of cause and effect—where I use these words in their widest sense, to include sequences in which the regularity which is laid down is only statistical. And no scientific theory exists until it has causal rules of this kind to fix behavior in time, even though all the times are past times, as in geology.

By what test is such a theory to be judged? Can we dispense with the test of prediction? Of course we can. We are at this stage not concerned with the future use of the theory, but with its success in bringing order to the record which we are given. Our test is therefore the ability of the model in its action to match the record. This is what made relativity in 1905 a more exact theory than the mechanics of Newton. When we enlarge the record by experiment, say by the eclipse of 1919, the added sharpness derives not from prediction but from decision: the experiment is designed to choose between two theories.

Yet clearly no experiment can decide between all theories. However full we make our record, it cannot decide between all possible models. For every record is finite, and can therefore be fitted by an infinite number of models. The record is only a sample, even of the history which it records. It is the nature of all experience that it only samples the universe.

If all our observations are only samples of nature, then plainly the way in which they match the scientist's model of her remains a rather loose test. We can fit the model to the facts only here and there; and anyone who has ordered a suit by sending his measurements through the post will know that this way of fitting leaves a large room for error. We try to cut down the error by experiment, that is by increasing the size of the sample.

Since we always have to experiment in the future, this may seem to beg the question that Hume asked. How do we know the future will be "conformable to past experience"? The answer is that we do not know; and we do not suppose it. We look at the whole of the enlarged sample when we have taken it: every experimenter knows that. We look for the effect of time—catastrophic or systematic—as we look for the effect of space or orientation or any other variable. In time, as in the other variables, we are concerned with relations; when we say that two days are the same, we may have to use that word as we do of the weather, to mean that both are changeable.

It is therefore proper to say that the purpose of experiment is to increase the size of the sample on which a theory is tested. In this, experiments are not all alike. Good experiments are more systematic than the random samples yielded by mere observation. And critical experiments are highly stratified samples in the variables under scrutiny. But however well the model fits nature at the sample points, the reasoning from there to its fit at all points can only be probable. It is in this sense that induction gives only a probable assurance of the rightness of a scientific theory, as Huygens well saw. All forms of sampling give only probable information about the population from which the sample is drawn. In testing a scientific theory by experiment, we try to get information about a population of natural events from a sample. We try to convince ourselves that this population matches the configurations generated by our model everywhere, by showing that they match at the sample points. A good deal of nonsense has been talked about probability in science by those who have missed this conception. Some philosophers speak of probable theories and some even speak as though facts can be probable. Facts are so or not so; observations are true or false; and theories are right or wrong. All that is probable is the assurance that we can have in extending what is known in experience to what is unknown—in arguing from a known sample to a larger unknown one.

But when I have said that our observations are only a sample of events, I have opened up a graver difficulty. We cannot now be sure that we have sampled all the properties of the natural objects we are studying. We must expect these objects to have properties which we have not observed or, what is the same thing, to which we have paid no attention. And we cannot expect these properties also to be consequences of a theory which has taken no account of them, and to be displayed by a model conceived in ignorance of them. This is a deeper criticism of the inductive method than those which are commonly made.

The aim of the inductive method is to reduce the description of the universe to a chain of deductions from a finite set of axioms. If this aim is to be reasonable, then all the properties of a natural object must flow from some set of defining properties. What makes an object unique also must make it behave precisely as it does. All the properties of iron must flow from its atomic structure; and all the properties of my dog must flow from a set of defining properties, on which the whole dog is to be, as it were, an elaborate tautology. I do not think that we can have any confidence that this is a possible program. And I am quite as much in doubt of its application to iron as to my dog. For we must base the definition of either class on those properties which are sampled. These may well suffice to make the class unique; but we cannot assume that they ever imply all its properties. The discovery of radioactivity, or of the black swans of Australia, should make us wary of generalizing about *all* the properties of a class.

I should add that any deductive system in mathematics also contains a regress of this kind. Gödel has shown that it will contain theorems which do not conflict with its axioms, yet which cannot be deduced from them. Such theorems are analogous to properties of a natural class which do not flow from its defining properties. I have remarked that we know in practice, from the sampling procedure, that it is rash to speak of all the properties of a class. Now Gödel's result warns us that it may be rash even in theory. I say "may be rash" and not "is," because Gödel's result holds for mathematical systems; it requires, roughly, that the system shall have available an infinity of numbers. But I am now not convinced that this is a demand that we need make among the axioms of a natural science; and I therefore do not press the analogy further.

I have been speaking so far as if the scientist who wants to make a theory has a task no more difficult than Euclid when he wanted to draw up a set of axioms. But the world is not so simple. Euclid's axioms were really simple experiences in geometry; that is why for so long they were thought to be self-evident. When Euclid defined a point and a line, he was in no doubt how his reader would picture them. It is only in modern times that perverse mathematicians have remarked that it works equally well to make these words mean the opposite of what Euclid meant by them. But the natural scientist has never been in Euclid's happy state of simplicity. From early times, he has been aware that the entities which underlie any axiomatic treatment of nature are not at all immediate to the senses. How on earth did anyone ever come to think of atoms? Or of genes? How did anyone think of chemical structure?

I have never seen these questions put by philosophers of science. Yet they seem to me the fundamental questions to be asked of scientific method. Here is nature, a jumbled puzzle of substances. They all turn out to be assembled from ninety-two elementary substances. How did anyone get on to that particular key to the puzzle, or rather to those particular pieces in the jigsaw—and before that to the notion that it is a jigsaw?

I think that the key to these questions lies in the word "puzzle." From the outset, the Greek mathematicians and the Greek atomists approached nature with the notion that there is something to be learned: she has a meaning. This belief was largely lost in the Dark Ages, which saw matter as a perpetual accident, kept in place from moment to moment by a new act of grace. Natural science did not flourish again until men like Alberti and Leonardo were ravaged by a new hunger for meaning. Like the Greeks, they were convinced that nature has a message. What we have been doing ever since is to look for the code.

I use the word "code" designedly and literally. It was Leibniz who likened the unraveling of nature by science to the reading of a cryptogram. I am not sure that he himself saw how powerful and exact this analogy is. Take any of the practical examples which I have quoted. From the seventeenth century, apothecaries knew that if you treat common salt with oil of vitriol, you make spirits of salt and that aid to digestion which, in their enthusiasm for Dr. Glauber, they called *sal mirabile*. We should now write the process

$$2NaCl + H_2SO_4 \rightarrow Na_2SO_4 + 2HCl.$$

This statement is precisely the result of breaking down my sentence about making Glauber's salts, and a thousand other sentences for chemical reactions, into the elements of the code. We break it down into code letters: the word "elements" and the word "letters" are both exact descriptions.

Now go on to ask of the code why these letters are associated. Why does S so often go with O_4? Why does the letter H move about in so many of these messages? You are well on the way to another stop in decoding: the counting of the relative frequencies of letters and of groups of letters. This count directly gives the theory of valence.

Go further. Join to your count a like process carried out on sentences in which physicists record their experiments. Put it that these valences describe a structure: the structure of what we shall call atoms. The theory you now reach gives each atom a nucleus with electrons arranged round it in shells. The atoms are the letters S and O and H and the like, and you are doing nothing else than to break them down in turn. The alphabet of the new code no longer consists of ninety-two letters or elements, but only of two; a stroke / and a letter x, say. The stroke is the electron, and the number of strokes which you string out for each letter is characteristic of it: it is the atomic number of the element. The x at this stage is still an unknown and variable component, and it would be more just to write it frankly as a question mark. But in fact, in the last twenty years this stage has already been passed, and we can decode the variable x into constituent symbols to make the message clear. These symbols are a dash – for the proton and a dot · for the neutron.

In this symbolism, we have broken down the letters of our code message into three constituents. They now read –/ for H, –·–·–·–·–·–·–·–·//////// for O, and so on. When we have found this code, we see from the complete table (which includes the isotopes) that the number of dashes – is always equal to the number of strokes / so long as we stick to the nonionized state of the atoms. We therefore discard the strokes as redundant, as nuclear theory in fact does, and we are left with the dots · and the dashes –. We write – for H, –·–·–·–·–·–·–·–· for O, and so on.

You are so familiar with the facts which I have developed that to read them as a code may seem an artifice. Even as an artifice, I ought to remind you, it is powerful; Morse made telegraphy possible precisely because he grasped its power. But it is not an artifice. It is the fundamental approach of the scientist to the problems set by nature. Modern chemistry derives from the periodic table, and that, I insist, is the discovery of the code in which nature writes the messages which we call chemical processes. What was the state of chemistry when the reaction for making Glauber's salts could only be described in words? When Humphry Davy showed that muriatic acid is H and Cl, he was breaking down the code in which nature has written all her sentences about it. Until the code was broken, chemistry was simply incoherent.

The process of building a scientific system is an awkward one, in which it is much clearer what not to do than what to do. Even this morning I have had to spend time in such negative preliminaries. There is, in fact, only one positive procedure to be laid down. It is to treat the processes of nature as messages, and to look for the code which shall make them most meaningful or (what in this context is the same thing) most informative.

The brunt of my procedure is carried by the demand that the code shall make the messages as informative as possible. It is again characteristic of the awkwardness with which scientific procedure is treated that this demand is usually made in its negative form. Occam did not tell us what to do but what not to do: we were not to multiply hypotheses. But consider two alternative theories to account for a series of experiments. If the experiments are read as messages on the symbols and axioms of the two theories, then they have in each case a content of information of the form

$$-\sum p \log p,$$

where the ps are the probabilities that the symbols occur in their places by chance. The demand that we shall maximize their information content is therefore identical with the demand that we shall choose the less restrictive theory, that is, the theory in which the symbols have more free choices for their occurrence or behavior. And this is exactly Occam's razor.

In summary, then, our procedure is this. We regard nature as composed of processes (and not of single objects or events). We regard the sentences which describe these processes as written in code. The scientific procedure is to break down the code into its constituent symbols and their laws of arrangement. So far, this is essentially the procedure for setting up an axiomatic system. But we add to it the requirement that the code is to make nature as meaningful as possible. That is: science is formally the search for that code which shall maximize the information content of the messages which record the processes of nature.

Both observation and description are limited in their fineness, and this sets a limit to the process of decoding. We can liken this to the presence of a basic level of noise under the message. We ourselves provide a grosser element of random noise in practice by our experimental errors. But these limitations apart, we assume that nature writes her messages free from noise: nothing in her processes is arbitrary. And nothing in her processes is meaningless; if we could only read them, her messages are everywhere dense with information.

These assumptions incidentally dispose of the difficulty, which has troubled logicians since the time of Laplace, that no experiment seems to add much to the probability, or I prefer to say the assurance, with which we can entertain a scientific theory. On the contrary, a good experiment is a challenge to nature to opt between one of two messages. Think of the great critical experiments of history: the apocryphal experiment which Galileo is supposed to have made from the tower of Pisa, the discovery of Neptune, the interference of light, the Michelson and Morley experiment, the work of Mendel, the charting of blackbody radiation, the eclipse of 1919, the atomic pile, the search for Yukawa's mesons. They were as decisive as the discovery in a crossword that "bezique" crosses "syzygy" at the right point—a discovery whose information content we can calculate, and show to be large. On the interpretation of the scientific process which I am putting forward, the analogy with the crossword is indeed close, for there too the clues are written in code. What is more important, we see that there is no distinction (such as R. G. Collingwood imagined) between the physical sciences and those interlocking puzzle sciences like geology and paleontology and archeology.

There is one oddity which will have struck you already. A code message is a linear arrangement of its symbols. It offers, therefore, only one dimension of structure; and even the simple chemical compounds and their atoms which I have presented in code do not fit well into this. Is it really sensible to speak of a code when we want to symbolize, not the mere formula for salt, but its crystal structure?

We must here beware of a confusion. What I have called a code sentence or message does not describe an object or an event: it does not describe a fixed structure. Such objects or events, such structures, are to be incorporated in the symbols themselves, and the internal arrangement of parts in a code symbol or group of symbols can be given as many dimensions as we find necessary. The code groups have a function space of their own. *What the message represents is always a process.* It is a sentence which summarizes an experiment. That indeed has a dimension imposed on it: and the dimension is time. The formula which describes how you make Glauber's salts says what you do first and what happens then. This is what I have called the causal structure, in its widest meaning; and it underlies our code. The messages of nature have to be read in the direction of time which we experience.

This is a critical function of experiment. If we are only given a record of the past, we can order it on a rational theory. But we cannot tell whether in that theory time should run one way or the other, by anything within the record alone. The record might have been written backwards, as a book of code messages can be written and read backwards. What we must contribute is the decision which way the record shall read. We cannot make that decision without adding at least one experiment of our own to the record. This experiment has to fix the direction which nature imposes on living beings, as rectifiers of time.

I have presented an experiment as a message; and a theory as a code, ordered by time, which is to read in the record of experiments the most information. This puts the axiomatic method in its most powerful form. But it cannot make the method all-powerful. We have no reason to suppose that it is so.

The limitations of the axiomatic method lie plain in the procedure of decoding. We break the sentence into words, the word into letters, the letter into Morse code—and so on for so long as we choose. But that apparently is what we must choose; we cannot escape the piecemeal structure of language. Language is made to give information, and gives it in what information theory tartly calls "bits." This is therefore the way we get information from one another. But it also constrains us to look for knowledge in nature by the same process of taking her to pieces. For we do not analyze experiments; we decode the sentences which record them.

It is today familiar that the fine behavior of matter is ill described by metaphors such as "wave" and "particle" which we carry from the world of gross behavior. Every metaphor is too tempting; it drags its context with it; we cannot resist pushing it beyond its relevance, to ask "particle of what?" and "wave in what?" This difficulty is familiar. But the difficulty which I now raise is more radical. I am questioning the application to nature of the bit-by-bit structure of language itself.

With this question I must leave you. I do not pretend to know the answer to it; no one does. Yet it has already had an influence in science. The growing scope of field theories is one sign of that influence. Another is the formulation of those powerful grand laws which Edmund Whittaker calls postulates of impotence, such as the principle of relativity and the principle that perpetual motion is impossible. In genetics and elsewhere in biology, the piecemeal models begin to look very bare. And it is plain that quantum theory has long been a search for a description of events which is not written in dots and dashes.

These are transformations which scientists will reach for themselves. In sum, they may make a major transformation of scientific method. But I end with them for another reason. The method of atomic models, the search for codes, has won great success for science. But it has left it helpless to contribute to those experiences whose meaning is not assembled from pieces. A work of music is not a succession of notes, but the scientist, like the music-writer, is trained to see it so. This is what put Goethe and Blake in a rage with Newton. Concepts like honor and beauty are not unreal; they give order to a field of behavior just as firmly as do concepts like momentum and world-line. But they are not atomic concepts; they can neither be taken to pieces nor put together. They do not fit well into language. No one has discovered how they can be handled. But if science moves away from particulate models, it may be taking a step toward that discovery.

My subject has been classical, and many other writers on it have stimulated me to think further. I should like to acknowledge two who have done so particularly; they are Donald Williams and D. M. MacKay.

7
THE LOGIC OF THE MIND

A man of my preoccupations, that is, a practicing scientist with a passion for literature, is often asked to write about the relation of science to literature. But usually he is constrained, by the broad nature of his subject, to write in very general terms about the play of the human mind in experiment and invention, in logic and imagination. I feel no such constraint here. That gives me the chance to write more searchingly and, as it were, more professionally about my subject than usual; and I take that chance gratefully.

In 1965 I gave a series of lectures at the American Museum of Natural History in New York on science and literature as modes of knowledge, which were published as a book under the title *The Identity of Man*. There are a few places here and there in the book (I think I count four) where I should have liked to speak more fully and more circumstantially, had I been speaking to a professional audience. I shall single out one of these places, which sketches what may be called the machinery of the mind, and make it the occasion for a larger analysis here. I hope to develop the others on other occasions.

The mind is an elusive entity, whose workings are not wholly confined within the brain. But because I am looking at the logical processes of the mind, it is fair that I concentrate in the first place on the brain as the organ in which these processes must be mechanized. The subject of how the mind works as a mechanism, what machinery we can imagine to operate within the brain, has its intrinsic interest in any case. We know that the brain is made of the same stuff as the rest of nature, and its atoms must therefore obey the same natural laws as other atoms do. In that sense, then, it is tempting and even reasonable to say that the brain must be some kind of a machine. But alas, to use the word "machine" in this catchall sense misses the crux of the question. The real question about the human mind lies deeper: it asks, Is the brain a machine with a formal procedure of any kind that we can now conceive? Let me quote a pertinent passage from *The Identity of Man*:

A machine is not merely a whirring train of gears or a humming set of electric circuits. These happy, busy strings of hardware are only the middle step, the visible link, in a procedure which has three steps, and to which the other two are as integral as this is. The machine is the procedure, and the whole procedure, all three steps of it. The first step is the instruction or input, which is the modern form of the button that starts the machine: and which must itself be precise and mechanical, an unequivocal set of holes or marks on a tape that directs the machine into one branch of its network of possible paths. Then comes the physical machinery which obediently carries out the instructions and turns them into actions. And the third step is the result or output, which is equally decisive and definite: in a computer, it is another set of holes or marks on a tape.

It is of cardinal importance here, and essential to my description, that the output from a machine must be exact and unambiguous as the input is. For a modern machine, like a man, is asked in part to regulate itself, and for this purpose it must be able to instruct itself. Such a machine, or a man, must be able to feed its output back into itself as a new instruction. Its output must therefore be as sharp, within the tolerance of the machine, as capable of symbolic expression, as well defined and as single-minded as its input.

Our field of inquiry is the grey region between the input to the brain and the output from it; that is, between the information that the senses send to the brain and the instructions or other decisions that issue from it. In this grey region, the brain manipulates the input and draws conclusions from it. During this process, the brain presumably uses some symbolism which translates and codifies its conceptions of the outside world. We do not know what this symbolic language is, but if it is indeed to be mechanical (on any system that we understand), its units must consist of configurations of atoms, and of changes in these configurations which are displayed as electrical signals. If, then, the brain reasons like a logical machine, these signs or units which it employs in its reasoning must constitute a formal language or series of languages which follow precise rules, just like the language of symbols in which we write out logical and mathematical arguments. The brain cannot be a machine in any sense that we understand unless its language is as strict and as artificial (in the logical sense) as any of our own marks on a magnetic tape.

The symbols with which the brain works, its language (or successive languages), are physical, chemical, and electrical. But this makes them no different from marks on a paper or on a tape. Provided that they are exact, and are always translated exactly in the same way, they constitute a formal logical language. What is to be said about them then, comes not from physics and chemistry and biology, but from symbolic logic. This is why I, a mathematician, presume to talk about it to physicists and chemists and specialists in biology.

We know a good deal now about symbolic languages and the logical procedures that they can express which was not known when I took the Mathematical Tripos at Cambridge in 1930. There were two of us who offered what was called Mathematical Philosophy that summer: Max Black and I. The man who had lectured to us had been the prodigious, prodigal Frank Ramsey. But he had died early that year, a month before his twenty-seventh birthday, and I imagine (though I cannot be sure) that we were examined in his place by his friend Richard Braithwaite. Whoever the examiner was, he blandly asked us on one of our papers to discuss the *Entscheidungsproblem*.

The *Entscheidungsproblem*, the problem of decision, was a startling question which David Hilbert had posed: whether it is self-evident—whether indeed it can be shown—that all mathematical assertions which make sense can necessarily be proved to be either true or false. The question had gone unanswered for a long time, and neither Max Black nor I was likely to settle it at short notice in an afternoon. I no longer remember what general arguments I produced in the examination room for and against the disputed possibility. For history caught up with us and our examiner in a spectacular way, ironically within a year.

Most professional scientists now know what happened. In 1931 a young Austrian mathematician, Kurt Gödel, proved two remarkable and remarkably unwelcome theorems. The first theorem says that any logical system which is not excessively simple (that is, which at least includes ordinary arithmetic) can express true assertions which nevertheless cannot be deduced from its axioms. And the second theorem says that the axioms in such a system, with or without additional truths, cannot be shown in advance to be free from hidden contradictions. In short, a logical system which has any richness can never be complete, yet cannot be guaranteed to be consistent.

That was in 1931. In the next few years, other unpleasant theorems were established. A. M. Turing in England and Alonzo Church in America showed that no mechanical procedure can be devised which could test every assertion in a logical system and in a finite number of steps demonstrate it to be either true or false. This is Hilbert's *Entscheidungsproblem* in its direct form. In a sense, Gödel's result is deeper than this; and Alfred Tarski in Poland proved an even deeper limitation of logic. Tarski showed that there can be no precise language which is universal; every formal language which is at least as rich as arithmetic contains meaningful sentences that cannot be asserted to be either true or false.

In order to leave no room for doubt, let me linger on the essential content of these extraordinary and far-reaching theorems. They are theorems in mathematical logic, and in one sense the mathematics cannot be removed from them. That is to say, any logical system to which they apply must include the arithmetic of whole numbers as a basic and distinguishable part. But with this proviso, to which I shall return, they apply to any system of thought which attempts to set up a basis of fundamental axioms and then to match the world by making deductions from them in an exact language—the language of physics, for example, or the chemical language inside the brain.

Such a system of axioms has always been thought to be the ideal model for which all science strives. Indeed, it could be said that theoretical science is the attempt to uncover an ultimate and comprehensive set of axioms (including mathematical rules) from which all the phenomena of the world could be shown to follow by deductive steps. But the results that I have quoted, and specifically the theorems of Gödel and of Tarski, make it evident that this ideal is hopeless. For they show that every axiomatic system of any mathematical richness is subject to severe limitations, whose incidence cannot be foreseen and yet which cannot be circumvented. In the first place, not all sensible assertions in the language of the system can be deduced (or disproved) from the axioms: no set of axioms can be complete. And in the second place, an axiomatic system can never be guaranteed to be consistent: any day, some flagrant and irreconcilable contradiction may turn up in it. An axiomatic system cannot be made to generate a description of the world which matches it fully, point for point; either at some points there will be holes which cannot be filled in by deduction, or at other points two opposite deductions will turn up. And when a contradiction does turn up, the system becomes capable of proving *anything*, and no longer distinguishes true from false. That is, only an axiom which introduces a contradiction can make a system complete, by making it completely useless.

The implications of these results for any theory of knowledge have long been stressed, for example by Rudolf Carnap and by Karl Popper. But in addition I am stressing here, as I have done before (in *The Common Sense of Science* in 1951), their implications for empirical science. For I believe that any exact science must include in its system the axioms of arithmetic, in the form of procedures which require us to distinguish all the whole numbers. For example, if we seek to reduce all the sciences to physics, then we shall need the theory of groups and the statistics of assemblies of particles; and both these operations are subject to Gödel's theorems. In the same way, the statistical limitations on the recurrence of physical systems which Henri Poincaré first demonstrated in ergodic theory are, in my view, another expression of Turing's and Church's theorem that it is impossible to decide for every instance whether it is a consequence of the axioms. And finally, Tarski's theorem demonstrates, I think conclusively, that there cannot be a universal description of nature in a single, closed, consistent language.

I hold, therefore, that the logical theorems reach decisively into the systematization of empirical science. It follows in my view that the unwritten aim that the physical sciences have set themselves since Isaac Newton's time cannot be attained. The laws of nature cannot be formulated as an axiomatic, deductive, formal, and unambiguous system which is also complete. And if at any stage in scientific discovery the laws of nature did seem to make a complete system, then we should have to conclude that we had not got them right. Nature cannot be represented in the form of what logicians now call a Turing machine—that is, a logical machine operating on a basic set of axioms by making formal deductions from them in an exact language. There is no perfect description conceivable, even in the abstract, in the form of an axiomatic and deductive system.

Of course, we suppose nevertheless that nature does obey a set of laws of her own which are precise, complete, and consistent. But if this is so, then their inner formulation must be of some kind quite different from any that we know; and at present, we have no idea how to conceive it. Any description in our present formalisms must be incomplete, not because of the obduracy of nature, but because of the limitation of language as we use it. And this limitation lies not in the human fallibility of language, but on the contrary in its logical insufficiency.

This is a cardinal point: it is the language that we use in describing nature that imposes (by its arrangement of definitions and axioms) both the form and the limitations of the laws that we find. For example, it may be held that if we can remove the arithmetic from physics, we may yet get an axiomatic system which is complete and consistent. I do not share this view, but it is arguable; yet it does not seem to me to bear in fact on our present formulation of the laws of nature. On present evidence, we must conclude (in my view) that the human mind is constrained to conceive physical laws in arithmetical language: the whole numbers are literally an integral part of its conceptual apparatus. If this is so, then the mind cannot extricate the laws of nature from its own language; our formal logic is not that of nature; and we are not at all, as Leibniz and others have thought, in a preestablished harmony with the language of nature. For it is then not true (As Leopold Kronecker proposed in a famous aphorism) that "die ganzen Zahlen hat Gott geschaffen—alles andere ist

Menschenwerk." On the contrary, the whole numbers are then exactly what man has imposed on God or nature, either as our mode of perception or of conceptualization. (And I ought to add that, with the whole numbers, man has also imported the fundamental theorem of arithmetic, which says that a whole number can be decomposed into prime factors in only one way. It is not clear that Gödel's construction could be made to work in a field of numbers which did not obey this fundamental theorem.)

Every scientific system as we understand that phrase now is incomplete: simply as a logical machine, it cannot cover all the phenomena of nature. It therefore follows, not merely in practice but in principle, that the system must be enlarged from time to time by the addition of new axioms, which cannot, however, be foreseen or proved to be free from contradictions. How does the outstanding scientist come to propose such a decisive axiom, while less imaginative minds go on tinkering with the old system? How did Gregor Mendel leap to conceive the statistical axioms of genetics? What moved Albert Einstein to make the constancy of the speed of light not a consequence but an axiom in the construction of relativity?

An obvious answer is that the great mind, like the small, experiments with different alternatives, works out their consequences for some distance, and thereupon guesses (much like a chessplayer) that one move will generate richer possibilities than the rest. But this answer only shifts the question from one foot to the other. It still remains to ask how the great mind comes to guess better than another, and to make leaps that turn out to lead further and deeper than yours or mine.

We do not know; and there is no logical way in which we can know, or can formalize the pregnant decision. The step by which a new axiom is added cannot itself be mechanized. It is a free play of the mind, an invention outside the logical processes. This is the central act of imagination in science, and it is in all respects like any similar act in literature; it can, in fact, be taken as a definition of imagination. In this respect, science and literature are alike: in both of them, the mind decides to enrich the system as it stands by an addition which is made by an unmechanical act of free choice.

As for the invention that is added, the new relation in science or the imaginative shift of vision in literature, its birth is always the same. It begins in the multiple meanings and overtones, the hidden ambiguities, which human language contains in spite of our best efforts to make it sharp. The language of thought consists for the most part of general words, and although such a work may be as matter of fact as "parallel," as solid as as "mass," or as down to earth as "table," there is always about it a penumbra of uncertainty and ambivalence from which new relations may suddenly become apparent. "Parallel" may become the beginning for non-Euclidean geometries, and "mass" may become equivalent to energy, for the universal reason that even a "table" cannot be defined in terms which allow us to say with absolute decision of every object in the universe that it is either a table or not a table. Frank Ramsey, of whom I spoke earlier, proved that this is an indispensable factor in the development of any science; and in this important sense, he anticipated some of the implications of Gödel.

It is characteristic of human language that it is made up of past metaphors and analogies, and they are a fertile ground for the exploration of ambiguity and the discovery of hidden likenesses. Here begin the unexpected links and conjunctions which literature (and all art) constantly produces; and the inventive ideas of science begin here too.

As to how these ambivalences are developed in science and in literature, that is the theme of *The Identity of Man*, and I can only summarize it here. In science, the aim is to disentangle each ambiguity, and to force nature to decide between the alternatives by a critical experiment. In this way, we progress in science (as it were) by turning the information from nature through the logical machine of the brain into an effective tape instruction. In literature, the ambiguities are not resolved, and the brain works or plays with the information without ever turning it into a machine instruction. But in both, the new invention is taken by the same kind of step, and at the moment when the step is taken, we are in no logical system: we have left one system and are about to enter and form the other, and are in a no-man's-land outside logic.

The first half of my theme, which I have now completed, has consisted of theorems in mathematical logic and their application first to the language of science and then, incidentally, to literature. What I have shown there, the surprising demand that they imply for a kindred imagination in both, is unsettling, of course, and awkward, because this is not at all how we wanted the grand panorama of knowledge to look. But there it is, we must come to terms with it; and so far, I have simply displayed what the terms are, as a matter of fact.

Now I turn to the second part of my theme, to discuss a sharply different aspect of the same problem. I shall still be concerned with these maverick theorems in logic, but with something else about them: not so much with their existence and implications as with their origin. For there is a common source from which all these theorems spring, and it is uncommonly interesting and revealing.

Specifically, the two theorems of Gödel, the theorems of Turing and Church, and Tarski's theorem say different things. Each of them establishes some limitation on a logical system, either on its completeness or its consistency, and these limitations are not quite the same. Yet they do form a common family of limitations, and this is because they all arise from a common difficulty in all symbolic language. The difficulty is that the language can be used to describe not only parts of the world, but also parts of the language itself. In each of them, the proof hinges on a construction by which a proposition *about* arithmetic is expressed as a proposition *in* arithmetic.

Many logical problems grow from this common root, namely that the range of reference of any reasonably rich system necessarily includes reference to itself. This creates an endless regress, an infinite hall of mirrors of self-reflection. And the regress comes sharply to a focus in all the paradoxes of logic, which are cousins of one sort or another to the classical contradiction that the Greeks knew: what they called the Cretan paradox. This is the contradiction implied by the statement of Epimenides the Cretan that all Cretans are liars.

There are many modern forms of this and its related paradoxes. One form is Bertrand Russell's definition of the class of all classes that are not members of themselves. Another is the paradox of Jules Richard, which (roughly) gives this a numerical dress: Gödel constructed his theorems on this pattern. Perhaps the punning, linguistic quality of these contradictions, their oddly literary playfulness, is best displayed by a remark in the same vein by Groucho Marx, who said that he would not think of belonging to a club that was willing to have him for a member. Yet these are not trivial matters: they face us whenever we contrast rules and exceptions, tolerance and intolerance, and all the human issues which join and divide us in argument at the same time.

The mathematical paradoxes, and the devices derived from them that Gödel and others exploited for their theorems, all have the same feature: they depend on the use of concepts whose range of reference includes the concept itself. In short, the model for them all is the Cretan paradox, the simple sentence, "What I am now saying is not true." This is obviously a self-contradiction: if the assertion is true, then by its own evidence it is not true; and if the assertion is false, then that tells us that what is being said must be true.

Bertrand Russell tried (with Alfred North Whitehead in the *Principia Mathematica*) to untie the knot in this kind of paradox, and to put an end to the infinite regress of assertions about assertions, by constructing a theory of types. This was intended to prevent us from using the same language to discuss our language as we use to discuss the things that the language names. A hierarchy of types was created, starting with simple sentences about things, going on to sentences about sentences which are themselves about sentences about things, and so on. No one could look on this infinite construction with anything but a suspicious eye, and so it turned out; the theory of types is an unhappy artifice. If as human beings we want to use human language, then we must accept that a part of its richness is in its capacity to refer to itself.

I stress, in what I have just said, the word "human." Animals use language to signal to one another, and what they have to say essentially refers to states of affairs (factual or emotional) and to nothing else. Such a language has no problems of self-reference: it is intended to pass information from one animal to another, directly and unequivocally as an instruction. In this sense, René Descartes was right to say that animals are machines and human beings are not. Human language is richer precisely because we think about ourselves. We cannot eliminate self-reference from human language without thereby turning it from a genuine language of information into a machine language of instructions.

In particular, all philosophy and epistemology operates by its nature within the field where the difficulties lie, the field of self-reference. I mean by self-reference the construction of sentences, in thought or in speech, whose range of application includes that very kind of sentence. On this definition, "I am hungry" contains no self-reference, but "I am troubled" does. All thinking about thinking implies self-reference: the first statement of principle in the philosophy of Descartes, *Cogito ergo sum*, refers to itself. It is this very cogitation, or the class of cogitations that includes it, which gives the speaker the right to assert that he is cogitating. Philosophy is not possible without the regress of cogitation about cogitation. Whatever could be thought by machines, philosophy certainly could not. Indeed, on my view of human language, philosophy could not even be thought about by animals.

It is clear enough that statements in philosophy are, by their nature, often dogged by self-reference, and that philosophy as a discipline is therefore limited even more severely than science by the logical gaps that the theorems of Gödel and Tarski have laid bare. In mathematics and science, it is a surprise to find oneself bounded by these theorems; it is not at all obvious, and indeed is unexpected, to learn that mathematical and scientific statements cannot be wholly cleared of self-reference (or of some equivalent recursive regress). But it is evident from the outset that philosophy is full of self-references, and therefore that, if the breakdown in the machinery of logic has its origin in self-reference, then philosophy is surely subject to it. Indeed it is clear that, while mathematics and science are subject to it only from time to time, when a new step has to be taken, philosophy is subject to it severely and constantly—because self-reference is built into its very method.

In the same way, we can see at once why psychology and psychoanalysis, regarded as sciences, are most severely subject to the theorems of logical limitation. There was a time when no clear boundary was drawn between philosophy and psychology; Thomas Hobbes, John Locke, and David Hume all wrote philosophy much of which was a study of the mind, and was, for its age, a form of psychology. Now that psychology has entered into less conscious fields of the mind, the logical problems that are created by self-reference are very patent. Many natural scientists complain that psychology, and other studies of human thought and behavior, lack the rigor of a true science. This is usually excused on the ground that such human studies are young, and have not yet developed the proper formal apparatus by which information can be turned into exact prediction. But I suggest that the logical theorems now show us that this excuse is mistaken. There is an essential difficulty in casting these disciplines into an axiomatic system; they are limited, more severely and more constantly than the natural sciences, by the self-reference that underlies them everywhere. And it cannot be got out of the system by the occasional addition of a new axiom, as in the natural sciences. The axiomatic method as such may be unworkable in these studies, and whatever machinery is discovered for them in the future will (I think) not be of this traditional kind.

This is illustrated by Karl Popper's account of how he became disillusioned with the psychoanalytic explanations of Sigmund Freud and Alfred Adler. In natural science, remarked Popper, a theory is expected to make a prediction, and one prediction only, about the outcome of an experiment; and it is discarded if this forecast is not fulfilled in the experiment. But the theories of psychoanalysis are not of this kind at all; as Popper found, they are constantly explaining that my neighbor on the right is polite because he has an inferiority complex, and my neighbor on the left is rude because he has an inferiority complex. If, therefore, I turn the concept of the inferiority complex around, I get the unhelpful prediction that it may cause my neighbors either to be polite or to be rude. This is not what we expect of a scientific theory. And indeed it is not: all arguments derived from Freud's invention of the unconscious have this paradoxical content, precisely because their use of self-reference creates paradoxes. The Cretan who said that all Cretans are liars was talking a classical form of the language in which the psychoanalyst frames such concepts as the unconscious and its inferiority complex. If he had lived not in Crete but in Vienna, he would have said that all Viennese have inferiority complexes.

Beyond these borderline fields stands, full face, the particular interest to which I am drawn: the art of literature. A work of literature is in the first place a description or a story: William Wordsworth's poem "The Daffodils" is a description, and the *Oedipus Rex* of Sophocles is a story. Neither a description nor a story need contain any overt self-references. For example, the description of my interests and the story of my career are neutral accounts which do not demand that you involve yourself in them by referring any part of them to yourself. Unhappily, when that has been said about his description and this story, nothing at all has been said either about "The Daffodils" or about the *Oedipus Rex*. Yes, it is possible to have descriptions and stories whose content does not draw us into them, and in which our minds do not reflect on themselves. But such accounts simply do not have the power of Wordsworth and Sophocles. Neither, I am afraid, will they have their immortality.

From these simple examples it is at once clear that literature is literature only when it demands and commands our personal involvement. It is insistent because it insists that the bland descriptions of flowers and the remote *Police Gazette* records of incest and suicide concern us. They become part of us and we of them, they draw us to the human race and the human condition, and they make us one with Wordsworth on his couch and Jocasta in her bed and the plague-racked men of Thebes all over the world.

What is true of literature is true of every art. The work of art is a constructed thing, and is so even when it happens to have been found in nature in the form into which we now read a human meaning. It has been made in essence, its meaning has been created, by a human being: it expresses his vision of the relation between man and nature, and it invites us not to like it or to dislike it but to be drawn into it. The work of art compels us (when it is compelling) to look at the world with it, and to look through it into the mind of its maker. We cannot dissociate the work from its origin, which is to be a made thing—a thing made by a man which expresses how the man sees himself in the world. It interests us only as it engages us, and asks us to see ourselves in the same world also. Although what is expressed in the work is another man's self, the reference is to ourselves because the reference is universally to the human self.

Let me be explicit in my meaning here. I am not merely remarking that there is self-reference in the moral reflections of the Greek chorus, or in the reflections, "in vacant or in pensive mood," that fill Wordsworth's inward eye in solitude. These are only of the same kind as the reflections of Descartes in philosophy and of an analyst interpreting dreams. But the self-references of literature, and of art in general, go deeper than these formal thoughts. My argument is that literature is composed essentially of self-reference, and takes its life from the dual tension between watching our own minds from the inside and watching someone else's from the outside. And this is one of the classical paradoxes in the theory of knowledge, how and when we know that others do indeed feel as we do, which Ludwig Wittgenstein, for example, discussed in the *Blue Book* long before I discussed it in *The Identity of Man*.

The force and meaning of literature is to present the lives of others to us in such a way that we recognize ourselves in them, and live them from the outside and from the inside together. We do not understand Wordsworth unless our heart also turns over at the golden host, and the tragedy of Oedipus differs from the gunplay in the Sunday paper only if we recognize ourselves in the characters. We have to see that Oedipus is us, capable of killing a stranger at the crossroads and blundering into a labyrinth of horror. We have to see that Jocasta is us, longing for the lost youth who so transparently is a part of herself in both senses: the son who is also the symbol of her own youth, that she longs to recapture and sense again in her leaping womb. And when we recognize that in Jocasta and in ourselves, it is more tender, more heart-breaking, more deeply human than the explanations of psychoanalysis. Of course Freud was right about the Oedipus complex; but Sophocles wakes deeper echoes than Freud, because he brings home to us the longing of Jocasta for herself—the self that she was and the self that she gave birth to—in the same hushed breath with the familiar and familial jealousy of Oedipus.

Literature and art live by, they come alive in, the sense of our own self stretching into the actions and disasters of someone else's self, and thereby mapping the human self as a whole. This is how I put this part of my theme in *The Identity of Man*:

> I hold that each man has a self, and enlarges his self by his experiences. That is, he learns from experience: from the experiences of others as well as his own, and from their inner experiences as well as their outer. But he can learn from their inner experience only by entering it, and that is not done merely by reading a written record of it. We must have the gift to identify ourselves with other men, to relive their experience and to feel its conflicts as our own. And the conflicts are the essence of the experience. We gain knowledge of our selves by identifying ourselves with others, but that is not enough—that only gives us the fantasies of sex and the parodies of power, the absurd strutting daydreams of Secret Agent 007 and *Butterfield 8*. We must enter others in order to share their conflicts, and they must be shown to have grave conflicts, in order that we shall feel in their lives what we know in our own: the human dilemma. The knowledge of self cannot be formalized because it cannot be closed, even provisionally; it is perpetually open, because the dilemma is perpetually unresolved.

Let me recapitulate the steps in my argument. I treated my theme in two parts: the first was concerned in the main with science, and the second with literature. In both parts, I was at pains to show that the brain as a machine is certainly not the kind of machine that we understand now. It is not a logical machine, because no logical machine can reach out of the difficulties and paradoxes created by self-reference. The logic of the mind differs from formal logic in its ability to overcome and indeed to exploit the ambivalences of self-reference, so that they become the instruments of imagination.

In the first half of my theme, I explained the limitations (they derive from self-reference) which circumscribe any axiomatic and deductive system of a reasonable richness, in mathematics and (I hold) in the natural sciences. The logical theorems which I quoted and explained show that this must be so, and they also show how these logical gaps have to be filled, and new theorems incorporated as added axioms in a system, at each step. The decision to take new matter into our systems, in science or in literature, has no analogue in any logical machine. It is an imaginative step of a kind that we do not understand, but that we can watch in the work of a great scientist or a great writer; and it is alike in science and in literature.

The second part of my theme goes further. Here I pointed out that human language, when it is specifically human, and is concerned with reflection and judgment about our own lives, is necessarily full of self-references. This is clear in philosophy and in psychology. But it reaches deeper in literature, because the essence of literature (and of all art) lies in the identification of ourselves with other human beings whose actions we are watching and judging as if they were our own. Here the self-reference is so integral that we cannot construct any of the provisional systems with which mathematics and science make do for a time, and which they then mend when the need arises.

In literature, there is no provisional description which can take the place of the work itself. We cannot replace it, as in science, by an axiomatic system which will do until it turns out to fall short and has to be enlarged. The references in literature by the writer to himself and others, and by the reader to himself in what he reads, penetrate the work through and through; and there is no way of getting around Gödel's theorems and Tarski's theorem and the others by any step-by-step procedure. In this respect, science and literature are different.

Neither science nor literature ever gives a complete account of nature or of life. In both of them, the progress from the present account to the next account is made by the exploration of the ambiguities in the language that we use at this moment. In science, these ambiguities are resolved for the time being, and a system without ambiguity is built up provisionally, until it is shown to fall short. This is why the results of science at any given moment can be presented on an axiomatic and deductive machine, although nature as a whole can never be so presented because no such machine can be complete. Whatever kind of machine nature is, it is different from this.

But in literature, the ambiguities cannot be resolved even for the time being, and no provisional system of axioms can be set up to describe the human situation as the writer and the reader seek to see it together. Here the brain cannot act as a logical machine even for the time being, by which I mean that it cannot take in the information, sort out its ambiguities, and turn it into unambiguous instructions. That is not what a work of art does to us, and we cannot derive such instructions from it. I will quote at the last the passage from *The Identity of Man* of which, as I promised at the beginning, this essay is a detailed exposition. It states for the machinery of the brain the same limitations that I have exhibited here in my account of the machinery of nature:

> I am asserting that there is a mode of knowledge which cannot be spelled out formally to direct a machine. It may be asked, Any machine? If this is a question in the present, then the answer is Yes. For example, we know (from the work of Kurt Gödel and A. M. Turing) that no machine that uses strict logic can examine its own instructions and prove them consistent. But if it is a question about the measureless future, then it cannot be answered. A machine is not a natural object; it is a human artifact which mimics and exploits our own understanding of nature; and we cannot foresee how radically we may come to change that understanding. We cannot foresee and we cannot conceive all

possible machines—if indeed the word *all* has a meaning in this sentence. All that we can say, and all that I can assert, is that we cannot now conceive any kind of law or machine which could formalize the total modes of human knowledge.

There is, however, one respect in which my exposition now goes radically beyond this passage, not merely in detail but in substance. That is in tracing the common quality of imagination in science and in literature to the logic of self-reference; and in showing that, within this common quality, the difference of mode between science and literature reflects the different extent to which self-reference enters their languages.

8
HUMANISM AND THE GROWTH OF KNOWLEDGE

One of the pleasures of writing an essay of retrospect and appreciation is that it makes an occasion to read afresh the books that one has been taking for granted for many years. So I have been reading again in a leisurely way *The Logic of Scientific Discovery*, which in one form or another is now well over thirty years old. I could not have found a more delightful task; the book reads as freshly today, and strikes as deeply and as directly, as when I first held it in my hand. There cannot be many books, at least in philosophy, which begin to become classics while they still surprise the reader with an unforced air of exhilaration and intellectual urgency. The only thing that makes *The Logic of Scientific Discovery* more pedestrian now than it was thirty years ago is the weight of notes and appendices that has been added; it was livelier to read, and more challenging to the reader, before it was cushioned in an apparatus half as long (and twice as solemn) as the text itself.

Before I review the content of *The Logic of Scientific Discovery* I ought to recall something of the setting of the 1930s in which the book appeared. The climate of the time in England (where I had just finished college) is still vivid to me—both the philosophical climate and the political climate. What Karl Popper had to say was very timely, because it came when the climate was changing, and it helped to change it; we were conscious of that at the time, in philosophy as well as in politics. Let me begin with the climate then.

In 1930 the model of the philosophical method in Cambridge was still the *Principia Mathematica* by Alfred North Whitehead and Bertrand Russell, and the *Tractatus Logico-Philosophicus* by Ludwig Wittgenstein. That is, the main current of English philosophy was indeed preoccupied (as it had always been) with the problems of science; and it was then convinced that the empirical content of science could be expressed in the formulas of classical mathematics, and would therefore be arranged ultimately in a closed system of axioms like the *Principia*—or like the system of Spinoza, on whose *Tractatus Theologico-Politicus* Wittgenstein had modeled his title. The final task of philosophy in science would be to establish a universal system of axioms from which all the phenomena of nature could be derived.

There were, of course, a number of grounds for suspecting even then that this program took too rigid a view of the machinery of nature. In the first place, it was already doubtful whether mathematics could be made quite as tidy as Whitehead and Russell had tried. Jan Brouwer long ago had thrown doubt on their approach to mathematics; and though he was shrugged off as a maverick, the doubt remained. Now David Hilbert had posed some unexpected and awkward questions, among which the *Entscheidungsproblem* in particular gave signs that it might become very uncomfortable. And so it turned out quite soon, when first Kurt Gödel in Vienna in 1931 and then A. M. Turing in Cambridge in 1936 proved what Hilbert had suspected, that even arithmetic could not be contained in a closed system of the kind that science was supposed to be looking for.

In the second place, it seemed perverse to lay down grand rules for the conduct of science and (by implication) of nature, at the very time when physicists were discovering every day that the traditional forms of natural law would not fit their findings. Physics on the atomic scale was manifestly in flux—a flux of concepts as much as of models. Louis de Broglie and Max Born were trying to reconcile the particulate properties of electrons with their wavelike behavior. Erwin Schrödinger and Paul Dirac were creating wave mechanics. Wolfgang Pauli had enunciated the exclusion principle for some particles, Bose-Einstein statistics had been proposed for others, liquid helium was displaying its first disconcerting properties, and Werner Heisenberg had recently announced the principle of uncertainty. In such busy times, it was natural to speculate about the laws of nature, but it was peculiarly unlikely that a universal formula would be found for them. Most scientists felt in 1930 that philosophers had just caught up with nineteenth-century physics, and were trying to make it the model for all knowledge, at the very moment when physicists had painfully discovered its shortcomings. (In the same way, biologists feel today that philosophers have at last understood quantum physics, and are anxious to make it the model for all processes in nature, just when the problems of method and concept in science are shifting to biology.)

In the third place, there were doubts even among philosophers whether the entities of empirical science could be formalized as rigidly as had been supposed. Russell had made it fashionable to define the number 2 as the class of all pairs; but could such logical and, so to say, operational constructions also suffice to define the units which we suppose to underlie the mechanics of nature? Could the electron really be treated with resolute punctilio as the class of all the observations from which its properties (and therefore its existence) were inferred, as a shorthand of organization? Does not this form of scientific behaviorism close the door to speculation, and (as it were) forbid us in advance to find unexpected extensions to the concept of an electron? Frank Ramsey who had been my teacher, and who died in 1930 before he was twenty-seven, had shown that this was indeed so: if the inferred units of a science are all defined as logical constructions, then the system which connects them cannot accommodate any new relations between them. In a less exact way, many young scientists felt that logical positivism was trying to make a closed system of science, when to them the charm and the adventure of science was that it was perpetually open.

But the first place, and the second place, and the third place too, had no influence at all on the program that philosophers of science doggedly went on following after 1930. Percy Bridgman as the apostle of operationalism, and Rudolf Carnap as the St. Paul among the survivors of the Vienna Circle, still planned a millennium in which everything worth saying would be reduced to positive matters of fact, in a universal language of science that had been scrubbed clean of all ambiguities. Carnap in particular left no doubt that (like Wittgenstein at the opening of the *Tractatus*) he thought of the world as a collection of facts, he thought of science as the description of these facts, and he thought that the ideal description would specify the coordinates in space and time of every factual event. Since this is essentially the plan that Pierre Laplace had made famous and infamous more than a hundred years before, it is not surprising that young scientists were indifferent to philosophy, and regarded it (for all its talk about probability) as solidly stuck in the last century.

The political climate among English scientists in 1930 and the following years, which is also relevant to my history, had some of the same sense of disappointment and impatience. There had been a time when Cambridge philosophers had set a standard of high liberal conscience which had inspired their students: G. E. Moore had done so in his writing and teaching, and Bertrand Russell in his unswerving conduct as a pacifist. But that had been in another age, almost in another world, which had run out a decade before. Now the world of 1930 was deep in economic depression; England had two million unemployed; in Europe private armies were sniping in the streets; and all the starched phrases about personal freedom and humane values were becoming more unreal every day. It was a time when young men knew in their bones that politics could no longer be left to gentlemen, or to mobs either, and that they would have to commit themselves to some canons of social right and wrong. To be told that nowadays philosophy did not trade in these chattels, that logical analysis offered no guide to conduct or even to conscience, and that any prescription for them was strictly nonsense, did not heighten the respect of working scientists for the philosophers of science. Scientists were actively trying to break out from the aura of impersonality and even inhumanity with which tradition had hallowed their work and awed the public. And here they were to be herded back to the ancient postures, because philosophers were trying to construct a system of science which positively aspired to be impersonal and inhuman.

Since young men yearn for a philosophy, most of the young scientists at Cambridge turned to dialectical materialism. This is really too grand a name to give to their new beliefs, which were rather what William Blake long ago called "a refuge from unbelief—from Bacon, Newton and Locke." They were looking for some coherent ground on which to build a consistent code of personal actions in face of a mounting set of social disasters—the Wall Street crash, the hunger marches, war in Manchuria, the rise of Hitler, Stalin's crusade against Trotsky, the civil war in Spain, the *Anschluss* with Austria, and the surrender of the Sudetenland.

I ought to quote a characteristic instance, and I will choose one which surprised me at the time. Wittgenstein had come back to Cambridge in 1929, and at first many scientists went to his lectures. But after a while it became plain the he was no longer tackling the systematic problems of the *Tractatus*. Instead, his lectures turned literally into what he called them, a language game, which seemed to us more and more formless and devoid of method. One of the best of the philosophy students who remained loyal to him was Maurice Cornforth, and he seemed to be chosen by Wittgenstein to become his future spokesman and interpreter. But then Cornforth broke with Wittgenstein abruptly and became a Marxist. This was the most dramatic and (it was said) violent desertion from the camp of philosophic contemplation in Cambridge. The break had almost a symbolic quality; from now on the followers of Wittgenstein took little interest in science. When Maurice Cornforth wrote a book of philosophy many years later, he called it *Science versus Idealism*, and aimed it specifically at Wittgenstein and Carnap as the two Janus faces of idealism.

Of course none of us supposed that philosophers were indifferent to tyranny, or to the fate of those whom it threatened. After war broke out in 1939 Wittgenstein went from Cambridge to work as an orderly in Guy's Hospital in London. But that was not the light that we looked for from philosophy. We did not ask philosophers to be martyrs, or to seek purification (as T. E. Lawrence of Arabia had done) in manual labor and monastic anonymity. We wanted philosophy to be engaged in the living world, and we were shocked that we got no human gesture from the philosophers of science: no sign that philosophy and science might express more of man than his rational intellect alone.

Instead, the works that brought science to life for us came from history. An essay by a Russian, B. Hessen, called "The Social and

Economic Roots of Newton's *Principia*" opened our eyes to a new view of science. Although it patently overstated its case, its effect on young scientists and philosophers alike was electric. From that time, the history and philosophy of science came to be spoken of in one phrase, almost as a single subject. The Chichele Professor of Economic History at Oxford, G. N. Clark, replied to Hessen in 1937 in a book called *Science and Social Welfare in the Age of Newton*; yet the very form of the title shows that science was now acknowledged to have social roots. The most influential book published in England came at the end of the decade, and was boldly called *The Social Function of Science*. Much of its influence (and its merit) certainly derived from the fact that its author, Desmond Bernal, was an active and original scientist.

I begin with this historical preamble because it describes the status of scientific philosophy when Karl Popper began to publish. And I describe how matters stood then in England because in the long run that is where his reputation was made. *The Logic of Scientific Discovery* was published toward the end of 1934, and though it was published in German (it was not translated into English for almost twenty-five years), its main points began to be known in England in the next few years. There is a reference to one of them in *Language, Truth, and Logic* in which A. J. Ayer gave currency to the ideas of the Vienna Circle in 1936. Popper is an indefatigable writer, and he started to publish papers in English in 1938. His views became fairly well known, and fairly well respected, by the end of the war. Considering what else was going on in the world, that now seems a reasonably short time.

The Logic of Scientific Discovery is at first sight a rather dense and forbidding package of ideas. I shall want to exhibit some of them one by one; yet I ought to say at the outset that one of the things which made them attractive to my generation is that they are patently the expressions of a single personality. I do not think that the personality struck us as attractive in itself; on the contrary, it seemed (if anything) a little tense and touchy; but it was a genuine personality, it breathed and argued and struggled with its thoughts (and its second thoughts, and its afterthoughts). There was no doubt that *The Logic of Scientific Discovery* was written by a human being, and that it treated science as a communal activity among human beings.

The sense of humanity will be the recurrent theme of my essay: more than anything else, it is what humanism means to me. It is implied from the outset in Popper's conception of the growth of knowledge. He does not write of science as a finished enterprise, and he does not think of it (even unconsciously) as an enterprise that could conceivably be finished. In his exposition, science is systematic, yet it is a perpetually open system; it is constantly changed and enlarged, year by year it grows to embrace more of nature, and yet there is no vision of an ideal system that might embrace the whole of nature. Here Popper's outlook differs radically from the vision of the positivist philosophers. Their eyes were always fixed (somewhere on the horizon) on a finished scientific system, and their analysis was always colored by the ideal relation between the parts that would be found on the day when the system was finished. Popper has no such god's-eye view. He sees science simply as a going concern—a growing concern, and very much the concern of everybody. Knowledge grows because human minds work at that, and it is a workaday job which we have to get on with; no stroke of luck will find knowledge for us, for it is not there to be stumbled on, ready-made, like a lost corridor. It is not even there to be put together from its parts like a prefabricated building. None of these metaphors describes the reality of scientific knowledge, because all of them suppose that there is somewhere a structure of knowledge which is closed. But knowledge is not a structure in this sense at all; it is not a building, or any piece of architecture; you could not put the roof on it, or close it with a keystone.

Popper was so anxious to disavow the idealized view of scientific knowledge that he excluded any issue that might raise it from *The Logic of Scientific Discovery*. This is most striking in the pains which he takes to avoid discussing the truth of a theory in science. The last section of the book (before the peroration) points this out with a note of triumph: since Popper has discarded the test by verification, and looks askance at most criteria of corroboration and confirmation, he can get along pretty well (he explains) without a formal demand that a scientific theory should be true. We shall see that he has not sustained this act of self-denial in the long run. Yet we can also see why Popper worked so strenuously (and ingeniously) to achieve it in his first book, at a time when the vision of science as a closed system dominated the formalism of other philosophers of science.

It is familiar that Popper discarded the crucial stipulation made by the Vienna Circle, namely that we should confine philosophy to the discussion of statements which can be verified, at least in principle. In its place Popper put the requirement that our statements should be capable of being falsified. On the face of it that looks like a formal difference only: but of course it is not, for two reasons. First, Popper's requirement is meant to apply to general laws, such as Newton's laws of motion, which can never be verified in every instance, but which could be falsified by a single instance. And second, the demand that we should be able to find a statement false has a different function from the positivist demand that it ought to be verifiable. The potential of being verifiable was put forward by logical positivists as a criterion of meaning; it was supposed to separate meaningful statements from utterances which are essentially meaningless. Popper did not claim to have a criterion of meaning; he proposed the requirement that a statement should be capable of being found false in fact only as a criterion of demarcation. Its function, he says, is to mark off statements that can be used in science from statements that cannot.

In a narrow sense, the distinction between demarcation and meaning is something of an artifice here, and it has accordingly given rise to a good deal of artificial debate. For either the requirement that a statement should be verifiable, or that it should be falsifiable, is at bottom a demand that it should have factual consequences, and therefore a factual content. Obviously this is a sound demand to make of a statement that purports to be scientific, on any modern characterization of science. But then the logical positivists who called it a criterion of meaning were not saying anything different from this, in essence. In essence, they were proposing that the requirements of science should be applied to all human discourse. Their thesis was that discussion is only meaningful if it meets the criterion for rational argument in science—otherwise it is merely emotional chatter or nonsense. This is a very grand claim, because it implies that logical positivism has the key to the underlying reality in all human problems; and positivism lost its hold on us in the troubled thirties because it failed to make the claim good. But in the strict application to science, there is not much to choose between the words "demarcation" and "meaning"; the advantage that Popper's word has is simply its firm clarity; and there would be no difference in principle if he had chosen instead to call his criterion a criterion of *scientific* meaning.

The appeal of Popper's formulation, and its strength, must therefore be seen in the broad sense of its human application; and here it is surprisingly and engagingly more modest than the program of positivism. It does not claim to be a system of life, or even a system of science; it is presented tidily as a book of practical rules for the conduct and interpretation of scientific research—the word *Forschung* in the German title, research, is even more modest than the phrase *Scientific Discovery* which translates it in the English title. What Popper puts forward is a method to guide our theorizing and help assess our experiments so that knowledge will be genuinely gained by them. For example, he carries on a running fight with induction as Francis Bacon pictured it; and though I think his objections miss the point of the inductive stratagem (say, in Mendeleev's periodic table), they express his constant concern—induction alone does not yield any genuine advance in knowledge. *The Logic of Scientific Discovery* is an account of scientific method. As a method, the demand that a statement should be falsifiable, and the use of this demand as a criterion of demarcation, belong together as a unit, for they are two parts in a single description of how a scientific theory is debated in practice. In this broad sense, demarcation is an important idea in Popper's methodology.

After what I have said about scientists in the thirties searching their souls, it may seem odd that Popper's philosophy should have appealed to them. I think that there were two separate grounds for this. One is that, having taken science for his subject, he treats it with the practical absorption of a professional. What he has to say is sensible, informed, enlightening, and (above all) realistic; it carries conviction because scientists recognize in it both what they do and what they conclude. They are therefore attentive and sympathetic to the reasoning by which Popper justifies the conclusions, for they know that these are indeed the conclusions that they draw.

The second ground for the respect which Popper earned among the scientists of my generation is that he does not claim too much for science. Consider again (for example) his demand that a statement is only scientific if it could be proved to be false. Popper stresses that this is to be treated as a criterion of demarcation and not of meaning; statements that fail this test are not scientific, but it is not asserted that they are meaningless; and we therefore retain the right to believe that there can be meaningful statements which do not have a scientific content. Of course there are scientists whom that reservation would outrage, but I imagine that they did not have the experience of philosophy in the thirties that we had. We learned then to be skeptical of the pretensions, and the reach, of scientific philosophy. In Popper we caught the sense that science is a marvelous mode of knowledge, but that at no stage does it claim to be the final or the only mode to guide human conduct. What we read in him most deeply was a passion for science, not as a system but as an activity—a method to foster the growth of knowledge.

The tone of *The Logic of Scientific Discovery* is one to catch the ear of a man actively working at research. It is systematic but not formalist—and neither, at the other extreme, does it move in a zigzag of happy improvisations, as the later work of Wittgenstein seems to do. It is concerned with scientific theories as intellectual entities, and not as heaps of instances: the way that Popper takes fire at the word "induction" is testimony to that. It treats experiments as a good experimenter tries to plan them, not as items of evidence but as decisive tests: this is why Popper insists that their practical aim must be to falsify a theory (or better, one of two alternative theories); and his advice is very practical, because the best experiments are classics in the history of science exactly because they fulfill this aim. It does not shirk the central difficulty in modern science, which is that this decisive aim cannot be wholly met when the theory under test does not predict a unique outcome for an experiment, but only one of several probable outcomes. It ventures unafraid into fields of contemporary science which are still in disarray, such as quantum mechanics, and says both wise and foolish things about them. It implies, not very loudly but persistently, that an original theory is a work of imagination, and is formed more in the mind than on the bench. In short, *The Logic of Scientific Discovery* is a book to quicken the mind (and I think the heart) of every research scientist who loves his work, and I believe that they have learned more from it about scientific method than from any formal treatise on the subject.

I must not end my assessment of the book, however, without giving notice of one criticism which I shall be making later. The strength of *The Logic of Scientific Discovery* is that it is, robustly, a manual of scientific method; and yet of necessity that is also its weakness. The book outdistances the more formal attempts (say, by logical empiricists) to analyze the content of science, because it makes no such attempt. It gives advice to guide our reasoning and to make our experiments productive, but in the end the advice is always about the testing of theories and not about their content. This is very timely and practical, but somehow it bypasses the question, why science deserves our attention—why it deserves even the small attention of these pages. The philosophers who tried to wrestle with such questions of principle have been less instructive than Popper, because they did not understand the practice of science as he does; and it is manifest now that we cannot divorce the content of science from its practice. But that does not make the questions about content irrelevant, and I shall pose them toward the end of this essay.

There are several problems which relate to the growth of knowledge to which Popper has returned since 1934. Indeed, his book of collected essays *Conjectures and Refutations* of 1962 has as its descriptive subtitle the phrase "The Growth of Scientific Knowledge." I shall single out the most important of these problems, in the discussion of which Popper has gone well beyond his first book, before I turn to what seems to me the central essay (and the central issue) in the collection.

The Logic of Scientific Discovery had contained a long and thoughtful analysis of the uses and abuses of the idea of probability, and the subject has rightly preoccupied Popper ever since. His main view here seems to me clear, steadfast, and wholly right. Probability on this view is a concrete property of physical systems in which the events overall fall out in a consistent way, but not in a unique way. In such systems, probability is an inferred or theoretical entity which we do not observe directly, much as an electron is—and it is real in the same sense. I share this view of probability as a physical property, and so I think do most physicists now; though I prefer to express it by saying that probability can only be ascribed to events which have a distribution, and must be read as a symbol for the distribution as a whole. On Popper's view and mine, then, probability is not a description of a state of mind, or a subjective expectation of how a future event will fall out: and in fact these personal experiences cannot be marshaled as distributions. More important, the status or plausibility of a scientific theory cannot be described by a probability, because there is no unique distribution in which it has its place. Of course the status of a theory goes up and down with the evidence for it, but that is not the same as having an assignable probability.

The concept of probability therefore cannot be separated from a probability calculus, and Popper has continued to work to give the sharpest possible form to both. The formal definition of probability which he now advances is not relevant to my purpose here, since in my view the content of probability lies in the distributions that the calculus generates. My purpose is to examine Popper's use of probability at two crucial places: in the testing of theories which predict events that are only probable, and in the formulation and assessment of theories of any kind.

When a theory predicts several possible outcomes of an experiment, it is hard to tell what set of outcomes is different enough from a predicted set to falsify the theory. Strictly speaking, we ought no doubt to say that it is impossible to tell. The predicted outcomes of a string of experiments are all the possible samples of that size from the postulated distribution; and whatever the actual outcomes are, they certainly form a possible sample. Of course the samples of a given size from the postulated distribution have a known distribution in their turn, and we can therefore calculate how improbable it is that we should have drawn our actual sample by bad luck alone. But this regress does not help us to make an absolute decision that the theory is false, yes or no, however far we continue it. The sample that we have drawn may be wildly improbable, but it is not impossible. How long ought we to watch a tossed penny come down heads before we can be sure that we are being cheated—the penny is bad? Strictly speaking, forever.

The Logic of Scientific Discovery met this difficulty (which it did not hide) by fixing an arbitrary limit to the process of decision. In effect, Popper proposed that if the collective outcome of a string of experiments is too improbable, we treat that as equivalent to falsification. (The mathematics is more elaborate, but this is what it says: "that extreme improbabilities have to be neglected" [p. 202].) This is a sensible way to interpret experiments in practice, and it is in fact the way that scientists use. But in principle it removes the test by falsification from the singular eminence to which Popper had raised it. In the first place, it makes the test arbitrary, by leaving us to fix the range of improbability that is to be accepted as zero. In the second place, it suffers from the usual regress implicit in such ranges (and in all measures of the probability of a probability) because the end points of the range have to be surrounded in turn by their own ranges, and so on. And in the third and chief place, it invites the same privilege for the test by verification that we have just allowed to the test by falsification. We can hardly make a scheme of approximate falsification, and elevate it (in effect) to a principle of sufficient falsification, without granting the same liberty to verification. Of course verification is only provisional; but the point is that in this scheme, falsification is also only provisional. In the language of mathematical statistics, as Jerzy Neyman and Egon Pearson have formulated it, we cannot escape errors of both kinds: errors of acceptance in verification, and also errors of rejection in falsification.

A theory that makes only probable predictions cannot be strictly falsified by any run of its alternative outcomes. For such theories (that is, for most modern theories) the test by falsification is therefore no more decisive than a test by verification. Popper rightly criticized verification because it must be inconclusive; but in the fundamental theories of modern science, falsification can do no better—and no worse. Both offer evidence, for or against a theory, and no more.

Thus the difficulties that I have exhibited undermine the unique character of falsification. Nature provides no decisive test to prove a theory false if it makes only probable predictions. We can only sharpen the test as Popper does, by doctoring it: by stipulating for ourselves that, say, tossing ten heads in a row is too bad to be true, and the game cannot be fair—no doubt the penny is loaded. But "no doubt" does not resolve the doubt; our rejection of the hypothesis that the game is fair remains open to doubt, and we must treat it as provisional; and if rejection is provisional, its standing is no better than that of acceptance. That is, the test by falsification has a privileged place only because it is decisive, and therefore only so long as it is decisive. Once it fails in this, it is back on all fours with the test by verification, and there is nothing to choose between them.

So if we have to fly in the face of nature, and choose (because we have no other choice) to make falsification decisive by doctoring the test—then we must do the same for verification. If we are allowed to decide, by a test that we have made for ourselves, that ten heads in a row is too bad to be true, then we cannot be forbidden to say that some other severe requirement (say, exactly 0.5×10^n heads in 10^n tosses) is too good to be false, and to conclude that we are not being cheated: the game is fair and the penny unloaded. (I ought to say, the game is sufficiently fair and the penny is effectively unloaded.) The rule that extreme improbabilities have to be neglected is exactly as reasonable, or as unreasonable, for positive assertions as for negative.

In practice, scientists do act in this way, and statistical tests in general (and sequential tests in particular) use the same kind of criterion for acceptance as they do for rejection. It may be argued that this is reasonable only because the hypotheses that they are testing contain statements of probability. On such a view, then, we should not be entitled to use a doctored criterion of verification when we are testing a theory whose predictions are unique—since here the criterion of falsification does not need to be doctored. I would be willing to respect this argument only if it were backed by the assertion that all theories ought to be free from statements of probability, and will be found to be so in the long run. Otherwise the distinction is an artifice, and the argument is casuistic. So long as we are allowed to doctor the criterion of falsification when we need, we cannot (I think) be forbidden to doctor the criterion of verification when we choose.

All this is very human and natural, and it is indeed how scientists behave, in accepting theories as well as in rejecting them—because there is no other practical way to behave. There is a limit to precision in all our actions, and if we are not to allow it to bring science lamely to a standstill, we must be willing to be decisive in the face of uncertainty. But what we have then is no longer a rigorous and foolproof method uniquely based on falsification. It is a stratagem for decision, but not a prescription.

Accordingly, Popper in his later work has more and more moved away from the sharp issues of scientific decision. He writes less about falsification and more about evidence; less about theories or hypotheses and more about problems; and he stresses the part played in science by argument and criticism. His picture of the scientist is no longer that of a man with an audacious theory, devising an experiment that challenges nature to prove him wrong. Rather he is pictured now as a skeptical but benign Socratic elder (no doubt looking a little like an Austrian professor) discussing a problem with his staff, and unraveling it strand by strand until they are rationally persuaded to prefer his explanation to another. The critical steps in the discussion which lead them to reject another explanation still rely on experiments, of course, but now the experimental results are accepted as convincing without being decisive.

What I have been saying implies that the proposal to test theories by falsification is powerful and original, but it does not relieve us of the need to attend to the positive evidence for a theory also. And we cannot avoid discussing this if we are to be practical, because in their practice scientists do it all the time. So it is not strange that Popper does discuss the confirmation of theories—or, as he rightly prefers to call it, their corroboration. As time has gone on, he has given more attention to it; and in the essay which I am going to single out from *Conjectures and Refutations*, he states two unexpected requirements. It is indispensable (the word is his) that a good theory when it is first proposed "must lead to the prediction of phenomena which have not so far been observed" (p. 241); and—the other requirement—some of the phenomena must then be observed. There is a footnote defending "a whiff of verification here" (p. 248) which would strike the practicing scientist as pedantic and indeed comic, were it not that respected writers on probability and confirmation (J. M. Keynes and Rudolf Carnap among them) have said that we give too much weight to prediction. Popper is on the side of the practicing scientist: he is not content to accept a theory as a passive register of known facts or effects.

A theory is an intellectual construction and not a passive register of known facts or effects. Since, like Popper, I am inveighing against all passive views of science here, I should explain my usage. I think it is misleading (and a perennial source of misunderstanding) even to say that science describes facts. Statements in science do not have the factual form of a predication, "snow *is* white." Such statements belong to natural history, not to science. The statements in science have the form "snow *melts* at such and such a temperature," and this is different in kind: it is an active statement and not a predication, it asserts that something changes, and often it derives the change from an action on our part—"when you heat snow, such and such happens." (But when you look at snow, nothing happens so long as you stick to the predication "is white"; something happens only when you take off from that to say "snow *reflects* white light"—which is to say, whatever color of light you shine on it.) In short, science does not deal in predicates but in actions; and to have a fixed melting point or a wide band of reflection is not a predicate or property in the same sense in which to be white is. In my view and usage, even a singular statement in science describes a dynamic effect, "when *u* then *v*," and not a static fact, "*A* has the property *b*."

A theory, then, is an intellectual construction and not a register of known effects. Nevertheless, when we form a theory we take account of the known effects, and in time we look for new effects which flow from the theory. The known effects are evidence for the theory, and indispensable evidence; and when a new effect which is predicted by the theory is confirmed, it adds a measure of evidence or corroboration.

Philosophers who have tried to quantify the weight of new evidence have often said that it increases the probability of the theory. But I have already remarked that Popper insists, and rightly insists, that we cannot assign a probability to a theory: for probabilities have to conform to a calculus which (he holds, and I hold) can only be made to apply consistently to physical events or logical statements about them. I put this by saying that probability requires the events which it subsumes to have a distribution, but a theory and all its possible alternatives do not have a unique distribution. It is true that a theory can contain a *param-*

eter whose possible values have a distribution, so that we can assign a probability to the hypothesis that the parameter has one range of values rather than another. But this is not the same thing as calculating a probability for the theory as a whole.

Since this is a fine distinction yet is fundamental, I will spell it out in an example. Johannes Kepler in 1609 put forward the theory that the orbit of a planet is an ellipse, with the sun at one focus. This theory contains a free parameter, namely the eccentricity of the ellipse, which may have any numerical value between 0 and 1. We can therefore ask what is the eccentricity of the ellipse traced by a particular planet, and we can gather evidence to this end by observing the planet. The evidence can be expressed in summary form as a probability that the eccentricity lies within such and such a range of numbers, and outside the remaining range. When we make more observations, the growing weight of evidence will then be expressed as an increasing probability. In this way, we can show with overwhelming probability (which we may choose to accept as decisive) that the eccentricity falls well short of 1, and therefore that the orbit is not that kind of ellipse which is a circle. When we have done this for each planet, we shall have given what (historically) engaged Kepler's mind most, namely decisive grounds for saying that the planets do not run in circles, and good grounds for saying that they run in ellipses.

So in general, when a theory contains a free parameter, the possible values of the parameter have a distribution, and we can therefore use the experimental evidence to assign a probability to estimated values of the parameter. This looks like assigning a probability to the theory, and it has been so represented in the writings of logical empiricists. The work of Carnap and his students on inductive logic and the confirmation of hypotheses is dogged by this error, which ascribes to a hypothesis a probability that in fact applies only to a numerical parameter embedded in the hypothesis. The parameter may itself be a probability (as when I was tossing pennies earlier in this essay) and this adds to the confusion. But my example from Kepler shows plainly where the confusion lies. We can assign a probability to a parameter, and thus decide whether a curve is a circle or some other ellipse. But we cannot assign a probability to the theory that the curve is an ellipse, when it might be any kind of curve. There is an endless crocodile of curves and their parameters waiting to be fitted to the orbits of the planets, and there is no valid assignment of probabilities that can help to single out the ellipse from the more sophisticated curves.

This point was well made by Popper from the outset, though he argued it differently; and I have chosen to illustrate it with Kepler's ellipses in part because he used that example in *The Logic of Scientific Discovery*. What I have said about theories or hypotheses and the parameters in them will, I hope, help to clear up the recurring puzzle in arguments about confirmation: why the weight of evidence for some hypotheses can be expressed as a probability, when in principle a theory should not be called probable or improbable at all. Popper raises these matters again in his recent proposal to define a measure that he calls verisimilitude, and I shall return to that toward the end of this essay.

Those who think that we can calculate the probability of a theory naturally recommend that we explain the known facts or effects by forming the most probable theory that will entail them. Popper takes fire at this, and points out repeatedly that any scientific theory which is worth having is highly improbable, in any sense of that word. He urges us instead to invent the theory which is most improbable, because it will have the largest number of new consequences, and can therefore be tested most stringently.

I am a little out of patience with this exchange of gestures, but that may be because I am plagued more than Popper by people who send me improbable and silly theories. The point of substance here is that the two advocates are framing their theories to different ends, and therefore have to use different strategies. Nothing follows from this except that there are different strategies in science: it does not even follow that they are incompatible in the long run, or that the words "probable" and "improbable" should not be used in either—though in fact they should not. The advocate of so-called probable theories is saying that we should stay fairly close to the known effects, because the further we guess beyond them the more likely we are to go wrong. It is extravagant to imply that this is just what we want, because falsification is the only test that we accept. It does not help us to be wildly wrong: we do not learn from our mistakes if they are gross mistakes; we are only sent back to the effects from which we started with nothing added. Yes, any theory worth having must take some risks, and go beyond the known effects—because it would not be worth having if it were unable to propose anything new. And it is true that some advocates of so-called probable theories (Carnap among them) are writing of science as a closed system, so that what they have to say has no bearing on the real practice of science, and is fundamentally misconceived. But it is possible to be an advocate of caution and still to talk sense. Caution here is induced not by the fear of straying too far from the known effects, but of getting too far ahead of the pattern or theory that they seem to follow. When we hesitate to speculate too far, it is because we then lack a guide to the shape of the new theory that we would like to imagine.

Popper says in his essay "Truth, Rationality, and the Growth of Scientific Knowledge" in *Conjectures and Refutations* that, well, we are not altogether helpless in shaping a new theory, "we *know* what a good scientific theory should be like" (p. 217). Certainly we do, in the sense that we know some of the requirements that it should meet, and the pitfalls to avoid. And in that sense, we know in advance whether a new theory that is proposed to us would be better than the old, if it turned out that it worked. But we do *not* know how to propose a new theory unless it is rather like the old; we have no method to guide us toward a different kind of theory from that; and when Popper says that we know "what kind of theory would be better," that is exactly what we do not know. It is the theory different in kind, the new viewpoint from which the effects arrange themselves in another way, the structure that departs from the old model, which we do not know how to project far ahead. Scientists who stick to a cautious strategy which does not venture beyond the known effects (such as the strategem of induction) do so not from lack of philosophic training but of imagination, for that is the only strategy that will propose a new theory if its structure needs to be radically different from the old. There is a letter from Albert Einstein to Popper which says just this: "dass Theorie nicht aus Beobachtungsresultaten fabriziert sondern nur erfunden werden kann."

Popper has devised a formula to measure the corroboration of a theory (in a new appendix to *The Logic of Scientific Discovery*), and he has applied it to compare Einstein's theory of gravitation with Newton's. It turns out that Einstein scores higher than Isaac Newton, because he explains more effects. This is fair enough, although it is not exactly a revelation. But the trouble is that a register of the effects would also get Einstein's score, and would equally beat Newton's theory. This cannot really satisfy us—either Popper or me; a theory that interests us must have more content than the sum of effects; and what is more is evidently the structure of the theory, the way it organizes the effects. What characterizes an original theory (relativity, or quantum mechanics, or Gregor Mendel's distribution of inheritance) is that it is structurally different from the old. The total content of a theory is larger than its empirical content, and includes its structure.

If this is accepted, it forces us to take a new view of the growth of knowledge. Popper himself has done so in a long essay on "Truth, Rationality, and the Growth of Scientific Knowledge" which he published for the first time in *Conjectures and Refutations*. The essay is something of a philosophical testament, and is also remarkable as a human account of the march of Popper's mind in thirty years. At some points, it is as challenging to the prejudices of the 1960s as *The Logic of Scientific Discovery* was to the 1930s. It will be seen that I should have liked it to go even further, but it is an absorbing document as it stands, and I shall end my assessment with it.

The question, what is the content of science, throws its shadow forward from the first page: "It is not the accumulation of observations which I have in mind when I speak of the growth of scientific knowledge, but the repeated overthrow of scientific theories and their replacement by better or more satisfactory ones" (p. 215). The central issue here is the meaning that Popper will develop to justify the description of one scientific theory as "better or more satisfactory" than another. But before we reach that, we have to examine his older favorite, "the repeated overthrow of scientific theories."

The overthrow of a scientific theory is accomplished when we show as a matter of experiment or observation that one of its consequences is false. This cannot be the whole story, for any theory can be patched up to save the phenomenon—so that if this were all, the theory of phlogiston would still be with us. But in principle, this had been Popper's original method: to challenge a theory by testing its empirical consequences, and discarding it if one of them failed the test. The growth of knowledge was to be promoted by clearing away the rubbish of mistaken theories or superstitions.

The trouble with this negative method is that it is preoccupied with the idea of testing. What it asks of a scientific theory, and the criterion by which it judges it, is that is shall stand up to test. Yet testing in science, as in any human activity, is by nature only a diagnostic procedure: it does not express the function of the activity—it only marks out conditions for it. Scientific theories are not invented for the *purpose* of passing tests, any more than motor cars and courses in philosophy. Whatever it is that we want theories for, it is not to test them; so that this certainly cannot be a criterion to show that a theory does what we want of it. The test by falsification will diagnose when a theory falls sick, but it does not reflect what we ask a healthy theory to be or to do.

Science is a human activity, in which the theories that we make for it play the part both of an account and of a general plan or brief. As in any activity, we make the plan to guide us: we want it to work, in some unwritten but positive sense—to inform and interest us, to show how things are and guess how they will fall out, to organize our outlook. And an inquiry into the nature of science must tackle these functional demands, because they are the issues of substance and the nub of the matter. Science is meant to work, not to be tested; and though it must be tested as a diagnostic or instrumental safeguard, to alert us when there is malfunction, we must not let that tail wag the dog. Even as a mere matter of language, we invite error if we constantly describe every scientific action as a test. The functional requirement is that a scientific theory should work, however we define that; and we shall surely lose this concept if we let the language of diagnosis distort it, and call every occasion when it is put to work a test.

Accordingly, the essay on "Truth, Rationality, and the Growth of Scientific Knowledge" does not stop at the overthrow of scientific theories. Fostering the growth of knowledge is now conceived as a more active undertaking than merely clearing away the older growth of mistaken theories. The real task is "their replacement by better or more satisfactory ones" (p. 215). Presumably a better theory is not simply any theory which can pass all the tests that have been tried so far; and Popper therefore squarely faces the question, What makes one scientific theory better than another?

What makes a theory better or worse, what makes it a theory at all (and not a register of effects), must express what we want from a theory. What we want stipulates the purpose or function of a scientific theory in our usage, and this points in turn to what we expect to read in it (or to read into it) as an integral part of its content. That is, a part of the content is the view of the organization of nature that it presents by the manner in which it arranges the effects; and this is expressed in the structure of the theory. Or so at any rate I see the problems, in sequence; and though Popper does not look at them quite in the same way, they are roughly the topics that now occupy him in "Truth, Rationality, and the Growth of Scientific Knowledge."

Popper does not ask explicitly how we see the purpose or function of science as a guide to conduct. But it is evident, and indeed self-evident, that he does not picture it simply as a book of rules for action. In the language that I use in *The Identity of Man*, science and other provisional modes of knowledge do not bluntly *instruct* our actions—they *inform* them. Both as an account and as a plan, therefore, a theory must attempt to guide us to effects which will be confirmed, that is, which will turn out to be as the theory implies. How shall we characterize this demand made of a theory, that it shall imply the effects truly?

Popper proposes in his essay that we do not beat about the bush, but say firmly that we want the theory to be true. Of course we do; but does not that postulate that knowledge will thereupon have completed its growth along this branch? There is no danger of that, says Popper; we can never reach the truth, or indeed know what it is; we can only push nearer and nearer to the truth.

This is a startling program, coming from a philosopher who took immense pains in the past to avoid using even the word "truth." Popper explains that he has been converted by the new clarity that Alfred Tarski has brought to the definition of truth. Thanks to Tarski, it is now possible to know exactly what we mean when we say that a statement is true, and therefore we no longer need use any circumlocution in saying what we all feel, that we would like scientific theories to be true.

I am an admirer of Tarski's work, and especially of his simple and searching analysis of the concept of objective truth. It has separated what can from what cannot be said about scientific statements in their own language. As a result it has proved once for all that there is an inherent contradiction in the Vienna program, which hoped to express all true statements about the world in a single scientific language. Much like Kurt Gödel, but more immediately, Tarski has shown that there is no universal language or system in which we can develop a formal way to say everything that is true. This is a deep finding, and Popper has been tireless in making it known and in his tribute to Tarski.

Tarski's achievement rests on his elucidation of a consistent logical basis for the realistic view that a statement is true when it corresponds to the facts. But in the nature of things, his analysis applies only to statements of fact: "snow is white." We need not read the phrase "statements of fact" too narrowly; plainly it can be made to include what I call statements of effect, "snow melts at such and such a temperature," and would be happier if it were confined to those. But there is nothing in Tarski's analysis that sanctions our applying to theories the concept of truth as correspondence with the facts. Quite the contrary. Scientific theories are not statements of fact; they are not even descriptions of effects; they are explanations, which means that only their consequences are open to inspection, and available to be compared with our experience. The theory as such, the explanation which it offers, is simply not accessible to any scrutiny that we can devise; so that there is nothing that we can put beside it in order to say with a pointing finger, "Yes, the theory as stated is true, because it corresponds to that." Neither is the theory as explanation accessible to Popper's preferred test: there is nothing that we can put beside it which would make us able to say, "No, the theory as stated is false, because it does not correspond to that." We falsify a theory by comparing its *consequences* with something that we can inspect—not by comparing the theory, for there is nothing that we can inspect (even in principle) that is comparable.

Popper is evidently exercised by this problem, for he discusses some versions of it elsewhere in *Conjectures and Refutations*, chiefly in an essay on "Three Views Concerning Human Knowledge." Nevertheless, the argument as I have stated it seems to me conclusive. I think that its conclusion can only be avoided if we suppose that the true theory, the ultimate theory, is different in kind from any theory that we make, and is open to inspection of every part. (We have to *look* at the bad penny to prove that it has two heads.) Such a theory would have to encompass all effects at once, and would no longer be an explanation as we understand that, but a gigantic register or description of them all. No doubt there are philosophers of science who picture nature in this way, as the memory store of a universal computer, but neither Popper nor I (nor Tarski) would accept that this is a necessary projection or model of scientific theory.

Yet strangely enough, it does not matter here whether we do or do not believe that nature is a closed mechanism. The argument that I have given against extending to scientific theories the correspondence view of truth is powerful if we do not, but it is not the strongest objection that can be made. For there is in any case a more practical objection, and I think a decisive one. It arises when we want to compare two theories, neither of which claims to be ultimately true. Which has the better claim to our confidence? The one that is nearer to the truth, says Popper: theories form a progression from less true to more true, and the growth of knowledge is an asymptotic approach toward the truth. Popper grants that we cannot know what theory will be true, and we cannot expect to reach it; nevertheless, he holds that we can measure which of two theories contains more truth than the other.

On the contrary, I do not think we know how to measure the partial correspondence to the truth of two theories, as theories. If we do not know what the true theory is, there is no way to assess that we are approaching it, as a theory. Indeed, it does not make sense to say that an explanation is approaching the truth when we do not know the true explanation and must therefore foresee that it may have an altogether different and unforeseeable form. How could we have anticipated that a better theory than Newton's would have the form of relativity? So long as we are comparing theories as explanations, the correspondence view of truth cannot give us a yardstick which will measure that one is closer to the unknown truth than the other.

Popper anticipates this objection, and he replies to it in advance that "there is no reason whatever why we should not say that one theory corresponds better to the facts than another" (p. 232). But this is not a legitimate use of the word "corresponds" in Tarski's scheme. A statement of fact is true if it corresponds to the fact; a theory is true if it corresponds to what it asserts—and what a theory asserts is not an array of facts, but their explanation. There is nothing in Tarski's work which justifies measuring the truth of a theory by counting the true and false statements of fact that can be derived from it.

Of course we all agree that it makes sense—more, that it is essential—to say that one theory is better than another if it accounts for more facts or effects. There is a yardstick here for measuring theories comparatively, one against another. But it does not measure their truth as theories, that is, as explanations, and gives no ground for saying one has moved closer to the truth than another. A criterion of distance from the true *explanation* cannot be derived from any definition of truth as correspondence.

When Popper in the same essay develops a count of true and false assertions of fact or effect, he is therefore returning to an older criterion—a formula for the confirmation of a theory, on familiar lines. He now calls the formula "verisimilitude" and offers it as a measure of the content of truth in the theory; but of course what it measures is the content of facts or effects. (Presumably the true theory would entail an unbounded set of consequential effects.) The criterion of verisimilitude distinguishes a more ample theory from a less ample one, and nothing more; and this the only ground which it advances for calling one theory better than another. All theories which subsume the same array of effects would rank as equally true and equally good—even if they did not look in the least like explanations.

The practice of science shows that scientists looking for explanations patently prefer some kinds of theory to other kinds. Popper does not miss this point. Having described science as the search for true theories, he goes on to say: "Yet we also stress that *truth is not the only aim of science*. We want more than mere truth: what we look for is *interesting truth*" (p. 229). He offers several glosses on the word "interesting," but I shall go straight to the practical criterion in his mind for thinking one of two theories better than another when they are equally ample. At the end of a list which repeatedly (and rightly) prefers a more ample theory to one that is less ample, he comes to a different kind of preference, namely for a theory which "has unified or connected various hitherto unrelated problems" (p. 232).

In the list in which it first appears, the criterion of unity is out of place (it does not increase the verisimilitude), but in the essay as a whole its position is cardinal. It becomes the first and, to my mind, the most searching of the three requirements for the growth of knowledge which Popper puts forward in the essay. The other two are still concerned with the tangible content of effect, and are really beyond dispute (even though I have quoted a funny footnote about them). But the requirement of unity includes a different constitutent in the content of theory: "The new theory should proceed from some *simple, new, and powerful, unifying idea* about some connection or relation (such as gravitational attraction) between hitherto unconnected things (such as planets and apples) or facts (such as inertial and gravitational mass) or new 'theoretical entities' (such as field and particles)" (p. 241). This is admirably conceived and said. In the most practical way, it leaves no doubt that there is something more in the human search for knowledge than the wish to get the facts right—basic as that is. We want to feel that the world can be understood as a unity, and that the rational mind can find ways of looking at it that are simple, new, and powerful exactly because they unify it.

It is also clear that the demand for unity in a theory goes outside the principle of correspondence, however this is applied. It is an appeal for coherence, and I myself express it by saying that a theory must be rich, by which I mean that it must contain a wealth of connections to other theories and to the effects that flow from them. Whatever words we use, they express the same conclusion, namely that a scientific theory has to combine the view which sees truth in correspondence with that which sees it in coherence. We cannot expect a theory to be true, but we cannot rightly assess its content unless we give weight both to correspondence, that is, to fact or effect, and to coherence, that is, to unity or richness.

Since Popper does not develop the concept of unity, let me say something about the concept of richness that I use. It starts from the same recognition that the organization or structure of a theory is a part of its content. However, Popper confines himself to single theories, while I think of the axiomatic system of a science as a whole. Popper has remarked (following Joseph Agassi) that systems of axioms are only provisional, and "should be regarded as stepping stones rather than as ends" (p. 221); and he has taken issue with Pierre Duhem and Willard Quine for involving the whole system whenever a single theory is challenged (pp. 238–239). Nevertheless, I hold that the state of a science can only be characterized by the set of axioms which govern it at the time, and the content of a theory can only be measured when we see it embedded in them. But a set of axioms in an empirical science is not a linear array of separate statements (even when they are formally independent). A set of axioms is a topological network, in which the knots or joints are the inferred or theoretical entities which the science has had to create so that it will hold together as a unity. The network is given its character by the pattern of linkages that it forms across the joints, and it is the topological invariants of connection that describe it which I call the richness of the system. A new theory changes the system of axioms, and sets up new connections at the joints which change the topology. And when two sciences are linked to form one (electricity with magnetism, for instance, or evolution with genetics), the new network is richer in its articulation than the sum of its two parts.

But this is only my own sketch of an extended concept of unity which will pinpoint the crucial place of the connections made by the inferred or theoretical entities in a scientific system. I close this essay with it as a reminder that the structure of scientific theories is still unexplored territory; that we know roughly what we mean by unity, but not how we mean it to work; and that "Truth, Rationality, and the Growth of Scientific Knowledge" takes a long look ahead toward its exploration.

It is a pride of the rationalist and empiricist tradition in England that it raises philosophers who combine intellectual power with liberality of spirit. Bertrand Russell has been an example in our lifetime, and Karl Popper was preordained to be a recruit to the tradition. Coming at a time in the 1930s when a generation of young scientists despaired of philosophy, he helped to reestablish its credit and its relevance in the face of authoritarianism. For he insisted in his philosophy as much as in his life that there is no final sanction and authority for knowledge, even in science; that only that is knowledge which is free to change and grow; and that a condition for its growth is the challenge by independent minds. An informal definition from the preface to *Conjectures and Refutations* makes the point: "by a liberal I do not mean a sympathizer with any one political party but simply a man who values individual freedom and who is alive to the dangers inherent in all forms of power and authority."

This is the humanist view which reaches from philosophy into conduct, because it derives the social responsibility of each man from his consciousness of human dignity. On this view, the growth of knowledge is indeed an organic growth. Like the evolution of a living species, there is no model in the mind of God toward which knowledge moves, and yet it moves from lower to higher forms by a process of selection which discards the errors, and step by step elevates those mutations that fit the world.

9
HUMAN AND ANIMAL LANGUAGES

The distinction between human language and animal communication has been debated by many writers; indeed, the main lines of the argument were laid down in the last century. Since then, a great deal has been learned about animal behavior which has given the topic a new and solid interest. At the same time, fossil evidence has been found which changes the traditional conception of the evolution of the human brain and the human gifts. These findings and speculations give a different philosophic depth to the discussion of human and animal nature, and I hope that I shall be forgiven on that ground for writing about them as an amateur (that is, an untutored lover). I hope that what I have to say will also throw some light on my special interests, namely the language of science and the language of poetry.

It is right to ask at the outset whether there are indeed two and just two distinct categories: human language, and every kind of animal communication. Here the evidence is very reasonable. Roman Jakobson has shown in a series of studies (collected in 1962) that the several thousand human languages all have a common character, which can be traced in the way that their structure is built up layer by layer from simpler units. By contrast, the means of communication which animals use lack this layered structure, and consist rather of a vocabulary of discrete signals. This distinction is only general, and will no doubt turn out to have borderline exceptions—for example, human beings certainly make some of the same gestures and exclamations to one another that animals do. It is not implied, therefore, that there is any break in evolution between human speech and its origins in animal behavior. Yet when these cautionary remarks have been made, there remains a plain division between human language as a structural system and the code book of signals that animals exchange; and we are justified in treating them as two distinguishable categories.

The distinction made here can be put in other terms, for it is one expression of a more general contrast between human and animal behavior. In almost every setting, the responses of animals are more rigid and stereotyped than those of human beings. So the animal's responses are both fixed in and served by the utterance of stereotyped signals, which are read as rigidly by the receiver as by the sender. Indeed, we know from the work of modern ethologists that many animals single out only one feature in a situation, which then works as a direct signal—and may become a superstimulus—to release their response. The robin, for example, sees in a rival male his red breast and nothing else (Lack 1939). Other birds will sit on absurdly large eggs (such as the cuckoo's) because they respond to a single obsessive signal (Tinbergen 1951).

By contrast, the layered structure of human language is both a facet of and an instrument for the expression of varied and flexible responses. What linguists call the productivity of human language, which allows us to assemble and recognize an endless number of sentences from a limited number of words, is not an accidental feature of the system. On the contrary, it reflects the plasticity of responses which human beings build up from a limited neurological output. We can therefore say, by way of summary distinction, that the signals that animals make are (like most animal reactions) too direct and total, too *immediate*, to make them capable of the constructive assembly which characterizes human speech and thought.

These general distinctions are clearer and better founded now than they were in the past, but they do not differ in principle from those that Müller saw (1872). In some sense, as Chomsky (1966) recalls, they were already present to Descartes (1637) when he asserted that the inventiveness of human behavior differs in kind from what he thought of as the mechanical routines of animals. There is no dearth of historical prejudice or of modern evidence to testify to the uniqueness of human language, in general terms.

The trouble begins when we try to translate the general terms into specific and, as it were, diagnostic details. This has been done very thoroughly by Hockett, who has made several itemized lists (1959, 1960, 1963) of linguistic heads in which most animal communication differs from human language. The shortest of Hockett's lists (1959) marshals seven heads, and it might therefore be supposed that there are at least seven critical features of human language which are absent from every animal language. But this is not so. The seven form a battery of tests which jointly characterize human language, but six of the tests are also passed by some animal language or other. Only one of the seven features is in Hockett's view probably absent from any animal language, and even there some ethologists think otherwise (Alexander 1960).

To show what are the difficulties, I will take one item from Hockett's list to discuss. This is the feature of human language which he calls "arbitrariness," and which most people will recognize as "symbolism." I choose this because it is widely and rightly held that the ability to command and manipulate symbols is a distinguishing gift of the human mind, which has enabled us to outdistance all the animals. Symbolization begins with fairly direct and realistic images (what Charles Peirce called "indexes" and "ikons"), but a true symbol in the end is quite arbitrary: it stands for something else only by agreement.

It might be thought that because only human beings think with arbitrary symbols, they are also alone in speaking with them. But once again, this is not so. Hockett rightly remarks that most animal cries are arbitrary, in the sense that they neither point to nor picture the agent that prompted them. An animal's call for help has no more resemblance to the need that it symbolizes than has a human SOS. It may be objected that the animal's mate recognizes the need in the call without prior agreement, and that this act of empathy (whether genetic or conditioned) shows that the symbol has the allusive quality of an image. But if this classification is accepted, the word "agreement" is restricted in effect to forms of understanding which could only be reached by using human language. In that case, we are arguing animal symbolism out of existence by playing tricks with the definition.

An animal recognizes a cry of pain or alarm as we do, directly. We must suppose that this ability has been conferred on it by the mechanism of natural selection, which presumably has favored the survival of individuals that heed the cry and of species whose members both utter and heed it. This is a procedure of communal agreement by evolution, and is as valid a definition as that which asks for a formal exchange of preliminaries. Animals understand one another's intention movements by the same inborn agreement.

Or consider that favorite example, the dance of the bees. It must be interpreted with caution, for Esch (1961) and Wenner (1962) have now shown that it includes sound as well as gesture, so that it is more composite than Frisch (1950) thought. (Wenner [1965] even proposes that there is some learning.) Yet the same explanation holds: when honeybees tell one another how to fly to a source of nectar, their symbolic ritual rests in whole or in part on an agreement which has been reached by evolution, and which is fixed in their genetic make-up.

Some of the steps in this evolution have been traced by Lindauer (1961) and further by Esch (1965). They find that the direction of the straight run in the waggle dance is a direct pointer among primitive and dwarf bees, which only dance on horizontal surfaces. The pointer is moved into a vertical plane in those species of bees which also dance on a comb. Thus the substitute pointer in the vertical plane is a symbol which has evolved from an index.

The example of the pointing bee shows how hard it is to give an unequivocal meaning to Peirce's three categories of signs. When the forager bee was first thought to navigate directly by the sun, the substitution of the vertical on the comb for the direction of the sun seemed to be a very abstract symbolism, and this is how it was understood by Kroeber (1952) and others. However, it turns out that the bee does not take a bearing from the sun as an object, but is sensitive to the polarization of the scattered sunlight—as other insects are (Carthy 1961, Waterman 1966). Thus the sun affects the bee overall, as a directional field or tropism, and there is therefore an evident analogy with the field of gravitation into which the bee translates it on the comb. Similarly the work of Esch (1961) implies that the duration of the sound that the dancing bee makes may be a measure of the duration (and perhaps of the effort) of flight from the source of nectar. If this is so, then the running in the dance is merely an intention movement.

In summary, I do not believe that we can draw a strict line to separate arbitrary symbols from signs that carry a hint of their meaning. Perhaps no symbol is quite arbitrary, if we could read the hints of meaning deeply enough. (Marler [1961] has also discussed this dilemma.) Human thought begins with images, and still projects them into the symbols with which it learns to work. It is certainly true to say that human language is largely symbolic, and that animal communication is not. But that is a general and not a diagnostic distinction. Human language is not made entirely of arbitrary symbols, and what is more important, animal language is not entirely void of them.

What is true of the use of symbols is true, I believe, of the other tests that have been proposed to distinguish between human and animal language. They are sound in principle and powerful in application, but it would be a mistake to think that any one of them can be made decisive. This is not to say that human language is only marginally different from the language of animals. On the contrary, it is radically different. But the difference does not lie in a human monopoly of this or that linguistic device.

For example, consider some suggestions made by others than Hockett. It has been suggested that animals encode only one instruction into a signal. But this is not always so, nor strictly so. The waggle dance of the bee is different from the round dance just because it gives two coordinates in place of one. And the cry of the cuckoo seeking a mate also announces that he has a territory of his own (Kainz 1961), and this is the message that other males read in it.

In the same vein, it is said that an animal can make only two responses to a signal: all or nothing. But this is to overstate the rigidity of animal behavior, and to freeze it solid. It is true that ritualization has the effect of sharpening the messages into a discrete code, and this tends to make the responses discontinuous too. So it is true that a mating call, for example, is usually either accepted or ignored. But there are hesitations in animal conduct, and courtships that begin and then break down. The primates in particular need to be won over by more than one signal, and a good deal of their social behavior is a form of sustained reassurance.

In short, we must not overstate the inflexibility of animal responses, and treat them as if they were absolutely fixed. Every response takes place in a context which is larger than the direct stimulus, and there are certainly occasions when the context modifies the animal's automatic response. This is particularly true when the context is a social group of animals. A single animal may perhaps be thought of as a Cartesian automaton, to a first approximation. But whereas a group of automata is simply a larger automaton, a group of animals is not. In a group of animals, the small individual fluctuations in response accumulate and reinforce one another, so that the group becomes a society with its characteristic tensions and uncertainties. As an example, Huxley (1963) remarks that ethological study has now shown that even the direct drive of sex is modified in the courtship of birds by mutual gestures of attack and of retreat. These social modifiers of signal and response may be absent in insect communities, but they exist in crustaceans and birds and become progressively more important in the higher mammals.

It is inevitable, therefore, that the different modifications by context which are familiar in human speech can also be found, one here and one there, in animal communication. Once again, animals are not totally unaware of context, and human beings are not totally aware of it. Human beings are influenced by and (as it were) live in an immensely larger and more intertwined context than animals, and as a result their utterances are modified almost constantly. By comparison, animal utterances are seldom modified; yet in principle, modification exists in animal and in human language, when the speaker is aware of a changed context. We must not mistake for a principle of language what is in fact a difference in range between human and animal consciousness.

For example, it is suggested that animals do not modify their signals to address one individual rather than another, and in this sense that they address no one in particular. This is certainly not true in specific instances, such as the exchange of calls between mating birds, or (to take a more elaborate relation) between the African honey guide and the honey badger that follows the bird. But even where it is true, in insect colonies and hunting packs, it is a characteristic of social organization and not of language. The animal addresses no one in particular because it addresses everyone in the community. The only individual that the animal does not know how to address is itself; so that its shortcoming is not that it cannot turn monologue into dialogue, but that it cannot turn it into soliloquy. The bee that tries to dance in an almost empty hive fails to read its context, but the dance remains a signal and not a private act. For the dance has been evolved by a process of natural selection whose effect is constantly to improve its social efficiency. The same pressure of selection has shaped all animal calls and gestures to make them, in general, signals that instruct the whole community.

Evidently many features that have been taken to characterize animal communication, and to differentiate it from human language, have no special bearing on either. Rather they are by-products of the social psychology and organization of animals, and reflect the general determinants which shape their communities. When these features are said to be different in animal and in human utterances, the difference merely transcribes differences in degree of social coherence and organization. It is therefore not surprising that these features turn out not to be diagnostic, and produce no decisive tests to show up the radical distinction which we feel to exist between human and animal languages.

This misconception is very general, and the examples that I have already discussed show how this comes about. Consider again the most important of them: the attempt to set up critical levels of abstractness or arbitrariness in the symbols in which human and animal messages are coded. As Peirce put it forward, the conception of different levels of signs is very apt when we describe the expression of human thought. We all understand the general difference between signs that point, signs that picture, and signs that are abstract, for the human mind; and we do not feel that we need to puzzle over the borderline cases there. But the conception is hopelessly anthropomorphic when we try to impose it on the behavior of animals. We have little idea how they point or index, and less of what constitutes their imagery or ikonography. On what human scale shall we mark the arbitrariness of their ritualized gestures (Blest 1961), which have now turned out to be so important? We find the rituals of birds more understandable and more attractive than those of many other animals, evidently because they sense the world as we do, by sight, and address it as we do, by sound.

In short, our interpretations come from the analysis of human thought, and they cannot be rationally applied to animal behavior. The whole conception of signs in Peirce's sense is out of place there, because it presupposes an activity of pure cognition which animals almost never show. It is wide of the mark to ask whether animals use symbols, in a human sense, when at bottom they do not use any signs, in the human sense: for they almost never make a gesture which is meant to guide their own future actions. (Hunter [1913] has reported some rare exceptions when rats and dogs have tried to fix an unseen light, and Koehler [1949] when birds have tried to keep count of how many seeds they may eat.) The critical test is whether an animal ritualizes any messages that are meant to inform itself; and because it fails this test, the animal cannot be said to form signs at all, in a cognitive sense. An animal language consists simply of signals, which act strictly as means of social communication.

Moreover, an animal language is a means of communication for action, not for reflection. When the speaker cries "Wolf!" the hearer bolts; he does not ask himself whether he has heard the cry too often. That is, animal signals have the force of instructions rather than information. They carry both general and specific instructions. For example, birds have general calls of alarm, and they also have calls which specify whether the danger comes from a flying enemy or an enemy on the ground. Some of these calls are shared and recognized by birds of quite different species, and are accepted by them as common warnings (Thorpe 1961). We should have to be very ingenious (and misguided) to argue whether the teleonomy of selection which evolved these complex understandings worked with ikons or with symbols.

There are two other questions that genuinely concern the essence of language and that ought to be asked here. I will ask them in the first place in simple human terms. In this form, the first question is, Does any animal language have figures of speech? And the second questions is, Does any animal language have a grammar or other structure?

In more formal terms, the first question asks whether an animal ever uses the same gesture in two different meanings. This is an interesting question because the answer is not straightforward, and throws light on how we ourselves couple the ambivalent meanings in human language. There are occasions when an animal transfers a standard signal to a new and essentially different situation. For example, black-headed gulls that nest on crowded rocks make a standard signal before they fly off: they go through the formal intention movements of flying, and these preserve them from attack by their neighbors whose territories they have to cross in the act of taking off. Therefore when a gull has to go into the territory of a neighbor, say to retrieve a rolling egg, she makes the same intention movements of flying (Tinbergen and Cullen 1965). In one sense, the meaning is the same: the signal says that there is no intention to occupy the territory. But in a deeper sense, the meaning is different: the gull has no intention of flying, and she stretches her poor vocabulary to convey her meaning because this is the only word of reassurance that she knows (like a schoolboy saying "Pax!" and crossing his fingers).

The second question, in formal terms, asks whether animals can build up complex messages by changing the arrangement of units which may have no particular meaning in themselves. This is a difficult question. Hockett, who calls this form of construction "duality of patterning," suggests (1959) but does not insist (1960) that it may be the single distinguishing feature of human language. Others think that there are units in the songs of birds (Lanyon 1960) and insects (Alexander 1960) which have the same atomic character. Marler (1961) discusses the possibility that, at a higher level, birds may put together some messages like sentences from words, and Kainz (1961) quotes evidence for this from Koenig (1951). None of the evidence here is very convincing; for though there are certainly composite signals (among the black-headed gulls, for instance), they seem only to have the additive character of a string of sentences. Human language has a more integrated structure than this. At the same time, the animal examples remind us that it is not enough to think of the layered structure of human language as merely a putting together of simple units to make complex messages. There must be an underlying intellectual analysis as well as synthesis, to create a true reconstitution.

Human language is remarkable because it is not only a means of communication. It also serves as a means of reflection, during which different lines of action are played through and tested. This can only happen if there is a delay between the arrival of the stimulus and the utterance of the message that it has provoked. I propose to treat this delay between the receipt of the incoming signal and the sending of a signal out as the central and formative feature in the evolution of human language.

There must be some biological mechanisms which produce this delay in the human brain, and I shall speculate about them later. At least some of these mechanisms have also been at work on other primate brains, in which there is evidence for delayed response, though the delays are much shorter. But at the outset I want to discuss the consequences that would flow from a delay in the circuit of the brain between input and output. These consequences are of four kinds, which I will call *separation of affect*, *prolongation*, *internalization*, and *reconstitution*.

The *separation of affect* is a subsidiary phenomenon, but it displays itself as a startling difference in the conditions in which human beings and animals send their messages most effectively. Animals do not separate the emotional charge which surrounds the message from its content of instruction. A forager bee that has found a rich source of nectar dances so vigorously that it used to be thought that it was merely communicating its general excitement to the rest of the hive. Yet it gives its directions just as precisely as after a poor yield. A chipmunk is as exact in the choice of its alarm signal (it has three) when the danger is close as when it is remote.

This unity of response, particularly in the lower animals, has not been remarked as much as it deserves. It can only be achieved when both responses are largely automatic—or rather, are two aspects of a single automatic response. The point is that the affect is an integral part of the animal's message, and to think of it as separable from the instruction is once again to impose on it an essentially human analysis.

The reason why the animal's signal is a single unit derives, of course, from its evolution. The signal begins as an automatic response by an individual when he sees a predator, feels hunger, prepares to fly, and so on. This private response comes to work as a social signal by the process of natural selection, which favors the survival of individuals who heed it. And they heed it, naturally, as a unit; they do not interpret or analyze it; it expresses for them the same response which the same situation would evoke in them, and that response is total.

This is evident in the experiments on the fixations of animals, as Bally (1945) discusses them. It is well known that a hen cannot go around a trivial obstacle in order to reach her chicks: she is fixed by their presence and their cheeping, so that she constantly runs straight at the obstacle. In the same way, a mastiff is fixed by food close to the bars of his cage, and cannot run around to it through the open door. The experiments of Wolfgang Köhler (1921), in which chimpanzees invented devices to reach food outside their cage, could not even be begun with lower animals, because they lack the basic and prerequisite ability to separate their estimate of the location of the food from some of its affects.

This separation is crucial in human language. We think of the content of a message as something separable from its emotional charge or affect. It is on this ground that we make the classical distinction between content and form in literature; and we know how to control the affect by changing the form. We should not be able to appreciate style, and to consider alternative forms of expression or encoding, if there were not a delay interposed between the stimulus in and the message out.

Most animal signals are total, and must be, because they are immediate. By contrast, we are conscious of the time that we take to frame a reply, particularly to a question that makes an emotional challenge. Many of us remember that we were advised as children to create a deliberate delay before we speak under emotional stress: to count to twenty, or to say a paternoster. The separation of instruction from affect in human language depends on this delay in the brain. Without it, it would not be possible to make neutral statements: to keep silent when angry, or to write scientific prose. Indeed, it would not be possible to make purely cognitive statements at all.

It is worth remarking that animals on occasion also make a response of silence, with a special meaning. This happens among some birds and insects (grasshoppers, for example [Faber 1953]) that ordinarily announce their intention to depart by an advance sound signal. If they depart without this signal, the other members of the group treat their silence as significant, and take alarm. This is an interesting and economical procedure: we are reminded of the dialogue in Arthur Conan Doyle's *The Silver Blaze*:

> "Is there any point to which you would wish to draw my attention?"
> "To the curious incident of the dog in the night-time."
> "The dog did nothing in the night-time."
> "That was the curious incident," remarked Sherlock Holmes.

Human beings at times have copied the procedure: the Automobile Association in Great Britain long ago instructed its members to stop at once if one of their uniformed officials did *not* salute, and was thus able to defeat the predations of the police making speed checks. But once again the animal use of silence is quite different from the normal human use: it is an immediate alarm signal, and not a response contrived by and for delay.

Of course it does not follow that a delay in response will lead of itself to a separation of linguistic functions. That requires that the delay be used to refer an incoming stimulus to more than one center in the brain or the nervous system. The delay must be used to make an internal loop in the encoding mechanism before a message is sent. It may reasonably be held that the delay merely makes ostensible the existence of an internal loop, and should be regarded as a by-product of it. I shall return to this point of view later, when I discuss the evolution of multiple reference centers in the brain: for this complexity in parallel (rather than in series) is certainly the most important property of a large brain. Meanwhile, it is enough to say that the multiplicity of reference, and the construction of internal loops, is not possible without a delay in response—and that is so, whichever of them is regarded as prior.

The delay in human linguistic response has a second effect or concomitant which I call *prolongation*. This is the ability to refer backward and forward in time, and to exchange messages which propose action in the future. Human beings can interpret these messages because they have a sense of the future: that is, they can recall the past and manipulate the imagery of recall to construct hypothetical situations. In one application, this is the gift of imagination; and in another application, it forms the concept of time—both of which are effectively absent in animals. In its application to language (Hebb and Thompson 1954), it makes possible the prolongation of reference, and the postponement of the instruction, which we recognize as a characteristic in many human messages.

There are classical experiments to show that most animals cannot relate past signals to future actions except by reflex or habit. For example, Hunter (1913) showed that dogs and rats can retain a signal only for seconds after it is gone. Perhaps the work of

Buytendijk (1921) is most direct and unforced here. He scattered several tidbits of food in full sight of a dog. The dog ate the first, and then looked around for the next; he did not recall its position. Even a small anthropoid primate reacts quite differently: he will attend to and remember where several tidbits are, and turn from any one to another with assurance without having to hunt for them. And Köhler (1921) has shown that a chimpanzee can carry memories of this kind for many hours.

The picture is now familiar: we see the same mechanism at work here that we had before. The dog cannot delay his response, and as a result he cannot fix the features of the situation which will enable him to recall it; he cannot retain the signals and revive them in the future. (For this reason, a dog stakes out his territory by going from post to post and leaving his physical mark.) Only when we approach man in the evolutionary hierarchy do we find the rudiments of memory in the sense in which it is required in order to use and to understand human language.

Memory is this sense is the storing of signals in some symbolic form, so that they may be used to revive our responses in the future. This is only possible if the initial response is not total, but is delayed long enough to separate some abstract marker and fix it in the brain. This is basically a linguistic mechanism, in which the delay loop is essential for the formation of a vocabulary. In fact, Hunter called his experiment a study of the "delayed reaction" in animals and children; but he used the word "delay" rather as I use "prolongation," with a long time scale, and his title should not be confused with my discussion of an inherent delay in human response.

The delay between stimulus and message in human language gives time for the stimulus to be referred to more than one center in the brain and the nervous system. It therefore has the effect of producing an inner discussion of alternatives before the outgoing message is formed. This is the *internalization* of language, and it establishes the most far-reaching and consequential difference between the way human beings can use language and the way animals do. It gives a special quality both to human thought and to human speech, which has been admirably described by Vygotsky (1962) but which remains neglected.

When language is internalized, it ceases to be only a means of social communication, and is thereby removed from the family of animal languages. It now becomes an instrument of reflection and exploration, with which the speaker constructs hypothetical messages before he chooses one to utter. In time, the sentences that he makes for himself lose the character of messages, and become experimental arrangements of the images of past experience into new and untested projections. We do not repeat old sentences to ourselves, even when we return to old fantasies. We make a new sentence, and one reason why we understand the unexpected sentences that others make is that we recognize our own practice and manner of making them. (So the kind of aphasic who loses his grammar has also lost his inner language [Jakobson 1964].) Even when someone produces a sentence (such as a new scientific or poetic form) which surprises us with a device that we had overlooked, we recognize that the device fits into our practice. A man who has not thought about science or poetry does not understand a new sentence in them, although it is made up of terms and words that he knows. In this respect, he is like an animal that is bewildered by an unconventional succession of conventional calls: he has not prepared himself by internalizing the language.

Human beings therefore live with two languages, an inner one and an outer one. They constantly experiment with the inner language, and find arrangements which are more effective than those which have become standard in the outer language. In the inner language, these arrangements are information, that is, cognitive assertions; and they are then transferred to the outer language in the form of practical instructions. The inner language of each of us is open, in the sense that its words are not unambiguously defined. The outer language which we all share is closed, but unlike the language of animals, it is only provisionally closed; we are constantly enlarging it by bringing in new distinctions that have been uncovered in the inner language.

In the nature of things, most of the words in any language stand for concepts, and do not name individuals but classes of objects or properties or actions. They are therefore subject to the ambiguities which blur the outline of almost any general concept. The process of experiment in the inner language amounts to a testing of these ambiguities in practice, and all our cognitive discoveries (for instance, in science) can be regarded as a progressive resolution of ambiguities. We are, as it were, always transferring to the outer language the stricter meanings that we have discovered to be hidden in the inner language. In this way, we are trying to turn the outer language into a formal description of reality in which we can communicate rigorously without ambiguity. If we were to succeed in doing this, the outer language would be finally closed, and our inner languages would have nothing to contribute to it except confusion.

We know that this is not an attainable end, even in principle (Bronowski 1966). This is because the inner language includes assertions about language as well as about nature; and this makes it impossible to construct a closed language from it (Tarski 1944). It is a cardinal feature of human thought that it can refer to itself, and of human language that it contains its own metalanguage. In a sense, this is the essence of internalization: that not only can we choose between different sentences (in the language) but we can give reasons for our choice (in the metalanguage). To us, the conformity of what we say to logical rules is as much a part of knowledge as is the orderly description of the world outside us.

The internalization of human language has impressed on it a special structure, which is expressed in two procedures that together I call *reconstitution*. One of these is a procedure of analysis, by which messages are not treated as inviolate wholes, but are broken down into smaller parts. The other is a procedure of synthesis, by which the parts are rearranged to form other messages.

Linguists have stressed the second of these procedures, and they have discussed the different layers of structure in which the meaningless phonemes (themselves analyzable into what Jakobson [1962] calls distinctive features) are built up to make meaningful morphemes, then morphemes are built up to make words, and then words are built up to make sentences. And this is indeed the most expressive (and impressive) order in human language, so that its elucidation is as exciting as discovering a natural law. No doubt we shall find in time that some animals can sometimes build up some alternatives in some messages from movable parts, and even from meaningless parts. Yet even so, we are clear that we have here the deepest explanation for the richness that human language unfolds from simple means.

This is right, and deserves the attention that it has had. And yet it is not the whole story, and what it misses is as crucial as what it says. For it leaves unsaid the startling truth that nature did not present us ready-made with the atomic units which we use to build up larger messages. Man created the units for himself by analyzing his own messages.

It is evident that the normal unit of animal communication, even among primates, is a whole message. Unless we are willing to imagine a leap in evolution, we must therefore suppose that human communication begins with complete messages. These messages are instructions, so that they have the character of sentences, not of words. It cannot be true literally that "In the beginning was the word": on the contrary, in the beginning was the sentence. The word as a symbol for a single object or action can only have been teased out of the sentence by a difficult procedure of simplification and analysis (Zhinkin 1963).

Of course we cannot suppose that any man sat down to analyze a message into its elements, as we would analyze a chemical compound. But somehow it came to be understood that reality can be construed as objects as well as actions, and that the objects can be named separately from the actions. It is as if a bird's warning of two kinds of danger, from the air and from the ground, were turned into the names "hawk" and "stoat," and were thereby separated from the instructions to take cover. The concept of the object becomes more specific, while the concept of the action becomes more general. The effect of this increasing polarization is one of analysis, by which the world comes to be pictured as having separable parts. We would not think of analyzing a chemical compound if we had not first formed that picture.

The stratified or layered structure of human language therefore presupposes a capacity for analysis as well as synthesis; it is a reconstitution from parts which do not exist ready-made in advance. I have explained that the procedure of analysis must not be conceived as a simple breaking into parts. It is a progressive redistribution of the message, so that its cognitive content becomes more particularized, and its hortative content more generalized. The speaker grows aware that he is naming a particular object, and asking for a general action—which becomes specific in the hearer's mind as a need to make it appropriate to that object. The effect is progressively to form in man a different picture of reality from that which animals have. The physical world is pictured as made up of units that can be matched in language, and human language itself thereby shifts its vocabulary from command to description or predication.

For our arrangement of words into sentences must not be thought to reflect an inherent and inevitable structure in the outside world, which we would be bound to detect even if we had no language. It is not implicit in nature that it is made up of objects, properties, and actions, and that it must be perceived in that way. We have come to perceive it so in the process of trying to command our actions on it by the use of speech. That is how we have come to think, for example, that reality is described by sentences which predicate. It is the complex procedure of analyzing our own messages which has produced a matching grammar of language and the world together, hand in hand. We separate reality into parts, and describe the parts by their functions, as a grammatical device which reflects its response to human actions.

For example, it is striking that the layered structure that man has given to language constantly reappears in his analyses of nature. He conceives the physical world also in hierarchies: an architecture in which (as it were) the primitive stuff is formed into bricks, the bricks are formed into houses, the houses into blocks, and the blocks into cities. At each level or layer, stable assemblies are formed from the subsets (what engineers call subassemblies) that were formed in the layer below; and these assemblies, because they are themselves stable, can now become the units for forming more complex stable assemblies in the next layer above.

So nuclei form stars, and stars form clusters, and clusters form galaxies. On another scale, the fundamental particles form atoms, atoms form the four basic biological molecules, they form the twenty amino acids, the amino acids form the proteins, and the proteins are the units for a new hierarchy that constitutes the architecture of the cell—which in turn is the unit at the base of the hierarchy that builds the living plant or body.

It may be that some hierarchical structure is indeed inherent in nature, conceived as an evolutionary process. But it is also clear that the combination of analysis and synthesis by which we seek for it, the dual procedure which I call *reconstitution*, is a fundamental human invention which begins in language. It has since been made, and continues to be made, over and over again—in the invention of the alphabet, of movable type, of automobile assembly, and even of the institutions of representative government.

The vocabulary of any animal that has been studied (say, the rhesus monkey) contains, in sounds and gestures together, fewer than a hundred basic signals—perhaps fewer than fifty. The rhesus monkey uses some signals in pairs (for instance, his facial expression and the posture of his tail) as a modified signal that announces a degree of inner conflict or indecision (Hinde and Rowell 1962, Altmann 1962, and Andrew 1963). Some linguists will interpret this as a primitive synthesis, a rudimentary form of the creative construction that they call productivity. But it is separated from the human form by the absence of any underlying analysis. A statement is truly a production or creation only if it has a cognitive content, and that implies that it contains conceptual units which have been isolated by analysis. Zhinkin (1963) has discussed this very cogently in his search for a formal calculus of substitutions among the signals of baboons.

It is the procedure of reconstitution as a whole, analysis as well as synthesis, which creates the potential for original productivity in human language. By this means human beings have provided themselves individually with a vocabulary roughly a hundred times larger than the rhesus monkey's, and communally another hundred times larger again. The grammatical rules for the combination of so many words (the rules of number and tense as well as the rules of predication) are themselves a conceptual description of the world as we act on it and picture it, and it is this which makes it possible for us to recognize their right use at a glance. We experiment with these units in our inner language, and make original sentences for the outer language, by a total procedure of reconstitution.

The state of affairs that I have been describing is this. There is a massive difference between human language and animal communication, and it is easy to see overall that they form two groups with quite distinctive characters. But when we try to isolate the differentiating properties one by one, as Hockett has done, we find that there are indeed a number which more or less characterize human language; but we also become aware that none of them is itself diagnostic, in the sense of being the monopoly of man. The likenesses are occasional and marginal, but they are there, and modern ethology will certainly find more of them. Human language is unique not in any one of its unitary characters, but in their totality.

This state of affairs is to be explained as follows. Human language is indeed evolved from animal communication, as Samuel Butler (1890) insisted. But the evolutionary process here is to be regarded as having two distinct components. One component is the physiological evolution of delayed and more complex responses by way of the brain, which appears in other primates as well as in man: the effect of this is to separate elements in communication which are inseparable in the signals of lower animals. The other component is a cultural selection in favor of individuals with hindsight and foresight: the effect of this is to internalize the symbolism, and thereby to turn it from a means for communicating instruction into a true language which can express cognitive information as well. The second component begins later in time than the first, and its selective influence is strong and rapid, as the evolution of the speech centers in the human brain shows.

It is not clear what started the first component in this double evolution. Somewhere near the level of the primates, a number of the direct response paths of lower animals were lengthened by being switched through the new brain: the most unexpected perhaps is the sexual response. The effect was both to delay and to divide the response, and both of these are important. Since this essay is concerned with language, I have treated the delay as the primary phenomenon, because we can observe it directly in linguistic response, and we see how outstanding its importance is there.

The delay may also come first in the biological sense; at any rate, there is a biochemical peculiarity of the higher primates and man which might have produced it. All other mammals make an enzyme, uricase, which oxidizes uric acid and so removes it directly from the cells. The higher primates, and man among them, have lost the ability to make uricase, and can only excrete the uric acid (which they form when they eat nucleoproteins). There is therefore always some residue of uric acid in their cells, and Orowan (1955) has conjectured that this has influenced the functioning of the cells, in the brain in particular. Uric acid is a purine and therefore acts in part as a stimulant, and this is how Orowan regards it. But its more lasting action may be to accumulate breakdown products in some cells. If so, the effect in the long run would be to slow down responses, particularly by interrupting and diverting their paths at individual cells which have been heavily affected.

All this is speculation, based on a single metabolic oddity. Its point, however, is to illustrate that it is not hopeless to seek a biochemical origin for the generalized curiosity of the higher primates, and their capacity to give attention to detail. They are not obsessed by single features in their environment (by super-stimuli, for instance), and this is part of an ability to delay the response, a rudimentary suspension of judgment, which is more fully developed in man. The work of Köhler with chimpanzees shows that they can in a primitive way read a signal without being dominated by its emotional charge, and this is the basic property which I call *separation of affect*.

The second component in the evolution of man as a user of language is selection for hindsight and foresight. Since these virtues would surely be an advantage to any animal, it might be thought that they will be selected for in every species. But of course they can be selected only where they exist, and they cannot exist as rational processes until some individuals in a species are able to separate the content of a message from its affect. This prior and, as it were, precultural condition has confined the selection for hindsight and foresight, for memory and imagination, to the primates and to man.

The earliest instance of foresight that we know is probably the presence of pebbles and worked stones in the limestone caves of australopithecus (Dart 1955, Robinson and Mason 1957, Leakey 1959, 1961). The pebbles are a true innovation, even though many of them are unshaped, and they disclose a new order of mind. For they are not improvisations, as are the tools that chimpanzees make from a stick (Goodall 1963) when they want to poke into an anthill. The pebbles were picked up by the australopithecus in the river gravel and carried some miles to his cave, and that implies a clear intention to use them as tools in the future. This display of foresight has rightly been taken by Oakley (1957), Washburn (1959, 1960), and others as a crucial step to the evolution of intelligence.

The australopithecus has some physical characteristics which are unexpectedly human, and it was in demonstrating this that I first became interested in him (Bronowski and Long 1952, 1953) and in my subject here. But his brain is certainly not human, for it is hardly larger than a chimpanzee's. We therefore know that the evolution of the human brain followed on his act of foresight, and his use of pebble tools, and not the other way about.

We cannot assume that australopithecus evolved directly into modern man. He lived from two million years ago until about five hundred thousand years ago, and grew markedly in size in that time. By five hundred thousand years ago, the species homo is established and will clearly lead to homo sapiens—though modern man is not fully reached until fifty thousand years ago (Campbell 1963). There is thus a crucial point about five hundred thousand years ago. Some anthropologists think that australopithecus evolved to homo then. Others think that homo was a cousin who displaced australopithecus: for example, Robinson (1962) holds that australopithecus was only a user of tools, and that the craft of making them came with homo.

(It should be said that new finds of fossils both of australopithecus and of very early homo continue to be made, and new evidence of their ages is now being obtained by potassium-argon dating. Hence the relations and dates outlined here are likely to be revised; but the overall picture of their evolution and of the place of tools in it is well founded. See the collection of articles by Tobias, Leakey, Robinson, and others [1965].)

Since australopithecus, the size of the human brain has more than doubled. But the growth has not been uniform. It has been largely in three regions: one commands the hands, another controls speech, and the third bears a large responsibility for hindsight and foresight. It is reasonable to think, as Washburn (1959, 1960), Bruner (1962), and others have done, that these three developments of the brain are the result of a common selective cause.

We can trace the connection in the single fact that australopithecus brought home pebble tools for future use. The advantage conferred by this piece of planning will make for selection in favor of those with foresight, with two ancillary effects. One effect is selection in favor of those who can organize and communicate plans for the future—for instance, for joint hunting. We can conclude from this that from australopithecus begins the characteristic of human language which I call *prolongation*. The other effect is selection in favor of those who handle tools well, which links australopithecus with homo.

Human memory and foresight depend in an important part on the ability to call up images, and the same imagery helps to fix plans for the future in a form which prepares for their communication to others. The development of imagery is, in effect, a progressive internalization of language. At the same time, it increases the number of centers in the brain to which incoming messages are referred; and this increase in the number of inner loops and their connections is itself an aspect of internalization.

It is not possible to reason from evidence without internalization—particularly from the recorded evidence of one's own actions. The most pregnant record that the toolmaker has is his own artifact, which documents the success or failure of each stroke, and in the end should be not only a tool by but a blueprint. The internalization of language is therefore a necessary accompaniment (and expression) of the change from the use of tools to the planned making and copying of tools. Robinson (1962) proposes this as a distinctive skill of homo, and the suggestion is plausible, whether we regard homo as a descendant of australopithecus, or as a cousin from the same stock. It is clear in either case that by the time homo is established, the *internalization* of language is established.

It remains to trace the last step in the growth of language: what I call reconstitution, which gives human language its stratified or layered structure. Here there are two possible paths. One has been proposed by Pumphrey (1953), who thinks that the last step is mainly toward economy and the division of operations into simple sequences.

Pumphrey therefore suggests that there is further selective pressure in favor of those who simplify their imagery, so that it no longer recalls totally but only allusively. The effect will be to change the internal imagery to more abstract and symbolic forms, which (like a caricature) try to seize the essence rather than the appearance. These inner changes will lead to the specialization of language and of tools, and they will also be reflected in painting and sculpture: the representation of men and animals will cease to be realistic, and will become sketchy and formalized. Pumphrey concludes that we can date the full use of language by the first appearance of symbolic paintings and sculpture. When he wrote, this was thought to be a hundred thousand years ago, but it is now dated less than fifty thousand ago (Pumphrey 1964). On this argument, full human speech is only as old as modern man, homo sapiens sapiens.

This reasoning is attractive, but I think it is directed to a side issue. Symbolic abstraction is not the most sophisticated feature of human language; it even has counterparts in animal behavior (in superstimuli, for instance). Nor is there any test (or sanction) for calling one set of speech sounds more schematic than another, or for matching them with paintings. In short, as I have argued earlier, the preoccupation with symbolism seems to me out of place in the analysis of language, and to lead away from its deeper structure.

I therefore prefer a second path, which has been proposed by Jakobson (1966). He suggests that the progression to a fully structural language is most like the invention of another artifact: the tool to make a tool. A rudimentary master tool of this kind, a hammer stone, has been found at Olduvai, together with flakes struck off the tools that it made (Leakey 1961). Thus the tool to make a tool begins at the transition from australopithecus to homo (Robinson 1962). We may assume that it was fully evolved by the time that men used fire, about three hundred thousand years ago; for making a tool to make fire is also a process at a remove, which also demands a second level of foresight.

The step from the simple tool to the master tool, a tool to make tools (what we would now call a machine tool), seems to me indeed to parallel the final step to human language, which I call reconstitution. It expresses in a practical and social context the same understanding of hierarchy, and shows the same analysis by function as a basis for synthesis. As in my definition of reconstitution, the analysis is made not as an abstract process but by a specialized application of familiar tools or familiar signals.

Indeed, this conception underlies Pumphrey's scheme also; he too was seeking to pinpoint the time in human evolution when the analytic faculty became a basis for synthesis. The difference is that Pumphrey (1953) postpones this to the time when general purpose tools "are replaced by a wide range of sketchy but adequate flint tools . . . of varying form and obviously of limited application . . . applied successively in a sequence of operations." Of this change he writes, "Here we have, for the first time, clear evidence of an objective reached through a planned and orderly succession of *different* operations."

In my view (which I take from Jakobson) this stage is reached in principle as soon as the master tool is conceived. For deliberately to make a tool in order to make other tools (including fire) in the future implies a similar analytic process—an ability to break a plan into a sequence of steps, and to foresee the total effect as a coherent sum of its parts. The commentators on the Old Testament were so impressed by the mystery and the mastery of the machine tool that they made it a special creation: at dusk on the sixth day, they said, God made the first pair of tongs so that man might be able to forge other tools. I take this parable to express the same unity of thought and action.

The scheme that I have proposed postulates two components in the evolution of human language: one biological and one cultural. The biological component leads to the separation of affect, and the cultural component selects for hindsight and foresight. The great distance from animal communication is explained by the strong selective pressure of the cultural component, for that has made human evolution very rapid. The drive in human evolution has been the use of tools, and selection has favored those able to use them: language is both a part and a product of their abilities.

In this sense, human language is an invention, as tools are, and is not an innate gift: the invention has to be renewed in every generation. It enables man to express himself in a way which separates the content of what he says from its emotional charge, and he is therefore able to convey information and not merely instructions. Thus he can see and describe the world cognitively and analytically, as a set of objects and processes outside himself; it is not entailed for him, as it is for animals, simply as the field of his actions. His language describes it by general concepts, and not (as the language of animals does) by specific commands.

It is sometimes supposed that only the language of science has this general character, and I ought not to end without contradicting that. The language of poetry is also general, and its words stand for concepts just as those of science do. Nor are the concepts in poetry essentially different from those in science: "Beauty is truth" is a statement much of the same kind as $E = mc^2$; what is different is the mode of reference by which we try to identify them.

The language of poetry attempts to transcribe directly into the reader's own inner language. Since inner languages cannot be made identical, the reader must try to trace the writer's concept within the larger area that the context provides for him. He must try to understand what Keats meant by "beauty" and by "truth" by considering what their equation can mean—what it can mean with the gloss "That is all Ye know on earth" and with the larger gloss of the whole ode.

When concepts have to be identified in this indirect mode, as it were by overlap, the writer must provide as large a context or overlap as possible. It is to provide this enlargement that the poet chooses forms of words which are surrounded by some emotional charge, and reach directly from his inner experience into the reader's. In this way, poetry has the puzzling effect of conveying general statements by specific images, when they are highly charged. The poet does not discard the affect, but neither does he reproduce it whole; he controls it. This is the deeper meaning of Wordsworth's remark that poetry "takes its origin from emotion recollected in tranquillity."

By contrast, $E = mc^2$ is written in the outer language which writer and reader share by their scientific education. But the discovery that $E = mc^2$ was not made in the outer language, and could not have been made in it. For to be useful as a means of communication, the outer language must try to be unambiguous; it must therefore be closed, at least in intention—and in science it is quite formally closed. When Einstein wrote in 1905 both E and m were defined as invariants. No equation which presented an exchange between them could be invented within that closed system; that had to be done by speculating in the open system of the inner language. At any moment, the language of science is closed, yet only provisionally closed; and what constantly reopens it and makes it productive is the human ability to experiment in the inner language.

10
LANGUAGE IN A BIOLOGICAL FRAME

The several thousand languages spoken in the world have so much in common, and are so different from the signals used by other animals, that is is evident that language as used by man is species-specific to him. In this respect, then, the capacity for language is part of the biological endowment that is unique in man. However, this truism (which is at least as old as Aristotle) needs to be looked at and understood afresh now that we know so much more biology than Aristotle and even Descartes (1662) did. The first requirement, naturally, is to examine the physiological component (in which I include the neurological component) in the production of speech; and I do so in the first part of this essay. When this is done, it is clear that none of the special structures that are involved in speech can conceivably have been induced by a single genetic mutation or rearrangement. Therefore two further problems arise, and need to be studied in modern terms. Since man has demonstrably evolved from a primate stock, how far is his language also a biologically mediated development of more rudimentary capacities in primates and other animals? And if language is not a simple and single biological step, in what way does it depend on and express the integration of a number of distinct human traits? One of these problems is engaged, roughly, with what I call the behavioral component in language, and the other with what I call the logical component; and I discuss them in the second and third parts of this essay under these heads.

The systems by which men communicate with one another are not all verbal, or otherwise dependent on sound. And one of the unique uses of human language, namely the mode in which a man communes with himself (for example, in thinking in a foreign language), does not require audible articulation. Nevertheless, it can be taken for granted that the elaboration of language has been dependent on a rich store of sound signals which can be arranged in many sequences. I shall not confine my discussion to spoken language—on the contrary, it is an important part of my thesis that artificial systems, such as those of the deaf and of scientific discourse, throw light on the logical structure of language. But in the unfolding of human development, in the individual and in the species, the modulation and arrangement of vocal noise into coded speech is clearly central, and must be treated first.

As a matter of physiology, then, the structural sophistication of speech demands a nice ability to modulate a sequence of sounds. (Some writers have been tempted to say that it presupposes this ability—Bryan [1963], for example; but such a presumption misunderstands the interplay of selective factors by which evolution proceeds, as Hockett [1963] has pointed out.) There are animal mechanisms for modulation that will generate human sounds and yet are different from the human mechanism, as the examples of the parrots and myna and other birds show. But there is good evidence, mainly in the studies of Lieberman and his collaborators (1968a, 1969), that species close to man, such as the primates, are not able, for reasons of anatomical structure, to modulate and make the sounds that adult humans do. Lieberman has extended this analysis in two directions, each of which is interesting in itself. He has given experimental evidence toward showing that the vocal apparatus in the newborn child is so shaped that (as a matter of anatomy) it is not yet able to make the speech sounds (Lieberman 1968b). And he further claims, from the measurements of two fossil skulls, that Neanderthal man had some crucial features in common with a newborn child, and was therefore not capable of full speech (Lieberman 1971). Both findings would underline the importance of development to speech, in the individual and in the species.

There are other modifications and special structures in the physiology of man that make a biological frame for language. The most extensive and far-reaching are in the central nervous system, and particularly in the brain. It is notable how large an area in the brain is given over in man to the innervation and the muscular control of the mouth (including the vocal cavity and the larynx) and related facial movements. Even more specific are some structures in the cortex which have been shown to play a direct role in the retention and recall of the particular language or languages that the subject speaks.

There is a fairly extensive region on the surface of the human brain whose association with speech has been classical for a hundred years. Its forward end is in one of the frontal lobes (almost always the left lobe) and is named after Paul Broca (1861) who discovered it; and its backward end is in the corresponding temporal lobe, where it was discovered by Carl Wernicke (1874). These two extremes are connected to form what is in effect a single speech area, which has been explored by electrical stimulation by Penfield and others (1959), but about which most information has been gathered by the study of patients with lesions in the brain. A surprising conclusion from these latter studies, which has been drawn by Luria (1970), Jakobson (1964, 1966), and others, is that the two extremes of the speech area appear to store and perhaps to encode different constituents in the processes of speech. When there is damage to Broca's area, the main loss is in sentence structure; this may be related to its location in the frontal lobes, which are most highly developed in man, and which play a part in governing the long-term organization of behavior. When there is damage in Wernicke's area, the main loss is in vocabulary; and this may be related to the proximity of this area to the auditory centers in the brain—as is suggested by Conrad's finding (1963) that errors in random words we read are translated into auditory errors. Jointly the two findings demonstrate, so far as any physiological evidence can, that normal language is equally compounded of structure and vocabulary, which are only separated in pathological conditions.

It is well to know, however, that even the total language area cannot be separated from the rest of the brain if it is to give a first-hand analysis of experience. There are two kinds of evidence for this. One is the evidence by Sperry (1964, 1965) and Myers (1961) from patients in whom the connections between the two hemispheres of the brain (through the corpus callosum) have broken down. These patients can describe experiences which feed directly into the left hemisphere: for example, what they see in the right field of vision, or touch with the right hand. But they cannot find either the words or the sentences for experience in the left field of vision, or of the left side of the body. This is a subject which deserves deeper study in its bearing on language. The division of the brain into hemispheres with different functions and dominance is virtually unique to man; and in this unique arrangement, the speech area occupies what is virtually a unique status. The speech area is independent of dominance: it is almost always on the left, even in those persons in whom the right half of the brain is dominant in other activities. And the match for the speech area, symmetrically, on the right cortex is an area which appears to serve for the analysis of the two-dimensional visual input to the brain so that it reconstitutes its three-dimensional structure. As I shall say later, there may be a fruitful analogy between this visual reconstruction and an important activity which I call reconstitution of language.

There is still stronger evidence for the dependence of meaningful speech on the brain as a whole. It comes from cases where the speech area has been accidentally isolated; such cases were first described by Goldstein (1915) more than fifty years ago, and more recently by Geschwind (1968, 1970) and others. The last case is most revealing, since the patient survived the isolation of the speech area (by carbon monoxide poisoning) for nine years. During this time, the patient "never uttered a sentence of propositional speech," or showed any understanding of what was said to her. Yet she was able to repeat quite normally sentences spoken to her, to complete unfinished sentences (for example, from songs that she knew) and to learn the words of new songs that had not been written when she fell ill. Her case is the best evidence that the speech area stores and controls the mechanics of language, including verbal learning, but is dependent on the brain as a whole to supply this performance with meaning.

One other neurological structure has been proposed, chiefly by Geschwind (1964, 1965), as being seminal in the development of audible language. This is the region associated with the angular gyrus, which is only rudimentary in the cortex of the large primates other than man; Geschwind also holds that it is enlarged on the left side of the human brain. The angular gyrus in man is a region in which it is possible to trace cross-connections between nervous tissues that carry different sensory responses —such as the visual mode and the aural mode. Geschwind suggests that it has therefore played a central role in language, by making it possible to associate the visual and other stimuli from an object with a unique aural stimulus, namely its conventional name. Washburn (1968) and Lancaster (1968) have taken this theme to support their view that there is a single basic faculty which distinguishes man as a speaker from the other primates, and that this is the faculty of giving names to objects. In this form, their contention and Geschwind's idea are certainly too simple, for many workers have now demonstrated in different ways that there are cross-modal connections in the behavior of other primates. Davenport and Rogers (1970) have done so by direct experiment, and Gardner and Gardner (1969), and Premack (1970), by proving that at least the female chimpanzee can be taught a consistent system of naming by association (with nonverbal signs and counters).

The analysis of this work, for example by Bronowski and Bellugi (1970), has had the effect of shifting attention from the one-to-one naming of objects, particularly of objects classified simply by visual appearance, to the total structure of human language. But this does not detract from the value of Geschwind's idea: the angular gyrus may well be an evolutionary trace and correlative of the growth of language, in which our different sensory experiences of the world are brought together. Early precursors of the angular gyrus exist even in small primates, as Pandya and Kuypers (1969) have now shown, and its elaboration in man is likely to be part of the integration of experience which the human cortex both mediates and expresses—as language itself mediates and expresses it.

Finally, there must be more general features of the central nervous system which influence the structure of language. For example, it is reasonable to see a connection between the one-way conduction of nervous impulses and the serial order in which we utter the sounds that make up a message. In every language, words are put together from a small number of phonemes arranged in a large number of different sequences. (A similar mode of serial synthesis is carried forward into written language, in the progression from glyphs to syllabic script and to a pure alphabet.) The reliance on serial arrangement to determine the meaning, a kind of one-dimensional architecture, does not stop at the assembly of phonemes into words—and indeed, I shall be saying that it does not even start there. In many languages it is the serial order which naturally expresses the syntactic structure of a sentence and thereby its general meaning, that is, the pattern of relations between things and actions which sentences of that shape embed.

Thus the serial organization of signals in the brain may underlie language, as Lashley (1951) suggested in a searching analysis of behavior. But we can go beyond Lashley's analysis by looking at the way that the order of words in a sentence matches what we suppose to be the order in nature: the order of cause and effect, for example, in which time has for us the force of a logical relation. Bellugi (1970) has illustrated this in the difficulty that children have in passing on from active to passive constructions. That is, children readily understand and apply the construction "The boy chases the cat," and treat it as the normal form of sentence reflecting a normal sequence in behavior. But they have difficulty in grasping the alternative construction "The cat is chased by the boy," which they consistently mistake to mean "The cat chases the boy" instead of the other way about. Yet the passive construction here actually represents the order in which the cat (first) and the boy (second) come into view. (See also Clark [1971].)

In developing a structure for language, then, man has also developed a number of conceptual classes and procedures which are now built into the language. The embodiment of time and with it of causation in the basic syntax of serial order in sentences is only one example. There are other structural and hierarchical concepts that both influence and express the manner in which we put sentences together. A persuasive usage, for instance, because it seems innocent, is treating the subsidiary clause as conditional— as in Thomas Gray's couplet about ignorance, bliss, and the folly of being wise. What Chomsky (1965) calls the "deep structure" of a sentence is at bottom a rearrangement of the parts according to these conceptual categories which endorse the natural way we use language to match our analysis of the world.

Yet these conjunctions are not specifically linguistic; they are part of a total intellectual development, in the individual and in the species. This is true of the most far-reaching and formative of the conceptual procedures that have been fixed in human language: the notion of predication as a cognitive statement. Human speech in general, and literary discourse in particular, has long had as its basic unit the sentence which simply predicates; it is designed to carry information without emotional charge or a call to action. The ability to store and integrate cognitive information for future use is a function of the large and diversified human brain, with its many reference centers and circuits; and it is specifically served by the predicative and propositional form.

The development of cognitive sentence forms as the preferred instrument for human knowledge is so important that, in my view, the word "information" should be reserved for the content of sentences of this kind. A different word should be used for the hortative forms and the demands for response or action that are implicit in most animal utterances: their content should be called "invitation" or "instruction." In this sense, the sentences that are passed from one part of a machine to another in computers are instructions, and it is misleading that the theory of these procedures is called information theory. Only the output of a computer is usually a sentence of information, and it is not information for the computer. But I am here moving toward a characterization of languages, and it is therefore timely to go on from the physiology to the structure of human language.

The special mechanisms that I have described in man in the first part of this essay are patently too complex to be the product of any single genetic mutation or rearrangement. It is therefore relevant in a biological study, and necessary, to seek a detailed characterization of human language, and to consider how it may be related to animal signals. The characterization of language that I propose has a behavioral component and a logical component. The behavioral component describes the ways in which men differ from animals in the procedures by which they launch their utterances. The total effect of these differences is to allow a different kind of utterance, namely (among others) a cognitive statement. But cognitive statements in addition have a different logic. That difference I shall explore in the last part of the essay.

It is apparent from these and earlier remarks that the biological frame and background for my discussion includes the evolution of man. This is because biology is not a self-contained and closed universe of discourse, as physics is. Physics is a description of the configurations that matter and energy can assume in all conceivable conditions, governed by laws which we believe to be universal in time as well as in space. By contrast, as Bernal (1965) and I (1969a) have stressed elsewhere, biology is a historical subject, which describes species as they are now and the machinery by which they function now, at this moment on earth. It makes sense to say that the behavior of (say) a dislocation in a crystal could have been described in the same terms five million years ago as today, even though there were no men to describe it then. But it does not make sense to say that any human behavior could have been described in the same terms five million years ago, for the sufficient reason that there were no men then *in whom* to describe it. Evolution is the one agency in nature which creates new phenomena.

The difference between the physical and the biological sciences is precisely that biological entities are particular; and are particular in their engineering structure by reason of their evolution. If we exclude from consideration the probable sequence of events by which an existing organism came to be what it is, and to work as it does, we effectively limit inquiry to questions of mechanics and engineering, and miss the true biological questions on the interplay of structure and environment. The effect is to regard the organism in advance as a ready-made machine; and it is foreseeable that those who confine themselves in this way will be led to conclude, often to their own consternation, that the behavior they are describing (human language, for instance) is not distinguishable from the procedures of a machine. This has been well observed by Wilks (1969) when he points out that the opposition between two contemporary accounts of language is unreal; they are "two alternative mechanistic theories: Skinner's the simple one, and Chomsky's the more complicated."

The bearing of history, that is, of development, on the organization of language is important at two levels. First, language in an individual is elaborated as part of the process of maturation, and it is therefore peculiarly subject to the interplay of genetic development with experience which characterizes maturation. And this is not just a matter (as in the experiments with young monkeys by Harlow [1962]) of safeguarding normal psychological growth and balance. For human speech, whatever connections may exist in the brain at birth have to be explored and reinforced by use to become effective; if the child does not learn a language early, he will not be able to learn any language later. It is therefore too simplistic and rigid to picture the human brain as prewired for language, as Lenneberg (1967) and others commonly do. Rather, the biological analogue is the consolidation of the visual system in animals that have binocular vision. Wiesel and Hubel (1965) have shown that the functional connections of the system (in the cat) are only prewired in a formal sense. That is, cells which can respond at birth to signals from both eyes cease to be functional, and acquire one-sided responses, if the animal does not practice the normal responses during its early growth. The genetic equipment does not become effective unless it matures in the proper context of experience.

Second, man is particularly a cultural animal (one might say, a Lamarckian animal), in whom the biological role of genetic change and adaptation has in part been taken over by learning: much of it learning during the long years of maturation. It is pointless to claim at one extreme with Chomsky (1968) that language has been laid down in man by a genetic blueprint, or at the other extreme with Sapir (1921) that it is cultural. Neither is true in itself, or indeed means anything in itself. Certainly man is a language animal, but he is not a language machine—language is not a mechanism like a private telegraph; it is part of a complex of human faculties which are expressed in all cultures, and yet are somewhat differently expressed in every culture. And in so far as culture is a preferred form of learned behavior, it has itself had a selective influence on the biological evolution of man. Men and women to this day seek mates who have abilities that they value in their own make-up—so much so that the correlation of intelligence quotients between husband and wife is higher than between parents and children. Selective mating for preferred skills (in making tools, for instance) may explain how man has been able to evolve genetically so much faster than other animals. In this sense, much of man's biological adaptation has itself been culture-driven.

So when Sapir says that "walking is an inherent, biological function of man. Not so language," he exactly misses the evolutionary likeness between them. Sapir had it in mind that a child can learn to walk simply by trying; at about a year of age he has the muscular and nervous equipment, and the example of adults is needed only to show that walking is possible. By contrast, the child later needs the example of adults to show how to talk: how a language is put together (the child learns a particular language, not language in general) to match the experienced world. Yet in the biological frame, this difference is less remarkable than the common feature, which is that the ancestors of man could neither walk nor talk, and evolved both from cultural (preferred) adaptations under the pressure of the selective advantage which each confers. In each case, the advantage is an added freedom in manipulating the environment. The upright gait frees the hands and so, by stages, the mouth and the head. Speech frees those who use it from the domination of what is immediate to the senses; it enables them to hunt together, to make joint plans, and to foresee imaginary choices. What struck Sapir was the high cultural component in language, which seemed to him absent from walking. But in fact the upright gait expresses, even in the child, a cultural pressure to reach and command the environment as much as does the urge to speak.

In discussing language in a biological frame, we are necessarily led to consider its evolution as a form of behavior. Arguments about the evolution of behavior are obviously more difficult and tenuous than arguments about the evolution of an organ; for example, transitional forms of behavior when they become extinct leave no visible fossil evidence. Yet this is a field of growing importance in biology, where the mutual interaction of behavior and organ has become more and more interesting as a unit for study. It may be that language is an ideal performance in which to test the apparatus that we have at present, and to explore what kinds of reasoning need to be developed, for tracing the different expressions of evolution. Evolutionary arguments are bound to move away in the future from the classical enumeration of steps in some bony structure—the horse's hoof, for instance, or the bat's wing. We are perhaps in the same position today as astrophysics was in 1939, when Bethe proposed a mechanism of physical evolution for helium in the sun, and thereby initiated the forms of reasoning that have since allowed us to conclude that all the chemical elements are evolved in the stars.

I must postulate some initial state of affairs in order to begin the evolutionary sequence. My postulate is that throughout their evolutionary time the higher mammals have had innate vocal responses to some basic stimuli and needs: to pain, for example, to food, to sex, to alarm, and so on. In general, these cries confer no advantage on the animal that utters them—on the contrary, often they are disadvantageous to him. The continued existence of these cries therefore implies that they confer an advantage on other members of the species. That is, natural selection has favored the formation and survival of species in which these responses do not remain individual, but are interpreted by other members of the species as signals. Thus the cry of pain has become a warning, the food cry an invitation, and so on. Four features are characteristic at this stage.

1. There is no time lag between the stimulus and the signal; as Hunter (1913) showed long ago, few animals below the primates are capable of delayed response.

2. There is no separation of affect from message; indeed the affect is the primary meaning for the animal that hears the cry as well as the animal that utters it.
3. The signal is interpreted as an invitation to action, or at least (in some primates) to social response; in my usage, it is an instruction and not a piece of neutral information.
4. The signal is a complete unit; as such, it is equivalent to what we should call a sentence, and is not separable into words—there are no synonyms for it or in it, as Zhinkin (1963) has shown even for primates.

While this is the basic pattern, there are refinements of the simple signaling situations in many species, and I have analyzed them elsewhere (1967). For example, there are birds and other animals that distinguish one kind of predator from another and utter different cries of alarm, so that the hearer can respond to them to take different actions: an overhead predator evokes a different cry, and so a different action, from a ground predator. Moreover, the call of alarm of some birds is correctly interpreted by birds of other species as well as their own, as Thorpe (1961) has shown. Though these modifications of signal and response are delicate and delightful, there is so far nothing mysterious or discontinuous about their place in the evolutionary scheme.

In an objective sense, the structural and visible difference between the bird's cry of alarm and that of a man is that the man separates the concept of danger from that of the specific predator. He puts together a signal from the parts, namely a danger cry and a particular predator cry, "Look out! It's a snake!" This is indeed crucial to human language, namely that the complete utterance has been analyzed and taken to pieces like a tinker toy, and that the parts are then assembled to make appropriate messages which are not unitary. In the process, the abstract concept of danger has been turned into an objective thing—has been reified by this usage. This is the logical structure of cognitive utterances, with which I shall be occupied in the last part of this essay. Here I have to show how this logical difference is reached by way of behavioral differences, as follows.

The behavioral differences are four in number:

1. There is a *delay* in man between stimulus and speech. The human brain is slow in formulating replies, presumably because it refers the input to several centers or circuits and balances the responses from them. (Only so can we decide *not* to heed the cry "Wolf!") This is an important and in some ways basic phenomenon. The speech area in the human brain extends over several regions of the cortex which have markedly different functions. Among them is a region in the frontal lobes, which are known to be crucial in storing and organizing cognitive information needed to make a delayed response. Jacobsen (1936) showed long ago that primates that have suffered damage to the frontal lobes continue to be capable of other kinds of learning but can no longer learn delayed responses correctly.

2. There is a *separation of affect* or emotional charge from the content (either of instruction or of information) that the message carries. Here is the origin of the Cartesian gap in human behavior. The results are so extreme that it is possible for a man to be speechless, for instance, either with rage or by cold design. By contrast, consider the conversation between Watson and Sherlock Holmes in Conan Doyle's *The Adventure of Silver Blaze*:

"Is there any point to which you would wish to draw my attention?"
"To the curious incident of the dog in the night-time."
"The dog did nothing in the night-time."
"That was the curious incident," remarked Sherlock Holmes.

The dog could only have kept silent because he was friendly to the intruder.

3. There is a dramatic *prolongation* of reference. Human speech is able, and is constantly used, to refer backward and forward in time, and to exchange messages which propose action in the future.

4. There is a new use, the *internalization* of language, so that it ceases to be only a means of communication, and becomes also an instrument of reflection and exploration with which the speaker constructs hypothetical messages before he chooses one to utter, and frames long-term plans and policies.

The effect of these differences, singly and taken together, is to distance or detach the human speaker from the immediate context that occasioned his utterance. The most telling and total characterization of the behavioral component in human language is *disengagement*. No other animal displays or even approaches this. Only the primates show some rudimentary beginnings under the four behavioral heads, as Bronowski and Bellugi (1970) have found in analyzing the way that the chimpanzee Washoe uses the sign language that she has been taught.

It would be idle to call the transition from primate to human behavior either continuous or discontinuous, as if these words stood for absolute measurements. What the primates show us, not unexpectedly, is the way man came—as Hockett and Ascher (1964) and Campbell (1966) have also demonstrated in different, global analyses of his behavioral evolution. It is a mistake to adopt a definition of language that automatically burns any possible bridge between man and animal. (This would be the effect, for example, of accepting Simpson's [1969] characterization of human cries as "antilanguage"; see Bronowski [1969b].) And it is equally a mistake to accept a definition that automatically treats all language as communication, and all communication as equivalent. The beginnings of the disengagement that characterizes man's cognitive use of language can just be traced in the primates; and the effect is to show in sharp focus that the total ability to use language as man does, practically and logically, is indeed unique.

The parts of the behavioral component of language that I have proposed are all concerned in the response (human or animal) to the total situation or experience which evokes an utterance. But when a man uses the occasion to make a propositional or other cognitive statement, he extracts from the experience some special features and stresses them at the expense of others, while finding in them similarities with earlier experiences. This is different from the total response that an animal makes: that a bee makes when it signals instructions about a distant source of nectar in its dance, say, or a baboon when he barks his cry of alarm. The different and distinctive action in the human response is an analysis of the environment into parts. It is possible to see in the separation of affect a behavioral precursor to this mode of dividing up experience. But the critical step further here is not behavioral but intellectual, because it makes a subjective division of experience correspond to an objective division of the outside environment.

Linguists are unanimous in distinguishing between the unitary nature of animal signals and the "atomic" construction of human utterances out of words. (Jakobson [1970] remarks that when Democritus said matter is made from atoms, he quoted as his model the way sentences are made from their parts.) In characterizing human language by its construction, however, linguists constantly treat the "atomic" units in our speech—either the words themselves, or the concepts for which they stand—as if they already exist ready-made in advance of speech. For example, Lenneberg (1967) explains concepts as conditioned responses such as animals acquire by repetition, independent of language; for him, therefore, words are names given to preformed concepts, and speech is generated by putting such names together. This view seems natural when we think of language as something that is made and acquired as a foreign language is learned, by combining a dictionary and a grammar. The forms of sentences are thereby treated as propositional functions or formulas defined over the field of words, and the words serve as variables to be substituted in the formulas. But it is self-evident that man did not invent language, and it is certain that children do not even learn their first language, by this kind of formal and pedagogic procedure.

Before I put a sentence or a thought together from its constituent words, I have to be able to take my experience apart into words or other images and symbols. The ability to use language has two components: an analysis of experience into parts (which acquire in their usage an objective status equivalent to things, that is, are reified), and a subsequent assembly of the parts into different imaginary constructions. This is the double activity of *reconstitution*, and we can see how it is carried on in contemporary practice—in the language of scientists, and of children—and then can project the process back to the beginnings of language.

By way of example, consider the way a scientist arrives at a new concept such as the electron. He finds himself with a series of observations, which could literally be described only as pointer readings; and he concludes, in the light of other phenomena and explanations, that the pointer readings are best interpreted as expressing aspects of the behavior of a new entity, the electron. This is equivalent to framing a number of sentences containing the word electron in its empirically permissible uses—and in a sense the electron is nothing more than the sum of these sentences, as Russell (1918) held. But in practice it is convenient to use "electron" as a reified concept, and to consider the sentences which describe its behavior as cognitive statements about an object: not so much an imaginary as a man-made object, an intellectual artifact. In this way J. J. Thomson in 1897 concluded from his experiments that the electron has the properties (that is, the behavior) of a particle; and the procedure was in no way changed when his son in 1929 concluded from his experiments that it also has the properties of a wave.

This mutual relation between an object and the sentences that delimit and define it is the characteristic form of cognitive statements in all human languages, and applies equally when what is described is a link between concrete or between abstract entities. The relation has the formal duality of an abstract plane geometry: the words are joined in sentences, and the sentences intersect in words in mutual definition like that between points and lines. And this mutual dependence cannot be gotten rid of; the words are not defined except by the sentences into which they fit, and fitting into a sentence means obeying a grammatical scheme which formalizes in the syntax the laws of behavior which the object obeys in our experience. Thus vocabulary and grammar are not separable in their origins, and in particular it cannot be held that there is a specific linguistic competence which underlies the syntax of all languages. The universal syntax is a human way of analyzing experience, not of putting together sentences.

The same analysis applies to the way a child learns to name a man-made object such as a chair, which (like the electron) is defined by its behavior or use and not by its appearance. Bronowski and Bellugi (1970) have analyzed this characteristic example, and concluded that the preoccupation with visible appearances is also misleading in general. If pointing at appearances were the primary human procedure for forming words, then all languages ought to be rich in color words. But quite the opposite is the case. Berlin and Kay (1969) have listed languages with only two color words, with three, with four, and so on up to a normal complement of eleven. An increase in the number of color words comes with the growing use of color distinctions in man-made contexts, and not the other way about. The paucity of color words in the Old Testament and in Greek literature, which made scholars in the last century suggest that the ancients were color-blind, is a cogent illustration of the principle (Gladstone 1858, Geiger 1880).

The acquisition of language by children is instructive also in the way that they learn to put sentences together. A child is not taught the grammar of his first language; he must discover the rules of construction for himself. He cannot do so by rote, but has to use an inductive process of generalizing from the particular examples that he hears. This is proved by the errors that children make when they extend the general rules to irregular cases —when they say "mans" for "men," for instance, or "goed" for "went" (Bellugi 1970). They have not heard these errors from their elders; on the contrary, they have heard these words said correctly very often because (in the historical growth of languages) it is usual for irregular cases to arise in common words. Bellugi (1971) reports that similar mistakes of generalization are made by deaf children in learning sign language. These mistakes have a sharp intellectual character; they reveal that the child is learning to recognize abstract structures in the real world (the notion of plurality, for instance, and of the past) at the same time, and as part of the same action, as the syntactical rules for describing them that he teases or extracts out of the sentences that he hears. At each stage in his language development, a child has a consistent syntax that he has discovered for himself, and its discovery as well as its use is part of his reconstitution of language.

An example of another kind will show how readily the child learns a complex usage when it expresses a characteristically human analysis of experience. This is the use of the words John, I, you, he, all to mean the same person. There is no linguistic reason for this multiplicity of words (which is avoided in scientific discourse) and it serves no practical purpose—the proper name John throughout would do as well and would be clearer. But the analysis of experience into inside and outside, self and environment, is the basic human form of consciousness as I have described it in *The Identity of Man* (1965). As a result, the child learns this obscure usage early and easily, as an intellectual habit which is only incidentally linguistic.

The creation of an inner world and its comparison with the outer world is also important in the child's practice of language. As the records of Weir (1962) show, a child when alone will experiment with language, will see how different kinds of words fit into the same sentences, try new constructions with the same words, and generally explore his growing skill. But as in other forms of play, what the child does is not aimless. He is confirming in his inner speech what makes sense and what does not in the empirical world outside: for example, his substitutions show that he is testing the difference in usage between words for objects, for actions, and for properties.

The play with language serves two related aims, and both are important in the process of thought in adults. One aim is simply to match the facts of the real world—but of course I ought not to call that simple when I am speaking of either the acquisition or the evolution of language. For the notion of an objective reality, and the search to recreate that reality as information in the exchange of speech, is the fundamental invention of man which has shaped language and thought together. Truth as correspondence to fact is tested in language, as Tarski (1936) has shown; and the universal value that we place on truth is a cardinal human invention (Bronowski 1966).

The other aim in the play with an inner language is discovery: not simply to match the truth, to crack the code, but to extend it. The child is taking the elements that he has found by analysis and is rearranging them in his imagination into new forms and patterns. He experiments in make-believe to see whether these arrangements have a meaning, and in the process he discovers —as the creative thinker does later in life—new facts about the world and new meanings at the same time. This is the essence of the process of reconstitution, which alone makes language productive. The child is beginning to explore those metaphorical likenesses from which all original thought grows, alike in science and in art (Vygotsky 1962).

All this demonstrates that a child learns to speak by a procedure which is different from trial and error, or conditioning and reinforcement. The difference is a logical one and derives from the specific design of cognitive statements—namely, to give information, rather than to invite, instruct, or share psychological set or tone. A bright animal, such as the chimpanzee Sarah in Premack's work (1970), can be trained by a sequence of behavioral procedures to carry out almost any particular task in linguistic manipulation, and to reach almost any level specified in advance in the hierarchy of language construction. But no form of training by stimulus and response can give the animal or the child the capacity to discover by induction rules in language, or laws in the real world, and to turn them into a syntax or a system of nature.

In stressing the special character of the acquisition of language by children, I do not imply that the child recapitulates the evolution of language. My argument is that human language, because it is designed to discover and to convey information, has a different logical form from the primitive systems in animals, and that we see this logic developing in the child by necessary steps. Language expresses a constellation of faculties, and its logical development in the human individual or the species marches with the development of these different faculties. It is in this sense that the child's progress throws light on the growth of human language.

At what point did man begin to move from signals to language? There are grounds for trying to trace that step to social and kinship relations in primitive societies. But I believe that the crucial context for it was the manufacture of tools, because they are visual, tactile, man-made objects in which both the manner of construction and the manner of use are reified. The stone tool, like the sentence, is both a record and a blueprint; that is, it fits into two kinds of context: one kind directed to the past and another to the future. And fitting into the context is the meaning, namely the rules for allowable constructions that are effective or useful. In this deeper sense, there is no distinction between competence and performance in understanding how to make or to use a tool, or a linguistic construction—because there is no distinction between coding and understanding, between structure and meaning.

Yet in describing a tool as a record and a blueprint, I have run ahead of the immediate visual image that it presents. What we see is a stone; often archeologists dispute whether the stone has been shaped or used by men; so that the description of the stone as a tool demands now, and has always demanded, a series of inferences. If a stone tool carried from one culture into another indeed spoke for itself, it was because how it was used and how it was made were both inferred in the mind from its visual and tactile appearance. A tool, like an utterance, only reveals its meaning to those who can infer it by reconstructing it in their own context (Oakley 1957).

We have an analogue in the visual system to inferences of this kind, from the immediate appearance to the whole. What the eyes conduct to the brain are two-dimensional pictures, even though they have already been elaborately processed and interpreted on the way to the brain. They are reconstituted into a three-dimensional structure in the brain by a process of inference which is not foolproof, as we know from the errors that are induced by optical illusions. Gregory (1970) has pointed out that there is a marked analogy between the inferences that are made to arrive at this three-dimensional reconstruction and those that are made when we reconstruct the meaning or "deep structure" of sentences. Moreover, it is remarkable that the area in the brain which carries out the reconstruction occupies the same position in the right hemisphere that the speech area occupies in the left. Levy (1969) has suggested that the area on the right arrives at its reconstruction by a more immediate act of total appreciation than that by which the speech area operates. But it would be idle to argue about different interpretations now, when the subject is new and research has only begun. What is important is that there is a biological as well as an intellectual analogy between the reconstitution of language and of three-dimensional structures in the mind, which needs to be explored.

The stone tool at one extreme and binocular vision at the other may provide analogies for reconstitution as a fundamental process in cognitive language. But both are analogies in the large; they may throw light on the overall logical and biological structure, but they do not provide a specific starting point. How did man develop a symbolic system at all? Those who have believed that man began by naming things, like Adam in the Old Testament, certainly take too primitive a view; but the question in their minds is fair. How did it come about, and seem natural, that man should accept the substitution of one action for another —of an utterance for an action, and an object, and a property?

At bottom, the answer must lie in the particularization and analysis of animal signals, as I have already explained it. This process is basic to my theme, and I must not end without describing it once more, now that we can appreciate its relevance to our own usages. I do so in words which I have written elsewhere (1967):

Of course we cannot suppose that any man sat down to analyze a message into its elements, as we would analyze a chemical compound. But somehow it came to be understood that reality can be construed as objects as well as actions, and that the objects can be named separately from the actions. It is as if a bird's warning of two kinds of danger, from the air and from the ground, were turned into the names "hawk" and "stoat," and were thereby separated from the instruction to take cover. The concept of the object becomes more specific, while the concept of the action becomes more general. The effect of this increasing polarization is one of analysis, by which the world comes to be pictured as having separable parts. We would not think of analyzing a chemical compound if we had not first formed that picture.

The stratified or layered structure of human language therefore presupposes a capacity for analysis as well as synthesis; it is a reconstitution from parts which do not exist ready-made in advance. I have explained that the procedure of analysis must not be conceived as a simple breaking into parts. It is a progressive redistribution of the message, so that its cognitive content becomes more particularized, and its hortative content more generalized. The speaker grows aware that he is naming a particular object, and asking for a general action—which becomes specific in the hearer's mind as a need to make it appropriate to that object. The effect is progressively to form in man a different picture of reality from that which animals have. The physical world is pictured as made up of units that can be matched in language, and human language itself thereby shifts its vocabulary from command to description or predication.

But it is worth remarking, as a closing footnote, that animal behavior is not wholly devoid of the rudiments of symbolism. What I have in mind are some forms of ritual behavior, and specifically of displacement behavior. In displacement, an animal (usually) abandons a purposeful action which is not reaching its goal, and substitutes an irrelevant though normal action: a gull that fails to recover a lost egg may fall back on a formalized action of plucking grass (Tinbergen 1951, 1953). In other examples, the animal displaces a standard action to an inappropriate context in which, however, it is effective: a gannet that wants to enter the territory of a neighbor makes the habitual intention movement that precedes flying, and this preserves it from attack. Displacement is not in general a signal; instead, in substituting one action for another, it has some claim to be called symbolic.

Displacement in animal behavior is not very specific; such actions as plucking grass or the intention movement for flight are used in many contexts. But this does not rule it out as a precursor for symbolic or figurative utterances—it gives it a metaphorical quality which also has a place in human language. That is to say, displacement is not a model for the strict substitution, one-to-one, of a symbol for a specific thing or action; rather it is a general likeness, a kind of blank check on a whole class of actions by the animal. This is much like the way we use such words as high, hard, bright, strong, broad, to describe many different actions which evoke in us similar states of mind or preparation. It is well to remember that human language is not exact, and does not try to be; rather it draws on generalized images and schemes which serve to discover the likenesses that they cannot describe. Poetry is as species-specific to man as science is, and though its forms lean more openly on metaphor than those of science, they are based equally on cognitive statement. It is not possible for language to be totally precise; if we attempt to make a scientific system both finite and complete, it turns out to contain irremovable paradoxes.

11
WHERE DO WE GO FROM HERE?

It is evident that we are living in a cultural reformation—a harsh and perhaps disruptive movement in which we are all engaged. The fabric of western culture, its tangled skein of social habits, artifacts, and values, is being pulled apart and made over—by us. We have set going the headlong changes in conduct and belief which now fill us with questions. Is there a single direction in these changes? Is there, in particular, an imaginative direction in the arts and sciences which points the way for a future culture? How shall we educate fresh generations, either to follow the changes or to lead them? What is the future of man? And is there any point in our wanting that future to conform to our own conception of man?

In a time of such grand uncertainties, which we all prompted and all share, we are naturally drawn to the social sciences; and they are naturally more voluble than ever. I have picked two books from the many published in 1964, for several reasons. My overriding reason, of course, is that Margaret Mead is, and Pierre Teilhard de Chardin was, outstanding in intellectual depth and in scientific vision. And they mark the two ends of the spectrum of speculation: Mead is searching for the smallest step of social change, and Teilhard de Chardin by contrast looked only for its cosmic direction. They are equally at extremes in the relative importance that they give to the individual man and to his society; it is ironic that Mead, the social anthropologist, stresses the part played by the individual, and that Teilhard de Chardin, the shepherd of souls, pictured a society without men. And I must not hide my last reason: both writers understand what makes a theory scientific, the demands for order and coherence that it must meet, and they hold to this scrupulous standard.

The scientific concept which they both share is that of evolution. Mead's *Continuities in Cultural Evolution* in particular tackles the heroic task of giving an exact and rational meaning to this, the oldest and, alas, the vaguest concept in social science. For the

This essay was originally published as a review of *Continuities in Cultural Evolution* by Margaret Mead (New Haven: Yale University Press, 1964) and *The Future of Man* by Pierre Teilhard de Chardin (New York: Harper & Row, 1964).

strange thing is that the ideas of evolution, in the modern sense, began in the eighteenth century in studies not of biology, but of human society. Charles Darwin was led to the critical step in the theory of evolution by something that he found in a work on social science. He had returned from his five-year voyage in the *Beagle*, and was patiently putting his notes and his thoughts in order, when, in October 1838,

> I happened to read for amusement Malthus on *Population*, and being well prepared to appreciate the struggle for existence which everywhere goes on from long-continued observation of the habits of animals and plants, it at once struck me that under these circumstances favorable variations would tend to be preserved, and unfavorable ones to be destroyed. The result of this would be the formation of new species. Here then I had at last got a theory by which to work.

Darwin said that he read Malthus for amusement because, of course, he did not take the social sciences seriously.

So also, when Darwin at last published the *Origin of Species* in 1859, the social sciences took up his theme and turned it into a general philosophy. Herbert Spencer spent the rest of his long life in elaborating a system which explained all human conduct and ethics by the processes of evolution. His influence was prodigious: for example, he gave the language the phrase "survival of the fittest," which (at the suggestion of Russel Wallace) Darwin put into later editions of the *Origin*. If no one now reads or prizes what Herbert Spencer worked out with such pains, it is precisely because meanwhile we have adopted it as self-evident.

There is good historical ground, then, for saying that evolution has been a persistent idea in social science for quite two hundred years, and that its entry into biology is an almost accidental offshoot from that tradition. The obvious question, therefore, is why evolution has been so much less useful an idea in the social than in the natural sciences. Darwin (and Wallace) revolutionized our understanding of the relations between the species of animals by arranging them in a family tree of evolution. Quite recently, physicists have revolutionized our understanding of the relation between the chemical elements by turning the periodic table of Mendeleev into a family tree of evolution. Yet the first of the sciences that recognized evolution, the study of society, has uncovered no such profound order in two hundred years.

One plain reason is that no one has been able to lay bare the mechanism which turns one network of social relations, one set of values, one culture, into another. The machinery of competition, which worked so well in biology, and which was a favorite of the nineteenth-century sociologists, has done nothing to explain the evolution of cultures. It remains today as shallow and as false a predictor as it was in Malthus and in the eighteenth-century rationalists from whom he took it.

Underneath this there is a deeper and basic reason. We do not know the mechanism for social evolution because we have not been able to pin down the units with which it works—which it shuffles and regroups, and whose mutations make the raw material for new cultures. In physics, the evolution of the elements works by building up more and more complex nuclei from two units, the protons and the neutrons. In biology, evolution has for its new units those stable mutants which Charles Darwin called "sports," and within which Gregor Mendel later found the genes. But no analysis has yet isolated an acceptable unit of social structure.

This is the central problem in the study of cultures which Margaret Mead's book sets out to solve. She is concerned very precisely with the machinery of social evolution. And she looks for it in the minutiae of cultural change, the small shifts between one society and its neighbor, and not in the grand panorama which anthropologists have often tried to assemble. In her own phrase, her subect is "cultural microevolution."

It has been suggested before now that the unit in such change, its smallest step, is a human invention: an artifact such as an axe or a map or, more elaborately, the Samoan house, which fixes and carries the fine detail of a culture. More recently, anthropologists have looked for this unit not in physical invention but in social innovation. Mead is at her best here; her account, for example, of the origin and growth of pidgin English is masterly. She is able to make the concept of innovation work more exactly and concretely than has seemed possible hitherto. This is because she boldly attacks the problem at the heart of cultural transmission: the human means by which an innovation is made or borrowed, is advocated, and, in the end, is disseminated.

As for this human means, her conclusions are downright. There must be a man, one man, who has an affection for the culture into which he was born, but is impatient with its timid adherence to old habits. And he must have around him a band of a few disciples, what she calls a cluster, who are attached to him, are excited by his vision, and get a personal satisfaction from spreading his ideas. Such a small intense leader is not a hero of history, yet he and his cluster are the means by which the interlocking changes in society are made, one by one. Mead describes a man of this stamp who in 1946 rallied three hostile tribes in the Pacific, made them build houses, docks, schools, a common treasury, and in three years "transformed" a Neolithic society into a very crude but systematic version of a mid-twentieth-century society.

Clearly this analysis fits many innovators, for example in the arts and even in science. It also explains why changes in our social organization in the large, changes in formal institutions and procedures, come so much harder and slower than in the informal communities of art and of science. We see how it is that evolution can make changes in culture as radical as those which only revolution can make in government.

In all this, Mead's analysis is absorbing, provocative, and often decisive. Moreover, she has given a new turn to the discussion of the place of the hero in history, which long ago puzzled Darwin and Herbert Spencer. She is splendidly sensible, in particular, in chiding those fanatics who think that the human heritage can only be preserved by breeding a race of supermen.

Yet, in fact, her vision fails when she looks forward to the future. Surprisingly, what she has found does not help her to predict. She confesses that there is no way to recognize a leader except by his success, and therefore that we do not know how to bring about the changes for which we yearn. When she leaves analysis and proposes action, her book suddenly falls flat. After all that I have said by way of commendation, I may be forgiven for quoting mischievously from one of her closing chapters, "Possible Forms of Centers with an Evolutionary Potential":

> Dotted over the campus of the several institutions are small rooms where coffee is served at more or less fixed hours, and here, with the breath-taking speed that is so characteristic of American life, plans are hatched, ideas are briefly challenged, a reference to some remote work is given and received. "I didn't quite understand what you meant the other day; can you give me a reference?" Later there arrives a large envelope on both sides of which are imprinted little boxes saying *To* and *From*, already half filled with names, so that one has a sense of being part of a network of communication.

I doubt whether small innovations in culture are carried in large envelopes marked *To* and *From*.

The speculations of Teilhard de Chardin are, I have said, at the opposite extreme to Mead's. His vision was of macroevolution, on a cosmic scale. Moreover, to still his own religious scruples and those of his superiors in the Jesuit order, he colored his vision with a rich mystic lacquer. But the essence of what he had to say is plain, and it is particularly plain in this book of essays, which collects what Teilhard thought as he thought it, over thirty years. *The Future of Man* says nothing unexpected, yet it is to me much the most interesting of Teilhard de Chardin's books.

Teilhard held that what his fellow biologists call the higher animals are higher, not only on the scale of biological complexity, but on any scale of values which makes sense to us. And on that scale we are, of course, highest among the animals. This is (in Teilhard's view) an absolute scale: evolution has labored most elaborately on God's behalf to produce man. The complexity which places man absolutely above the other animals is expressed in his possession of mind. So far (apart from the religious intrusions) few biologists would find fault with Teilhard.

Man's mind enables him to form concepts, use language, build societies and cultures; above all, it enables him to work in intellectual community with others. Human groups are not mere packs of wolves or monkeys (in whose communal habits Teilhard was not interested), but are societies in which knowledge is fixed and handed on, and in which the intellectual and emotional life of each man is sustained by his unity with others—for the glory of God. So far (apart from the religious intrusions) few anthropologists would find fault with Teilhard.

What Teilhard did now was to project the direction of evolution forward, beyond man as he is to that which his endowments seem to design him for. He concluded that the social use of the intellect is the peak of man's talents, and would become their ultimate realization:

> The era of active evolution did not end with the appearance of the human zoological type: for by virtue of his acquirement of the gift of individual reflection Man displays the extraordinary quality of being able to totalize himself collectively upon himself, thus extending on a planetary scale the fundamental vital process which causes matter, under certain conditions, to organize itself in elements which are ever more complex physically, and psychologically ever more centrated. Thus (provided always that we accept the organic nature of the social phenomenon) we see being woven around us, beyond any unity hitherto acknowledged or even foreseen by biology, the network and consciousness of a Noosphere.

Teilhard foresaw a universal community of men who no longer have individual minds, but flow into one all-embracing mind, "an envelope of thinking substance" around the world. It was as if all mankind would become a single clone of cells—or a single insect colony, informed by a common unity of mind instead of common instincts.

This is of course a cultural, not a biological dream: what Teilhard called "an irresistible physical process: the collectivization of mankind." Nor did he balk at its totalitarian implications:

> My answer is that I do not think we are yet in a position to judge recent totalitarian experiments fairly: . . . it is not the principle of totalization that is at fault but the clumsy and incomplete way in which it has been applied.

It has been thought that Teilhard was silenced by his superiors, and died in 1955 with his work unpublished, because they would not acknowledge that man has evolved as the other animals have, without a special act of creation. But it seems to me that they must also have shuddered at his picture of the future, in which man will lose his identity in a God who has become a sort of queen bee of mind. Indeed, they cannot have approved his wish to see man saved by collective rather than personal grace.

Teilhard de Chardin was, beneath the faith and the hallelujahs, a pessimist about the fate of man; Margaret Mead, pouring her torrential prose over the coffee tables, is an optimist. I am on her side. But I am conscious that when any one of us thinks about the future, what we see is still hopelessly vague and idealized. I fear that, at bottom, we are handicapped by a shortcoming of scientific method. We find it hard to analyze culture and society because they are not things but activities. For we are all, as scientists, thing-directed; the method of the natural sciences (biological as well as physical) is to manipulate things which persist through time and which, if they change, change into other things. This search for things as the units of science may be slackening, and it may be that another generation will be more process-directed than we are. (Perhaps a prophetic example is the later work of Konrad Lorenz on the evolution of animal gesture, such as the courtship poses of different species.) If so, the social sciences will have a better backing in scientific method, and may become the leaders in discovery. But meanwhile we lack the conceptual habits to handle the units of behavior, the fluent actions and innovations, from which social conduct is compounded.

The other conclusion that I draw from these two remarkable books is larger. Every discussion of culture, and every projection of it, in the end must confront the importance that we give to the individual man and the importance that we give to society as a whole. This was clear to Jean-Jacques Rousseau when he first conceived the evolution of society back in the eighteenth century. Now it is clearer that this confrontation, this balance, hinges on our conception of the nature of man. What makes a man, any man, specifically human? How does he differ from the other animals, first biologically and mentally? What are the talents which are truly human, all the way back to the Stone Age and before? And how have the successive ages nourished them to become the human gifts of today?

This is a bold program of analysis, both in biology and in culture. And only when we know all that this asks—the essential identity of man—have we earned the right to look forward. We can say with confidence that our projections point along the line which is fixed by the human talents, and will help to fulfill them. It is not what we think society is that counts, but what we think man is. The only meaning for culture is the fulfillment of man as the very special and gifted, the unique animal: the social solitary.

12
TOWARD A PHILOSOPHY OF BIOLOGY

The new biology has been built in the decades since World War II, in large part by young men whose careers the war had interrupted, and who had to make a fresh start at the end of it. Many of them had been employed on physical problems during the war, and physics had come to seem rather barren to them, surrounded with unpleasant hints of regimentation and secrecy. By comparison, biology looked invitingly like open country. Leo Szilard characterized his unspoken belief and theirs simply, as "What I brought into biology was an attitude: the conviction that mysteries can be solved. If secrets exist, they must be explainable." And the word was out that they were beginning to be explained: the chemists Linus Pauling and Desmond Bernal were already doing impressive work on the structure of proteins, and the physicist Max Delbrück led a program which might unravel the genetic tape or blueprint within the cell.

In moving to biology from physics, the newcomers naturally brought with them the habits of thought that had been successful in physics. For example, it had become commonplace in physics to think of any material body as an arrangement of large numbers of atoms, repeated in some regular way; and to explain the behavior of the body and derive its properties by going back to these basic units. Anyone now coming into biology was sure to look for a similar unit of structure there. Evidently, this unit of structure in living matter was the cell.

The most arresting discoveries that have been made in the biology of the cell concern the inborn instructions which regulate it—that is to say, the genetic material which goes from one generation to the next, and acts as a blueprint or program to direct the sequence of chemical processes that makes up the life cycle of each cell. The facts are now well known: the main activity of a cell is the manufacture of many specific proteins, and the instructions for the manufacturing process are carried in simpler material in the cell nucleus, the nucleic acids.

In 1950 bold men were asking themselves what could be the structure of the nucleic acids which would give them the power to copy themselves when the cell divides in two, and supply each daughter cell with an accurate copy. And in 1951 James Watson and Francis Crick revealed the starting simplicity of the double helix of the DNA molecule.

Since there are many varieties of living creatures, and many genes in each, there are many different forms of DNA, in each of which the sequence of bases is different and is characteristic for some chemical process to make a protein in that creature. Crick and his colleagues have since shown that the sequence of bases in a molecule of DNA spells out the twenty amino acids, which in turn make the proteins. We have a simple hierarchy: the four bases are the four letters of the alphabet, each set of three letters makes up a word which is a fundamental amino acid, and the twenty words in their turn are assembled into different sentences which are the different proteins.

A cell is not at all a simple unit: and the very fact that there are creatures that consist of a single cell shows that it is effectively a microcosm of life. Since life is evidently not a thing but a process, it follows that we have to study the cell not merely as a structure, but as a changing structure. The cycle of events that follow one another within the cell is a life cycle, but more than that, it *is* life. But the basic structures and sequences of life follow from those of dead nature without the intervention of any special powers or acts. I want to make this point clearly and with force. There is no place for vitalism in the analysis of the cell. Certainly life, the perpetuation of form and process from generation to generation, is extraordinary: but whatever is extraordinary about it is not at the level of the atoms, or the molecules, or the genes and chromosomes and enzymes and electric discharges, the interlocking sequences of instructions and communications which actually make the body and the brain work. All that is understandable in physical terms, without the intervention of any mystic principles.

From the time of Henri Bergson and before, philosophers have been wrongheaded when they have tried to find a special sanction for the uniqueness of man in the mystery of life. What makes man unique is his command of cognitive knowledge, and that is not a property of life in the individual cell; on the contrary, it is precisely what man does not share with a cell—even with any other assembly of cells. The mystery is not in the cell: the mystery is that the cell is not a mystery to us—the mystery is that man can understand so much of nature.

None of this is to deny that life as a process has a different character from the other processes of the natural world. Life is a very specialized and accidental phenomenon: it derives its character (as well as its mystery) from the fact that it is improbable. I would put this forward as a philosophical principle, *that life is unique, and the forms of life are unique arrangements of matter, precisely because they are accidental.* I shall return to the statistical reasons and implications of that in good time.

If an arrangement of matter is unique, it must be accidental —that is, it must be singled out from all the other possible arrangements by an action which is arbitrary and highly improbable. Erwin Schrödinger took a similar idea from Max Delbrück, and Delbrück in his turn had been inspired to turn to biology by an essay on *Light and Life* by the greatest of all the quantum physicists, Niels Bohr.

Delbrück has recorded frankly what troubled him about physics in the 1930s and what he hoped to find in biology. Physics was exploring the behavior of matter on the minute scale of quantum changes. It seemed to Delbrück that there was something logically (and aesthetically) wrong in the disproportion between the tiny quantum effects and the vast apparatus which was required to demonstrate them. He hoped to find in living matter a kind of quantum resonator or multiplier, which would express new physical laws because it would display in visible form the impact of single quantum events.

In any simple sense, Delbrück turned out to be mistaken in his hope. Yet the crucial thought in Delbrück and Schrödinger is exactly right; as so often in science, the wrong guess is better and more creative than no guess at all. The cell is sensitive to single and unpredictable events which abruptly change its potential and that of the generations of cells that derive from it. The development of life from one form to another is unlike that of the rest of the physical world, because it is triggered by accidents, and they give each new form its unique character. Life is not an orderly continuum like the growing of a crystal. *The nature of life is only expressed in its perpetual evolution, which is another name for the succession (and the success) of its errors.*

Since I began this essay by analyzing the cell, I should now round it out by discussing the process of evolution. There are five distinct principles which make up the concept of evolution, as I interpret it. They are:

1. family descent
2. natural selection
3. Mendelian inheritance
4. fitness for change
5. stratified stability.

I shall present them in what is in effect their historical order. For evolution was not formed as an explanatory concept all in one leap; it grew by degrees from distinct strands, which came together one after another. The logic of evolution requires all five strands, in my view.

This first and central strand is simply the idea that the likenesses between different species of plants and animals are, literally, *family likenesses*; they derive from the fact that the species have a common family tree and ancestry. This idea is older than *The Origin of Species*, and goes back at least to Charles Darwin's grandfather Erasmus; yet (as a matter of history) this is what gave the book its shocking and decisive impact in 1859.

The principle of *natural selection* is the second strand in evolution; it is what gives the observations a structure and turns them into a theory. Selection is not strictly a causal mechanism, but a statistical one; and evolution is therefore the work of chance. Darwin was in no doubt about that—"Heaven forefend me from Lamarckian nonsense of a 'tendency to progression' "—and neither were his readers. We think of them now as outraged simply by the implication that man had not been specially created, as the Old Testament recorded, but was descended from the same stock as the apes and other mammals. But they were more deeply outraged, in their religious and their moral convictions, by the central place of chance in Darwin's theory of evolution.

Darwin had no theory of inheritance that could account for the persistence of a variant form from generation to generation. In this respect, his trust in natural selection as an agent that could form permanent species was an act of faith, backed only by the known experience of plant and animal breeders.

In essence, this difficulty was resolved by Gregor Mendel in the decade that followed the publication of *The Origin of Species*, and Darwin should have known that. Mendel guessed and then proved that every heritable trait is governed by a pair of discrete units, what we now call genes, one from each parent—of which one may mask or dominate the expression of the other, but both of which will be preserved and handed on to some of the offspring. This theory of *Mendelian inheritance* is a third and essential part of a soundly based theory of evolution.

In my view, it is necessary to add to a realistic account of evolution two further principles which govern its operation as we witness it. These two strands are *fitness for change* and *stratified stability*. That is to say, they are concerned, the one with the variability of living forms, and the other with their stability; and between them they explain how it comes about that biological evolution has a direction in time—and has a direction in the same sense that time has. The direction of evolution is an important and indeed crucial phenomenon, which singles it out among statistical processes. For in so far as statistical processes have a direction at all, it is usually a movement toward the average— and that is exactly what evolution is not. There is therefore something profound to be explained here, which goes to the heart of the mechanism of life; and it is natural that the disputes about the nature of life center on this. For the direction of evolution, which can be traced for about three thousand million years, gives it the appearance of a planned program: and the question is, How does this come about if there is no plan?

We need to be clear here what might be meant by a plan. For example, a vitalist who thinks it inconceivable that the orderly tree or pyramid of living forms could have evolved without a master plan might be content to say that the plan was conceived by a creator who simply understood the laws of chance better than we do. Indeed, he may claim (and no doubt he will, in time) that the two principles of variability and stability which I shall develop below demonstrate that the statistics of evolution have a scientific structure which an all-seeing creator understands at least as well as I do, and could employ to plan the future with perfect foresight.

Nevertheless, it is clear that such a statistical definition of a cosmic plan can satisfy no one, and is fundamentally pointless. For in the end it says no more than that the laws of nature take their course undisturbed, and move to their outcome with no other guidance than the edict which made them laws on the day of creation. Accordingly, we must suppose that those who believe that life follows some larger plan than the laws of physics constitute have in their minds a more literal picture of a plan.

For example, it is suggested that a living creature goes through a complex of cycles which are so matched to its environment that they have the manifest plan or purpose, they are patently *designed*, to preserve the life of the individual. But the fact that a living cell (for instance, a bacterium) is geared to go on living in the face of disturbance is no more supernatural than the fact that a falling stone is geared to go on falling, and a stone in free space is geared to go on moving in a straight line. This is its nature, and does not require explanation any more (or in any other sense) than does the behavior of a ray of light or the complex structure of an atom of uranium.

Therefore the vitalist must have some more sophisticated idea of a plan than the mere persistence of a cycle, or even of a linked sequence of cycles. Michael Polanyi, who claims that perpetuation of life cannot be understood except as an overall plan or purpose, uses a telling illustration. He says that to explain the machinery of a cell is like explaining the machinery of a watch; and that this misses the most important thing about a watch, which is that its machinery is planned for a purpose—to tell the time.

The design of a watch is the classical illustration for God's design in man that deists introduced in the eighteenth century. So what is telling is not that the illustration is fresh, but that it is oddly old-fashioned. Polanyi now gives the argument a new turn by saying that just as the design of the watch points to and is only understood in its purpose, so the design of the machinery of life points to and is only understood at a higher level of explanation by purpose.

However, the plan by which the watchmaker coordinates the totality of the machine from its subassemblies is not different in kind from the plan on which he forms a subassembly from its parts. They are all equally plans that are *closed*, in the sense that they describe the complete course or cycle which the operation runs. A closed plan is a rational sequence of instructions; the different levels of organization within it are merely levels of convenience; and there can be no level of design above the running of the machine, no overall purpose, unless there is an explicit designer outside the machine for whom it is a means to that purpose. We should have to believe in a creator with a conscious purpose, like a watchmaker who wants to tell the time.

Since I have stressed the character of what I call *closed* plans, it will be evident that I intend to contrast them with *open* plans. It is valid to regard an organism as a historical creation whose "plan" is explained by its evolution. But the plan of life in this sense is an open plan; only open plans can be creative; and evolution is the open plan which has created what is radically new in life, the dynamic of time.

So it is timely now to consider evolution as an open plan, and to ask what are the additional principles that are needed to make it capable of creating the new living forms that we know. For it is essential that we recognize these forms as new and as genuine creations. They arise naturally in and from the course of evolution, as a work of art or an ingenious move at chess arises naturally in and from the march or play of each successive step. Yet the work of art is not implied in its beginning, and the elegant mate at chess does not sleep like a seed in the first move of the game. They are open creations, and so is life; it is not a closed plan like that which runs its rigid course from the seed to the full-grown plant.

Put in this way, the issue is clear. There is a relation between the direction of evolution and the direction of time. In a history of three thousand million years, evolution has not run backward. Why is this? Why does evolution not run at random hither and thither in time? What is the screw that moves it forward—or at least, what is the ratchet that keeps it from slipping back? Is it possible to have such a mechanism which is not planned? What is the relation that ties evolution to the arrow of time, and makes it a barbed arrow?

The paradox to be resolved here is classical in science: How can disorder on the small scale be consonant with order on the large scale, in time or in space? Evolution must have a different statistical form in which there is an inherent potential for large-scale order to act as a sieve or selector on the individual chance events. The principle of a potential of order in the selection of chance events is clear, but what is never clear in advance is how it works. It is here that we need two additional mechanisms in evolution to turn the principle into natural selection as we know it, that is, with a natural order in time.

The first of the two additional mechanisms which we now see to underlie evolution is *fitness for change*, or (in more formal language) *selection for adaptability*. This important and unexpected process gives a special character to the variability which is inherent within any species. It is of course evident to our eyes that the members of a species are not identical; and in addition to this visible diversity, we know that there is an invisible diversity hidden in the mutant genes. This pool of hidden diversity supplies the variants which nature can select in order to modify the species. Thus we see that hidden diversity is an instrument for adaptation in the future.

But what is less easy to see, and is new and important, is that hidden diversity is the instrument for *adaptability* now, in the present. In order that a species shall be capable of changing to fit its environment tomorrow, it must maintain its fitness for change today. If this is to be done in the present, without some mysterious plan for the future, it must be by natural selection, not for this or that variant, but for variability itself.

And in fact it is evident that there is natural selection in favor of genetic variability. The selection is made by the small changes, up and down and up again and down again, by which the environment flutters about its mean. So the critical step in the conception of an open plan is certainly this: that "the survival of the fittest" must be understood as the *selection of those fitted for change* as part of the total concept of fitness to a changing environment.

Adaptation has to match the changes in the environment, but adaptability has to match the rates of change: it is (so to speak) the differential coefficient of adaptation, and expresses the second order of difference in the organism and its environment. It is of course characteristic of cooperative phenomena in nature that they involve higher orders of relation, and therefore the matching of higher orders of difference, than do isolated phenomena.

It is evident that we cannot discuss the variability of organisms and species without also examining their stability. We have therefore also to trace a mechanism for stability, as the second of the two balanced mechanisms that are needed to complete our understanding of evolution. I call this, the fifth and last strand in my analysis of evolution, the concept of *stratified stability*.

Evolution is commonly presented, even now, as if it required nothing but natural selection to explain its action, one minute step after another, as it were gene by gene. But an organism is an integrated system, and that implies that its coordination is easily disturbed. This is true of every gene: normal or mutant, it has to be incorporated into the ordered totality of the gene complex like a piece in a jigsaw puzzle.

Yet the analogy of the jigsaw is too rigid: we need a geometrical model of stability in living processes and the structures that carry them out which is not so landlocked against change. Moreover, the model must express the way in which the more complex forms of life arise from the simpler forms, and arise later in time. This is the model which I call *stratified* stability.

There are evolutionary processes in nature which do not demand the intervention of selective forces. Characteristic is the evolution of the chemical elements, which are built up in different stars step by step, first hydrogen to helium, then helium to carbon, and on to heavier elements. The most telling example is the creation of carbon from helium. Two helium nuclei which collide do not make a stable element, and fly apart again in less than a millionth of a millionth of a second. But if in that splinter of time a third helium nucleus runs into the pair, it binds them together and makes a stable triad which is a nucleus of carbon. And every carbon atom in every organic molecule in every cell in every living creature has been formed by such a wildly improbable triple collision in a star.

Here then is a physical model which shows how simple units come together to make more complex configurations. The stable higher forms cannot be reached in one leap: they have to be built up layer by layer, and each layer must be a stable form at which evolution can pause and accumulate enough raw material so that improbable encounters can happen to create still more complex stable forms.

The stratification of stability is fundamental in living systems, and it explains why evolution has a consistent direction in time. For the building up of stability in organization has a direction —the more complex stratum built on the next lower, and so on —which cannot be reversed.

There is therefore a peculiar irony in the vitalist claim that the progress of evolution from simple to complex cannot be the work of chance. On the contrary, as we see, exactly this is how chance works, and is constrained to work by its nature. The total potential of stability that is hidden in matter can only be evoked in steps, each higher layer resting on the layer below it. The stable units that compose one layer are the raw material for random encounters which will produce higher configurations, some of which chance to be stable. So long as there remains a potential of stability which has not become actual, there is no other way for chance to go.

It is often said that the progression from simple to complex runs counter to the normal statistics of chance which are formalized in the second law of thermodynamics. But this interpretation quite misunderstands the character of statistical laws in general. The second law of thermodynamics, for example (which is often quoted), describes the statistics of a system whose configurations are all equal, and it makes the obvious remark that chance can only make such a system fluctuate around its average. There are no stable states in such a system, and there is therefore no stratum that can establish itself; the system rests around its average only by a principle of indifference, because numerically the most configurations are bunched around the average.

Time in the large, open time, only has a direction when we mark and scale it by the evolutionary processes that climb from simple to more and more complex by steps. It is evolutionary processes that give time its direction; and no mystical explanation is required where there is nothing to explain. The progression from simple to complex, the building up of stratified stability, is the necessary character of evolution from which time takes its direction. And it is not a forward direction in the sense of a thrust toward the future, a headed arrow. What evolution does is to give the arrow of time a barb which stops it from running backwards; and once it has this barb, the chance play of errors will take it forward of itself.

Yet there is still a deeper question to be asked about time. It concerns our two experiences of time, one of which is the inner time of our body as an organism, and the other is the outer time of evolution. How does it come about that these two times, inner and outer, closed and open, have the same direction? Why does our sense of growing old and of going toward death point the same way as evolution, when we might well have expected the two to point in opposite directions?

The answer lies in the common mechanisms of life, which drive both the closed cycles of the organism and the open plan of evolution. In a living organism, growing old is not a thermal decay, and death is not a fall into the average such as the second law describes. As we understand old age, the cells in the organism age individually when they happen to make errors in their internal copying and when these errors are of a kind which repeat or perpetuate themselves. This is also and precisely the mechanism which underlies evolution. The cell cannot accommodate the errors because they do not fit into its organization, which is closed. But in the open field of evolution, the errors which are able to repeat or perpetuate themselves are the stuff of creation. The organism experiences the accumulation of errors in its cells as the direction of time toward its death. Evolution goes the same way because its mechanism is the same; and we perceive cosmic time as running the same way also because its direction is pointed by evolution.

Life as an evolutionary process is open, with no cycle in time; and it derives this openness from just such accidents or errors, at least in kind, as kill the individual. Here the mechanism is evolution, and evolution is that quantum resonator or multiplier, the exploitation of an accident to create a new and unique form, for which Delbrück was looking when he came into biology. *The closed cycle of an individual life and the open time of evolution are dual aspects of life, driven by the common mainspring of quantum accidents,* which are only properly understood when they are put side by side as complementary parts or processes of life.

The living creature and its evolution are the two matched faces of life. In this pairing, evolution is the creative partner: it does not solve a problem, as the cycles of the organism do, but makes a genuine creation—a creature. We can say of it what Piet Hein said of a work of art, in a penetrating phrase: that it solves a problem which we could not formulate until it was solved.

13
NEW CONCEPTS IN THE EVOLUTION OF COMPLEXITY

Vitalism is a traditional and persistent belief that the laws of physics that hold in the inanimate world will not suffice to explain the phenomena of life. Of course it is not suggested, either by those who share the belief or by those like me who reject it, that we know all the laws of physics now, or will know them soon. Rather, what is silently supposed by both sides is that we know what kind of laws physics is made up of and will continue to discover in inanimate matter; and although that is a vague description to serve as a premise, it is what inspires vitalists to claim (and their opponents to deny) that some phenomena of life cannot be explained by laws of this kind.

The phenomena that are said to be inaccessible to physics are of two different kinds. One school of vitalists stresses the complexity of the individual organism. The other school of vitalists asserts that physical laws are insufficient to explain the direction of evolution in time: that is, the increase in complexity in new species, such as man, when compared to old species from which they derive, such as the tree shrews. The two grounds for finding physics to fall short are therefore quite distinct, and I shall discuss them separately. I begin with a summary sketch of each.

The first ground, then, is that the individual organism (even a single cell) functions in a way which transcends what physics can explain, and implies the existence of laws of another kind —what Walter Elsasser calls biotonic laws. Elsasser argues that the development of an organism is too complex to be coded in the genes, and that there must be larger laws of biological organization that guide it overall. Eugene Wigner argues that development and reproduction are subject to so many statistical variations that there can be no certainty that the organism will survive them unless it is controlled by higher laws.

These arguments do not differ in principle from the classical argument, put forward (for example) by Bolingbroke early in the eighteenth century, that an organism is at least as complicated as a clock, and that we cannot imagine a clock to have come into being by accident. True, neither Elsasser nor Wigner speaks of origins, but both imply that the configuration of parts and the sequence of functions in the cell require a higher coordination than is provided by the laws of physics—by what one might call the simple engineering rules between the parts of the clock. Bolingbroke ascribes this higher coordination to God, and Elsasser and Wigner to biotonic laws, but this is only a difference in nomenclature.

The second school of vitalists finds another ground for claiming that the laws of physics are biologically incomplete, namely in questions about the evolution of organisms. Michael Polanyi asks questions of this kind, though he lumps all levels together—origins, functioning of individuals, and the sequence of species. He claims, as vitalists have always done, that there must be an overall plan which directs them all, and I shall criticize the confusion of meanings in his idea of plan or purpose. I shall distinguish between two concepts, the usual concept of a closed or bounded plan (that is, a tactic or solution for a defined problem), and a new concept of an *open* or *unbounded* plan, that is, a general strategy.

But beyond these concepts, there remains the crucial question raised by Polanyi—and others before him, of course, in earlier forms. Evolution has the direction, speaking roughly, from simple to more and more complex: more and more complex functions of higher organisms, mediated by more and more complex structures, which are themselves made of more and more complex molecules. How has this come about? How can it be explained if there is no overall plan to create more complex creatures—which means at least, if there is no overall law (other than evolution as a mechanism), to generate complexity? In particular, how do we square this direction with the second law of thermodynamics, which (as a general description subsuming ordinary physical laws) predicts the breakdown of complex structures into simple ones? This is the constellation of questions to which I shall give most attention.

The course of my argument will incidentally reveal what additional physical laws we expect to discover as we continue to unfold the chemistry of life. In essence, they can be expected to be laws of specific relations between a few kinds of atoms which govern the *stability* of the structures that can be assembled from them. These are indeed laws of cooperative phenomena or ensembles, but they are highly particular and empirical, being simply accounts of the stability to be found in different conjunctions of matter under the conditions we know on earth.

I shall assume that the reader is familiar with the way in which heredity is mediated by genes, which are molecules made up from four fairly small chemical bases that are strung out on two paired strands of DNA. Since there are many varieties of living creatures, and many genes in each, there are many different forms of DNA, in each of which the sequence of bases is different and is characteristic for directing some chemical process in that creature. The sequence of bases in a molecule of DNA spells out the twenty amino acids, which in their turn make the proteins. We have a simple hierarchy: the four bases are the four letters of the alphabet, each set of three letters makes up a word which is a fundamental amino acid, and the twenty words in their turn are assembled into different sentences which are the different proteins.

The book of heredity is not the whole book of life. It records only those instructions which make a species breed true, so that the child is revealed as a copy of the parents. Yet this is far-reaching, because the living child, the living cell, is not a static copy, but is a dynamic process in which one action follows another in a characteristic pattern. We only dimly understand how the process of maturation unfolds this inborn ability. Nevertheless, we have made a beginning by seeing how the processes of making one protein after another are programmed from the vocabulary of life so that they develop a stepwise, coordinated sequence.

Elsasser has argued that the development of living creatures (some of which consist of only a single cell) is too complex and too closely integrated to be directed by the genetic machinery. To this fundamental and, so to speak, primitive claim a biologist can only reply that there is absolutely no evidence to support it. No counting of constants, no calculation of the content of information in a set of chromosomes, can give any ground for it, because we simply do not know what the inner relations and restrictions between the parts of a complex molecule are. We do not even understand yet why a long protein molecule folds into the specific geometrical configuration which is its own, and not into any other. But we expect to find these laws, and we expect them to be no more esoteric or biotonic than, say, the laws which inform us that some assemblies of fundamental particles in physics make up stable atomic nuclei, and others do not.

In the same way, there is no evidence at all that the interaction of genes, either on the same or on different chromosomes, requires any kind of master law. In general it is mediated by local relations in the organ that is being shaped, just as the growth of a set of normal cells on a microscope slide is controlled in a regular array by chemical content between the walls of neighboring cells. It may be that there are some places on the chromosomes where master controls reside, but if so, they can be expected simply to have the character of special genes. We already know that there are some master genes which control groups of other genes, for example by making them all more mutable or more stable.

A single-cell bacterium goes through its life cycle on an exact schedule, and every step in the sequence is a rearrangement of and within the molecules which compose it. So the machinery of the cell, the clockwork that drives and demonstrates its life, is a constant shaping and reshaping of its molecular material. It is suggested by vitalists that these cycles are so matched to its environment that they have the manifest plan or purpose, they are patently *designed*, to preserve the life of the bacterium. Of course this cannot be simply on the ground that the processes of life are cyclic: for there are plenty of physical actions, say in gravitation, which are cyclic—from the tides to the seasons. Nor can it be on the ground that there is something mysterious about the resistance of a cycle against disturbing forces: for that is displayed by any cycle—for example, a spinning top. The fact that a living cell is geared to go on living in the face of a disturbance is no more supernatural than the fact that a falling stone is geared to go on falling, and a stone in free space is geared to go on moving in a straight line. This is its nature, and does not require explanation any more (or in any other sense) than does the behavior of a ray of light or the complex structure of an atom of uranium.

Therefore the vitalist must have some more sophisticated idea of a plan than the mere persistence of a cycle, or even of a linked group of cycles. Usually what he does is to propose a distinction between different levels of explanation (and, by implication, of action). He says that we may well explain the mechanics of each cycle, but that this still misses the point of what they achieve as a totality; and that this achievement, namely the perpetuation of life in general, cannot be understood except as an overall plan or purpose.

I shall return to the discussion of the concept of plans later. Here I will content myself with repeating again that though there is much about life that we do not understand, there is no evidence at all that this is because there is a mystery in its basic processes. Living matter is different from nonliving, but not because it follows different rules. The rules of organization by which the parts of a cell work together, the sequence of procedures which make it live, are understandable in the same terms as any other molecular process. The basic structures and sequences of life follow from those of dead nature without the intervention of any special powers or acts. There is no evidence for vitalism in the analysis of the cell, or of any simple assembly of cells that we know: a microorganism, a limb, or a cancer.

A different and deeper question has been raised by Eugene Wigner. He remarks that living cells go through their life cycles by taking nourishment from the environment, and incorporating it either into their own structure or into that of daughter cells. During this transformation, he argues, quantum effects make it impossible to ensure with certainty that the cell will make an accurate copy of itself (or of some specified modification of itself); and therefore the laws of physics cannot suffice to explain how living matter perpetuates itself. Wigner calculates in detail how the manufacture in the cell of exact or similar, specified copies can be shown to be (in his phrase) "infinitely unlikely." Even if we treat the calculation as only indicative (as Wigner himself does at the end of his paper), the indication is that copying of any specific molecule (a strand of DNA, for instance) must produce an unacceptable error, as a result of unpredictable quantum events. And this, Wigner implies, flies in the face of our daily observation of the process of reproduction.

The argument is strange because it uses the same quantum effects that Max Delbrück and Erwin Schrödinger used long ago, to arrive at exactly the opposite conclusion. Schrödinger reasoned that quantum effects are essential to explain the uniqueness of a living form. Wigner turns this reasoning upside-down, and concludes that no living form can maintain its identity in the face of quantum disturbances.

When we examine the argument which leads Wigner to his conclusion, its limitations are evident (and are acknowledged by him). Wigner's procedure is to transform the quantum state vectors of the cell and its nourishment, taken together, into the state vectors of the two similar cells that are to result (and of the rejected part of the nourishment). It appears that the number of equations to be satisfied is far larger than the number of unknowns at our disposal, if it is assumed (as in the absence of any more specific knowledge Wigner has to assume) that the Hamiltonian matrix which represents the transformation consists, apart from its symmetry, of *random* elements. But of course this begs the whole question, because it necessarily disregards all relations within the matrix of transformation—that is, the organized inner structure of the process of ingestion and cell division. So long as we do not know the relations between the elements of the matrix, the counting of unknowns and variables at our disposal is quite inconclusive, and can be wholly misleading.[1]

But in fact Wigner's procedure is (as he admits) even less realistic than this first criticism implies. For it is the nature of any

[1]For example, it is a familiar paradox in projective algebraic geometry that an argument like Wigner's can be used to prove that every conic section is a pair of straight lines.

argument that proposes a count of unknowns and variables that it can only assert or deny the existence of a solution that makes the outcome of the process certain. Even if we were to accept Wigner's assumptions, therefore, we could only conclude that the process of cell division as he idealizes it cannot be guaranteed to yield a second similar cell with certainty. But nothing is asserted, or could be concluded, about any process of cell division which has only a probability of producing viable offspring —even if the probability is as high as 0.99. The reasoning is not applicable to probable outcomes, however high or low.[2]

However, experience shows that no biological process works with certainty, and that few organisms produce similar and viable offspring with as high a probability as 0.99. We must therefore recognize that Wigner's argument misses the essence of biological processes, namely that they do not function with certainty. Indeed, the evolution of more highly organized forms of life than the cell would not have been possible if they had done so.

A cell in its task of simply living makes proteins over and over again from the same blueprint, and now and again it also replicates the blueprint when it divides in two. No conceivable machinery, within the known laws of nature or any that we might think of, can carry on this endless work of copying with zero tolerance—which means, without making individual mistakes from time to time. We put these mistakes down to quantum effects, and that is right; yet in a sense quantum physics is simply a formalization of our well-founded and much wider conviction that no natural process can work with zero tolerance and so be immune from error. Just as we know that perpetual motion is impossible, and can derive a great part of classical mechanics from this Law of the Impossible, so we know that perpetual accuracy of reproduction is inconceivable, and we can regard

[2]For example, if Wigner's reasoning here were applied to nuclear fission, it would persuade us that a chain reaction is impossible—because we can never stipulate that the entry of a neutron into a specified nucleus will certainly release two neutrons.

quantum physics as a specification of that knowledge: the specification of a nonzero tolerance, namely Planck's quantum constant, below which we cannot press.

The discrepancy arises because life has two separate components, and Wigner ignores just that creative component which is characteristic of life and is absent in dead matter. Life is not only a process of accurate copying: that is carried out quite as neatly in the geometrical scaffolding of a dead crystal. Life is also and essentially an evolutionary process, which moves forward only because there are errors in the copy, and every so often one of these errors is successful enough to be incorporated as another step or threshold in its progression. It is important to understand that the living creature combines both procedures, and to see how it does so.

The accumulation of individual errors is certainly a handicap to a cell: but we have to distinguish between two kinds, or better between two places, of error. Errors made now and again in producing a molecule of a protein which is merely a momentary step in the metabolism of the cell are not likely to be important, for the next molecule of the protein can be expected to be normal again. But there are some proteins which play a basic part in the productive machinery of the cell, and act as jigs or machine tools to help make copies of other proteins. When such a master molecule is wrongly made, it will in its turn cause errors in the making of other copies, and as a result the error will be cumulative. Leslie Orgel has suggested that errors in such master molecules may be the cause for cells breaking down, and the suggestion is supported by recent experiments. Moreover, if Orgel's picture is right, every cell must break down sooner or later when it accumulates errors in some master molecule. There can be no immortal cells. Indeed, Leonard Hayflick has found in careful experiments that by the time a cell has divided about fifty times, the clone of cells formed from it all fail to divide. *The machinery of life ensures the death of individuals.*

But exactly this machinery also ensures the evolution of new forms. *The errors which destroy the individual are also the origin of species.* Without these errors, there would be no evolution, because there would be no raw material of genetic mutants for natural selection to work on. There would only be one universal form of life, and however well adapted that might have been to the environment in which it was formed, it would have perished long ago in the first sharp change of climate. When Wigner and Walter Elsasser say that there must be some biological law different from the laws of physics in order that copying in the organism shall be free from error, and the storage of the instructions which govern its exact form and development from the cell shall be perfectly accurate, they are asking for the immortality of the individual but ensuring the destruction of species. We have only to look about us to see that the evidence is against them, on both counts.

Evolution is crucial to any discussion of biology, because this and only this makes biology a different kind of subject from physics. A recent survey by Desmond Bernal of what is known about biological molecules begins with a chapter on "The Nature of Biology," and he opens it with a section whose title bluntly asks "Does Biology Exist?" The question is meant to remind us abruptly that biology is a different kind of study from other sciences, because it studies a very specialized and, as it were, accidental phenomenon. Bernal puts the distinction precisely:

> I believe there is a radical difference, fundamentally a philosophical difference, between biology and the so-called exact or inorganic sciences, particularly physics. In the latter we postulate elementary particles which are necessary to the structure of the universe and that the laws controlling their movements and transformations are intrinsically necessary and in general hold over the whole universe.
>
> Biology, however, deals with descriptions and ordering of very special parts of the universe which we call life—even more particularly in these days, terrestrial life. It is primarily a descriptive science, more like geography, dealing with the structure and working of a number of peculiarly organized entities, at a particular moment of time on a particular planet.

Perhaps Bernal is too narrow when he compares biology with geography, which is mainly a description of space. The comparison that comes to my mind is rather with geology, which like biology deals with configurations in space and traces their behavior in time. But essentially the distinction that he makes is well grounded; life has a more accidental and local character than the other phenomena of the physical world.

I would go further, and say that life has a *more open and unbounded* character than the other phenomena of the physical world: it is incomplete and unfinished in a way that they are not. That is, biology has a different character from physics at every point in evolutionary time. The biological universe that we are discussing today is different from that which we could have discussed three million years ago—when indeed there was no homo sapiens to discuss it. And we must expect that the biological universe of three million years hence may be quite as different again.

Let us make this distinction explicitly. The development of life from one form to another is unlike that of the rest of the physical world, because it is triggered by accidents, and they give each new form its unique character. Life is not an orderly continuum like the growing of a crystal; it creates new expressions, and remains constantly open to them, as a succession of errors which can only occur because life is accident-prone. The nature of life is only expressed in its perpetual evolution, which is another name for the succession (and the success) of its errors.

The molecules that make up a cell or an individual form a physical system with many states. If we map all possible states (disorderly as well as orderly) by the points of an abstract space, there is a narrow sequence of points which maps the sequence of steps in the life cycle of the cell, or the sequence of states of the individual before he returns to (approximately) the same state—say, waking in the morning. Since the cycle of states returns on itself, the sequence of points forms (virtually) a closed loop. Thus, on the scale of the cell and of the individual, life is a process which is topologically closed. It runs over more or less the same loop again and again, and in time it runs down.

Yet life does not run down in the way in which natural processes run down, by the general leveling of energy peaks which is called the second law of thermodynamics. The death of a cell or of an individual is not a leveling out, a falling apart of the architecture, as decay after death is. Instead, death is a failure of the metabolism to continue its cycles, and it begins in a failure to repeat the cycles accurately. It seems likely that the cell or individual is clogged by errors which are inevitable and become cumulative: whatever the underlying cause proves to be, the topological loop wavers and comes to a stop.

But life as an evolutionary sequence is not a closed loop. On the contrary, life as evolution is topologically open, for it has no cycle in time. Yet it derives this openness from just such accidents or errors, at least in kind, as kill the individual. The mechanism of survival for a species is its evolution, and evolution is that quantum resonator or multiplier, the exploitation of an accident to create a new and unique form, for which Max Delbrück was looking when he came into biology.

In summary, the closed loop of an individual life and the open path of evolution are dual aspects of life. The common mainspring of quantum accidents (that is, of errors in the copying of biological molecules) may be responsible for individual death, and is certainly responsible for evolution. Both are only properly understood when they are put side by side as complementary parts or processes of life.

I will make this distinction in another form by examining the different arguments for vitalism which have been advanced by Michael Polanyi, first at the level of the cell, and then at the level of evolution. At the first or lower level, Polanyi simply says that to explain the machinery of a cell is like explaining the machinery of a watch while missing the most important thing about it, which is that a watch is planned for a purpose—to tell the time.

The design of a watch is the classical illustration for God's design in man that deists introduced in the eighteenth century. Henry St. John, Viscount Bolingbroke, and William Paley in the *Evidences of Christianity* used it to claim that man is a more ingenious machine than is a watch, and must therefore be supposed to have been designed by a more ingenious creator. Polanyi now gives this argument a new look by saying that just as the design of the watch points to and is only understood in its purpose, so the design of the machinery of life points to and is only understood at a higher level of explanation by purpose. He calls this the boundary condition for any mechanism, but these words only restate the requirement which he proposes, namely that it must fit into and serve some overall plan outside itself. In essence, the argument remains in the eighteenth century: we know that the watch is ingenious because we know the purpose for which it is planned.

Perhaps it is easiest to see what is wrong with this argument by deriving a paradox from it, as follows. The argument is intended to show that man (and any other living form) is not simply a machine. In order to show this, he is compared with a typical machine, namely a watch; and it is concluded that he is more sophisticated, namely more purposeful, than the mechanism that drives the watch. How is this concluded? By showing that the watch itself, as a machine, is more sophisticated, namely more purposeful, than the mechanism that drives it. In short, even a machine is not merely a mechanism, or what we usually call a machine. Man, therefore, is not a machine because he is a machine, and it has already been shown that a machine is not a machine.

How does this paradox come about? Evidently, by confusing the external function for which the machine has been made (by the watchmaker, for example) with the inner plan which the living creature follows as its natural and species-specific sequence of operations. To claim that this inner plan means anything more can only be justified by appealing to a quite abstract, classical tenet of philosophy, that the reduction of a sequence to its parts is not a sufficient explanation of their totality. But the implication is out of place here, where it merely restates the analogy of the watch which is designed to tell the time. There are indeed contexts in philosophy in which reductionism is not enough. But reductionism is valid and sufficient when it is a historical explanation, so that it presents a temporal and logical sequence of steps by which the result has been reached. (Indeed, all causal explanations are of this kind, and can only be challenged if we challenge the first cause.) To reduce a whole to its parts is a valid exposition of its plan if in fact the parts have come together in time, step by step, in building up a sequence of lesser wholes. So it is valid to regard an organism as a historical creation whose plan is explained by its evolution. But the plan of life in this sense is unbounded. Only unbounded plans can be creative; and evolution is such a plan, which has created what is radically new in life, the dynamic of time.

So it is timely now to consider evolution as an open and unbounded plan, and to ask what additional principles are needed to make it capable of creating the new living forms that we know. For it is essential that we recognize these forms as genuine creations, which have not been formed on a bounded plan like that which runs its rigid course from the seed to the full-grown plant.

The distinction here is between a sequence of actions which is fixed in advance by the end state that it must reach, and a train of events which is open and unbounded to the future because its specific outcome is not foreseen. Any bounded plan is in essence the solution to a problem, and life as a mechanism has this character. By contrast, the sequence of events that constitutes an unbounded plan is invented moment by moment from what has gone before, and the outcome is not solved but created. Life as an evolution is a creation of this kind.

In this analysis, the vitalist's question becomes directed to a different issue: the relation between the direction of evolution and the direction of time. In a history of three thousand million years, evolution has not run backward—at least, by and large, and in a definable statistical sense, it has not run backward. (The existence of some lines of regression, such as those which have produced the viruses, does not change this general characterization.) Why is this? Why does evolution not run at random hither and thither in time? What is the screw that moves it forward—or at least, what is the ratchet that keeps it from slipping back? Is it possible to have such a mechanism which is not planned? What is the relation that ties evolution to the arrow of time, and makes it a barbed arrow?

The paradox to be resolved here is classical in science: How can disorder on the small scale be consonant with order on the large scale, in time or in space? If this question is asked of the molecules in a stream of gas, the answer is easy: the motion imposed on the stream swamps the random motions of the individual molecules. But this picture will not help to explain evolution, because there is no imposed motion there. On the contrary, if we were to assume an imposed motion, we would be accepting the postulate of vitalism. Evolution must have a different statistical form, in which there is an inherent potential for large-scale order to act as a sieve or selector on the individual chance events. There are such cooperative phenomena in physics: for example, in the structure of crystals, which we understand, and perhaps in the structure of liquids, which we do not. The existence of a potential of order in the selection of chance events is clear, but what is never clear in advance is how it will express itself. It is here that we need two additional principles in evolution to give it a natural order in time.

There are five distinct principles which make up the concept of evolution, as I interpret it. They are:

1. family descent
2. natural selection
3. Mendelian inheritance
4. fitness for change
5. stratified stability.

The first three are familiar, and I need not elaborate them; they make up the standard account of the mechanism of evolution that has been accepted since R. A. Fisher first formalized it in *The Genetical Theory of Natural Selection*.

But in my view, it is now necessary to add the two further principles which I propose, namely, fitness for change and stratified stability. They are concerned, the one with the variability of living forms, and the other with their stability; and between them they explain how it comes about that biological evolution has a direction in time—and has a direction in the same sense as time. The direction of evolution is an important and indeed crucial phenomenon, which singles it out among statistical processes. For in so far as statistical processes have a direction at all, it is usually a movement toward the average—and that is exactly what evolution is not.

Of the two new principles that I propose, the first is only peripheral to my theme here, and I shall deal with it quite briefly. In order that a species shall be capable of changing to fit its environment tomorrow, it must maintain its *fitness for change* today. The dormant genes that may be promoted tomorrow when they become useful must be preserved today when they are useless. And for this they must be held now in a setting of other genes which makes it possible to promote them rapidly. If this is to be done in the present, without some mysterious plan for the future, it must be by natural selection not for this or that variant but for variability itself.

It is evident that there is natural selection in favor of genetic variability. The selection is made by the small changes, up and down and up again and down again, by which the environment flutters about its mean. A long-term trend in the environment which lasts a hundred generations or so will in that time select a new adaptation. But the short-term fluctuation which goes one way for a few generations and then the other way for a few generations will meanwhile select for adaptability. That is, the short-term fluctuation favors the establishment of an arrangement of genes that will help mutant genes to express themselves.

Indeed, we know now that there are single genes which function specifically to enhance variability. For example, there are single genes which increase the rate of mutation in several other genes at the same time. Their action could explain the tendency for genetic change in one part of an organism (particularly, and in the first place, a haploid organism) to keep pace with change in other parts. A master gene of this kind, which increases mutation, is a mechanism that opens up the future, not by foreseeing it but by promoting the capacity for change.

I turn now to the crucial part of my argument. It is evident that we cannot discuss the variability of organisms and species without also examining their stability. We have therefore also to trace a mechanism for stability, as the second of the two balanced mechanisms that are needed to complete our understanding of evolution. I call this, the fifth and last principle in my analysis of evolution, the concept of *stratified stability*.

Evolution is commonly presented, even now, as if it required nothing but natural selection to explain its action, one minute step after another, as it were gene by gene. But an organism is an integrated system, and that implies that its coordination is easily disturbed. This is true of every gene: normal or mutant, it has to be incorporated into the ordered totality of the gene complex like a piece in a jigsaw puzzle.

Yet the analogy of the jigsaw is too rigid: we need a geometrical model of stability in living processes (and in the structures that carry them out) which is not so landlocked against change. Moreover, the model must express the way in which the more complex forms of life arise from the simpler forms, and arise later in time. This is the model of *stratified* stability.

There are evolutionary processes in nature which do not demand the intervention of selective forces. Characteristic is the evolution of the chemical elements, which are built up in different stars step by step, first hydrogen to helium, then helium to carbon, and on to heavier elements. The encounter of hydrogen nuclei makes helium simply (though indirectly) because they hold together: arrangements are briefly formed which in time form the more complex configuration that is helium. Each helium nucleus is a new unit which is stable, and can therefore be used as a new raw material to build up still higher elements.

The most telling example is the creation of carbon from helium. Two helium nuclei which collide do not make a stable element, and fly apart again in less than a millionth of a millionth of a second. But if in that splinter of time a third helium nucleus runs into the pair, it binds them together and makes a stable triad which is a nucleus of carbon. Every carbon atom in every organic molecule in every cell in every living creature has been formed by such a wildly improbable triple collision in a star.

Here, then, is a physical model which shows how simple units come together to make more complex configurations; how these configurations, if they are stable, serve as units to make higher configurations; how these higher configurations again, provided they are stable, serve as units to build still more complex ones; and so on. Ultimately a heavy atom such as iron, and perhaps even a complex molecule containing iron (such as hemoglobin), simply fixes and expresses the potential of stability which lay hidden in the primitive building blocks of cosmic hydrogen.

The sequence of building up stratified stability is also clear in living forms. Atoms build the four base molecules, thymine and adenine, cytosine and guanine, which are very stable configurations. The bases are built into the nucleic acids, which are remarkably stable in their turn. And the genes are stable structures formed from the nucleic acids, and so on to the subunits of a protein, to the proteins themselves, to the enzymes, and step by step to the complete cell. The cell is so stable as a topological structure in space and time that it can live as a self-contained unit. Still the cells in their turn build up the different organs, which appear as stable structures in the higher organisms, arranged in different and more and more complex forms.

Two special conditions have assisted this mode of climbing from simple to complex. First, of course, there is the energy which comes to us from the sun, which increases the number of encounters between simple units and helps to lift them over the next energy barrier above them. (In the same way, simple atomic nuclei encounter one another reasonably often, and are lifted over the next energy barrier above them, by the energy in hot stars.) And second, natural selection speeds up the establishment of each new stratum of stability in the forms of life.

The stratification of stability is fundamental in living systems, and it explains why evolution has a consistent direction in time. Single mutations are errors at random, and have no fixed direction in time, as we know from experiments. And natural selection does not carry or impose a direction in time either. But the building up of stable configurations does have a direction, the more complex stratum built on the next lower, which cannot be reversed in general (though there can be particular lines of regression, such as the viruses and other parasites which exploit the more complex biological machinery of their hosts). Here is the barb which evolution gives to time: it does not make it go forward, but it prevents it from running backward. The back mutations which occur cannot reverse it in general, because they do not fit into the level of stability which the system has reached: even though they might offer an individual advantage to natural selection, they damage the organization of the system as a whole and make it unstable. Because stability is stratified, evolution is open, and necessarily creates more and more complex forms.[3]

There is therefore a peculiar irony in the vitalist claim that the progress of evolution from simple to complex cannot be the work of chance. On the contrary, as we see, exactly this is how chance works, and is constrained to work by its nature. The total potential of stability that is hidden in matter can only be evoked in steps, each higher layer resting on the layer below it. The stable units that compose one layer are the raw material for random encounters which will produce higher configurations, some of which will chance to be stable. So long as there remains a potential of stability which has not become actual, there is no other way for chance to go. It is as if nature were shuffling a sticky pack of cards, and it is not surprising that they hold together in longer and longer runs.

It is often said that the progression from simple to complex runs counter to the normal statistics of chance that are formalized in the second law of thermodynamics. Strictly speaking, we could avoid this criticism simply by insisting that the second law does not apply to living systems in the environment in which we find them. For the second law applies only when there is no overall

[3]For a fuller account, see my Condon lectures for 1967 at the University of Oregon, published under the title *Nature and Knowledge*. Recently David Bohm has put forward a similar scheme for an inherent hierarchy of complexity, in which he calls "levels of order" what I call "strata of stability."

flow of energy into or out of a system: whereas all living systems are sustained by a net inflow of energy.

But though this reply has a formal finality, in my view it evades the underlying question that is being asked. True, life could not have evolved in the absence of a steady stream of energy from the sun—a kind of energy wind on the earth. But if there were no more to the mechanism of molecular evolution than this, we should still be at a loss to understand how more and more complex molecules came to establish themselves. All that the energy wind can do, in itself, is to increase the range and frequency of variation around the average state: that is, to stimulate the *formation* of more complex molecular arrangements. But most of these variant arrangements fall back to the norm almost at once, by the usual thermodynamic processes of degradation; so that it remains to be explained why they do not all do so, and how instead some complex arrangements establish themselves, and become the base for further complexity in their turn.

It is therefore relevant to discuss the second law, which is usually interpreted to mean that all constituent parts of a system must fall progressively to their simplest states. But this interpretation quite misunderstands the character of statistical laws in general in nonequilibrium states. The second law describes the final equilibrium state of a system; if we are to apply it, as here, to stable states which are far from equilibrium, we must interpret and formulate it differently. In these conditions, the second law of thermodynamics becomes a physical law only if there is added to it the condition that there are no preferred states or configurations. In itself, the second law merely enumerates all the configurations which a system could take up, and it remarks that the largest number in this count are average or featureless. Therefore, if there are no preferred configurations (that is, no hidden stabilities in the system on the way to equilibrium), we must expect that any special feature that we find is exceptional and temporary, and will revert to the average in the long run. This is a true theorem in combinatorial arithmetic and (like other statistical laws) a fair guess at the behavior of long runs. But it tells us little about the natural world, which, in the years since the second law seemed exciting, has turned out to be full of preferred configurations and hidden stabilities, even at the most basic and inanimate level of atomic structure.

The second law describes the statistics of a system around equilibrium whose configurations are all equal, and it makes the obvious remark that chance can only make such a system fluctuate around its average.[4] There are no stable states in such a system, and there is therefore no stratum that can establish itself; the system stays around its average only by a principle of indifference, because numerically the most configurations are bunched around the average.

But if there are hidden relations in the system on the way to equilibrium which cause some configurations to be stable, the statistics are changed. The preferred configurations may be unimaginably rare; nevertheless, they present another level around which the system can bunch, and there is now a countercurrent or tug-of-war within the system between this level and the average. Since the average has no inherent stability, the preferred stable configuration will capture members of the system often enough to change the distribution; and in the end, the system will be established at this level as a new average. In this way, local systems of a fair size can climb up from one level of stability to the next, even though the configuration at the higher level is rare. When the higher level becomes the new average, the climb is repeated to the next higher level of stability; and so on up the ladder of strata.

So, contrary to what is usually said, the second law of thermodynamics does not fix an arrow in time by its statistics alone. Some empirical condition must be added to it before it can describe time (or anything else) in the real world, where our view is finite.

When there are hidden strata of stability, one above another,

[4]It should be remarked that von Neumann's quantum-theoretical proof of the second law, like Wigner's argument above, assumes that the behavior of a system to which it is applied can be represented by a random symmetric Hamiltonian matrix—that is, it contains no hidden inner relations.

as there are in our universe, it follows that the direction of time is given by the evolutionary process that climbs them one by one. Indeed, if this were not so, it would be impossible to conceive how the features that we remark could have arisen. We should have to posit a miraculous beginning to time at which the features (and we among them) were created ready-made, and left to fall apart ever since into a tohubohu of individual particles.

Time in the large, open time, takes its direction from the evolutionary processes which mark and scale it. So it is pointless to ask why evolution has a fixed direction in time, and to draw conclusions from the speculation. It is evolution, physical and biological, that gives time its direction; and no mystical explanation is required where there is nothing to explain. The progression from simple to complex, the building up of stratified stability, is the necessary character of evolution from which time takes its direction. And it is not a forward direction in the sense of a thrust toward the future, a headed arrow. What evolution does is to give the arrow of time a barb which stops it from running backward; and once it has this barb, the chance play of errors will take it forward of itself.

14
A MORAL FOR AN AGE OF PLENTY

On August 2, 1939, Albert Einstein told the president of the United States that his scientific colleagues had evidence to show that an atomic bomb might be made. Five years later, in February 1945, Klaus Fuchs met a Russian agent whom he knew by the code name "Raymond" and passed on to him what he knew about making the bomb. Was one of these men right to disclose his terrible knowledge, and was the other wrong? Or were they both wrong? Do scientists have a sense of right and wrong?

Questions like these haunt the minds of many people today. Our age of plenty has produced such an expansion of knowledge —from birth control to bombs—that it overwhelms the common judgment. How can I decide what is good and what is bad? asks the honest citizen. Moreover, why should I decide? Has science abandoned its own responsibility, because it has lost its moral judgment?

These fears in the public mind are understandable, but I think they are mistaken. On the contrary, I have found that the conscience of scientists is the most active morality in the world today.

When Einstein told the president that he thought that an atomic explosion could be produced, he did what a moral man in a democracy had to do: he told the elected representative of the people what he knew. To have withheld the information would have been to deny that representative a choice of action. If Einstein, knowing what he did, had not written to the president, he would have been as disloyal to his own democracy as Klaus Fuchs was later when he passed his knowledge to another state. If we ask a scientist to decide himself whether to withhold or to disclose a discovery, we are asking him to flout the rights of the community.

Here I should say something personal, because I have great sympathy with those people who feel that there are some lines of research on which a scientist ought to refuse to set out at all. I spent the war years in operations research on work which was designed to make British and American bombing more destructive. This is how I came to be sent to Japan at the end of the war in order to report on the atomic-bomb damage there.

When I saw the inhuman desolation of Hiroshima and Nagasaki, I was convinced that the development of atomic weapons could lead to the destruction of mankind. I therefore resolved to take no further part in the making of weapons of mass destruction. But I do not therefore regard myself as morally superior to any one of my fellow scientists who made a different choice. I know that he dislikes weapons as much as I do, and if he works on them and I do not, I do not despise his reasons. I think that the gravest threat now is to human survival, and another scientist thinks that the gravest threat is to human independence. Both judgments, if they are honestly made, deserve equal respect. Each of us no doubt thinks the other mistaken, but neither of us thinks the other wicked. We know that we have each searched a long time before we have reached our own convictions.

I have found that the conscience of scientists is the most active morality in the world today. This is a strange thing to say at a time when few believe that science has a conscience. Most people think themselves generous if they allow that science is neutral and that its findings can be used either for good or for evil. These people imply, of course, that what is good and what is evil cannot be judged by the standards of science. Science, they say, tells us only what is true and what is false; and they insist that true and false are quite different standards from good and evil. True and false, they say, are matters of fact; but good and evil are matters of conscience which lie on a different plane.

This separation of the true and the false from good and evil is destructive of sound morality. For it removes morality from the tests by which we judge the things that happen around us every day, and makes it something remote from our practical lives. This is most dangerous now, when the setting of our lives is being changed by discoveries in medicine, in mental health, in psychology, and in social science in ways which most affect the relations between human beings. Our habits, particularly our habits of thought, are shifting profoundly. In every field of human welfare, from nationalism to sex, and from race relations to delinquency, we learn that we can truly judge the actions of others only when we understand their motives. In such a time it is a disaster to think that the difference between knowledge and ignorance is somehow more trivial than the difference between good and evil. True humanity is understanding—understanding nature and understanding man. This is why there is no human warmth unless wisdom and goodness are linked together and are seen as facets of our character which cannot be separated.

There is a deep moral lesson in the practice of science, which has been missed only because most people never see science as it is practiced. They never see the pains, the care, the patience, the humility, the bewilderment, the long hours spent in trying to see all the facts in focus, the agony of rejecting an explanation which seemed plausible but which fails to fit one obstinate fact, the illumination of at last finding the thread through the whole maze. Most people see nothing but the finished discovery, dispassionate and neutral. How can they guess what devotion, what singleness of mind is needed in the pursuit of truth—whether the truth is as subtle as relativity, or as matter-of-fact as getting a rocket into orbit?

Of course a discovery—a fact or a theory—is neutral. There is nothing moral or immoral about the theory of relativity; a rocket can be used for good as well as for destructive ends; and even the inventions of medicine can be used to kill as well as to cure. But this does not mean that science is neutral. That idea is a misunderstanding of what science is and substitutes semantic confusion of language for thought.

Science is not a mere collection of discoveries, an album of facts and theories that have been established once and for all. Science is the process of discovery itself, a living process. It is not what scientists know that matters to them, but what they do not know; and what drives them is the urge to know more.

In short, knowledge is a form of experience for the scientist—as, indeed, it is for all of us. And as for all of us, what matters is not the experience that we have had but the experience that we are having. This is the essence of life, which has always been as decisive as a marriage and as delightful as a honeymoon; but our life is dead if once we let last year become more important to us than this year.

In the same way, what is important in science is not the initial act of discovery, but the continuing search for truth. Discoveries themselves are neutral because they already belong to the past. The practice of science is moral because it goes on without pause looking for what is true and rejecting what is false.

It may be thought that truth is too big a word to describe what science seeks—that "truth" can mean nothing as profound in science as in our moral judgments. Science seems to be about matters of fact, and when it says that something is true, it seems to tell us no more than that the facts are so and not otherwise. But this is not really how science works. If it were, there would be no debates in it and no new theories; and we should still believe today in the physics of Newton and in the biology of Lamarck—we should have heard neither of relativity nor of evolution. In reality, science is always an arrangement of the facts; and our preference for one arrangement rather than another is a continued attempt to find the truth behind the appearances of nature. This new truth may break with all our commonsense notions of how things happen, as quantum physics did. It may even set limits to what we conceivably can know, as the principle of uncertainty did. In any case, it is a profound reorientation of our outlook on nature. The truth we are looking for in science is something at the center of things: it has to fit the facts, but it has to be much deeper, more coherent than the mere facts.

Scientists have no other value by which they judge what they do; and their success as a community derives from this acknowledgment of a single objective. We saw in World War II how our own communities forgot their private ambitions and rivalries when threatened by a common danger. So the community of scientists has been sustained for over three hundred years now, ever since the Inquisition broke the spirit of the aged Galileo, by the common acknowledgment that nothing matters as much as the single-minded pursuit of truth.

When a community is directed to a single objective, its code of conduct becomes simpler and more severe than the easy-going code of compromises which does duty for most people. In daily life few of us are entirely rigid about white lies and tax-deductible expenses and other small evasions. We accept, even if we do not condone, such venial sins. But the professional morality of scientists allows no compromises. It tells each man that he must report what he believes to be true, exactly and without suppression or editing. Nowhere in a research journal is a scientist allowed to minimize an awkward discrepancy or to stress a comforting confirmation. Nowhere is he allowed to put what seems expedient in place of an unpalatable truth. A scientist takes it for granted that when another scientist reports a finding, he can be believed absolutely—by which we mean, that we can be certain that what the man reported is exactly what he thought he saw or heard, no less and no more.

This absolute trust of each man in the word of every other man is remarkable in the society of scientists. Yet it is not by itself the whole of scientific morality. For a morality embraces not only the individual and his trust, but a whole community, and it therefore has to provide for all the subtle relations between the members of the community. The morality of science is subtle in this way, but it has grown from a simple principle—the principle that the community of scientists shall be so organized that nothing shall stand in the way of the emergence of the truth.

Here we see how shallow is the belief that science tells us only what is the case, and morality tells us what ought to be. Of course, the facts of science, the discoveries already made, only tell us what is the case. But the search for the truth imposes a morality on those who share in it and tells them what they ought to do if they are to succeed in finding out what is the case. As soon as science sets what is true, at any cost, it also imposes on those who practice science an obligation of how they ought to behave. Science tells us, quite simply, that we ought to behave in such a way that we can all find out what is true.

We ought to behave in such a way that we can all find out what is true. From this basic principle the whole organization of the scientific community flows. For it means that the body of scientists has to create a code of behavior which shall tame the prejudices, the foibles, and the vanities of individuals for the sake of reaching the truth, not by dictatorial imposition, but by the agreement of free minds. It follows that science gives a special value to some forms of behavior which the everyday world finds tiresome. For example, the everyday world likes people to conform and not to find fault with the accepted beliefs of the past. But scientists assume that the beliefs of the past are not final and that they remain to be corrected by the present and the future. Therefore, science gives particular value to original thinking and to its outspoken expression. Independence of mind and reasoned dissent in speech are virtues in the world of science, though in many polite circles they would be regarded as vices.

A society which sets special store by independence of mind and freedom of expression must cultivate habits of humility. This sounds paradoxical, but it is necessary to the community, for without humility no one would give close attention to the opinions of others. Truth is not reached merely by the utterance of new ideas; it requires the study of those ideas. Therefore, scientists have cultivated a habit of listening to others and of thinking about what they say that is unusual. Science requires that each man shall respect what others tell him, whether it is a new idea or an old one. Truth is not reached by momentary flashes of individual illumination, but by the careful consideration of many minds. This is why the society of scientists is a model of democracy. It honors the new ideas of the young and it also honors the old ideas even when they have been overthrown, because it recognizes that the old ideas were not necessarily foolish, but simply lay further back along the road to the truth.

There is, therefore, inherent in the practice of science a set of values, without which it would be impossible to carry it on at all. Science could not be carried on without complete trust among all scientists. It could not be carried on if there were some other end besides the truth, and if this other end justified deception or the imposition of a belief by authority. Science could not be carried on if it did not implant in all those who practice it the faith that originality of thought, independence of mind, and freedom to dissent from established opinion are to be valued, because without them it is not possible to discover new parts of the truth. At the same time, science could not be practiced if the new ideas and the old were not examined and debated with tolerance, with respect, with honor. If these values did not exist in the world, then science would have to create them before it could make a single discovery, because nothing can be found, nothing can be learned, unless men prize the truth above all else.

The conditions which I have shown to be necessary to the practice of science are clearly not a set of neutral rules. On the contrary, they make up a stern morality whose undertones call to mind the Old Testament: the morality of truth, justice, and integrity.

To be sure, this scientific morality is not the whole of morality. It lacks what, by contrast, I may call the New Testament values: love, kindness, family loyalty, human charity. These are the values which inform the personal relations of people and which in our civilization preoccupy most writers and artists.

Human beings need justice and they also need affection. These are two different sets of values, and neither set of values is complete without the other. We have associated the more kindly values with religion and art, and have behaved as if somehow they belonged to a different life from the sterner values of science. But this is an unbearable division, and our society will perish if it persists in it.

The moral problem of our century is to make the values of science as much a part of our lives as are the values which religion and literature have long glorified. We must learn to build a complete morality, in which love no longer fights against truth in our unconscious thoughts. For our weakness is that we think that love and even goodness are threatened by truth, and that it is kinder and more comforting to be dishonest. It is this opposition between what we think of as the kindly values of family and national life on the one hand, and the stern values of science on the other, which threatens to demoralize society in the age of plenty.

The civilized world is, indeed, threatened with destruction by the physical impact of science on our lives. And it is characteristic that we are threatened as much, for example, by overpopulation as by radioactive death. For what threatens us in both cases is not the scientific discovery, but our own failure to weigh all the consequences honestly and without compromises. We are threatened by overpopulation because we refuse to face honestly —that is, to face actively—the need to control human reproduction. And we are threatened by atomic bombs because we refuse to face the necessity for a new age of trust among nations. Somehow we think it remote from morality to face the facts; somehow we think it possible to be good without being wise.

Nearly two hundred years ago the poet William Blake wrote this about the morality of the prophets in the Bible: "Every honest man is a Prophet; he utters his opinion both of private & public matters. Thus: If you go on So, the result is So. He never says, such a thing shall happen let you do what you will." William Blake was not a scientist, but a great religious mystic; yet he saw our problem more honestly than we do. We live in a technical age of plenty and are frightened because we try to control this abundance by a morality which shuts its eyes to the consequences of our acts. We are simply not thinking through to the end the implications of the changes that we are making in our lives and in the lives of other nations, and we hope that somehow we can make up for ignorance and compromise by an appeal to universal goodness. We are being less truthful, less tenacious in our self-analysis, than the men who made the inventions which both delight and trouble us. We want the body of science without its spirit.

There is no reason why the morality of science should not become part of our outlook, fruitfully joined to the morality of love. Foreseeing the consequences and facing the facts can help to create a complete and generous morality. Loyalty, tenderness for others, even heroism is not stifled because we are honest with facts.

Let me end with one example.

On May 12, 1946, Louis Alexander Slotin was carrying out an experiment in the laboratories at Los Alamos with seven other men. Slotin was good with his hands; he liked using his head; he was bright and a little daring—in short, he was like any other man anywhere who is happy in his work.

At Los Alamos, Slotin, then aged thirty-five, was concerned with the assembly of pieces of plutonium, each of which alone is too small to be dangerous, and which will only sustain a chain reaction when they are put together. Atomic bombs are, in fact, detonated in this way, by suddenly bringing together several harmless pieces of plutonium so that they form a larger, explosive mass. Slotin himself had tested the assembly of the first experimental bomb which had been exploded in New Mexico in July 1945.

Now, nearly a year later, Slotin was again doing an experiment of this kind. He was nudging toward one another, by tiny movements, several pieces of plutonium, in order to ensure that their total mass would be large enough to make a chain reaction; and he was doing it, as experts are tempted to do such things, with a screwdriver. The screwdriver slipped, the pieces of plutonium came a fraction too close together, and suddenly the instruments which everyone was watching registered a great upsurge of neutrons, which is the sign that a chain reaction has begun. The assembly was filling the room with radioactivity.

Slotin moved at once; he pulled the pieces of plutonium apart with his bare hands. This was virtually an act of suicide, for it exposed him to the largest dose of radioactivity. Then he calmly asked his seven co-workers to mark their precise positions at the time of the accident, in order that the degree of exposure of each one to the radioactivity could be fixed.

Having done this and alerted the medical service, Slotin apologized to his companions, and said what turned out exactly true: that he thought that he would die and that they would recover.

Slotin had saved the lives of the seven men working with him by cutting to a minimum the time during which the assembly of plutonium was giving out neutrons and radioactive rays. He himself died of radiation sickness nine days later. The setting for his act, the people involved, and the disaster are scientific: but this is not the reason why I tell Slotin's story. I tell it to show that morality—shall we call it heroism in this case?—has the same anatomy the world over.

There are two things that make up morality. One is the sense that other people matter: the sense of common loyalty, of charity and tenderness, the sense of human love. The other is a clear judgment of what is at stake: a cold knowledge, without a trace of deception, of precisely what will happen to oneself and to others if one plays either the hero or the coward. This is the highest morality: to combine human love with an unflinching, a scientific judgment.

I tell the story of Louis Slotin for another reason also. He was an atomic physicist who made a different choice from mine: he was still working on bombs when he died, a year after the war ended. I do not think the less of him because he took one view of a scientist's duty and I take another. For the essence of morality is not that we should all act alike. The essence of morality is that each of us should deeply search his own conscience—and should then act steadfastly as it tells him to do.

15
THE HUMAN VALUES

For fifty years now, philosophy in England has been in reaction against the metaphysics of the nineteenth century. Under the influence of Bertrand Russell and Ludwig Wittgenstein, it has returned to the empirical tradition which goes back in British philosophy to Thomas Hobbes, to John Locke, and above all to David Hume. This is a tradition which looks for the material and the tests of philosophy in the physical world; the evidence which it seeks is, roughly, that which a scientist seeks, and it rejects evidence which would not pass muster in science. It is, of course, familiar that both Russell and Wittgenstein were trained in scientific disciplines.

Nevertheless, the later work of Wittgenstein has a very personal, even an introspective air. In his early writing he held that a statement makes sense only if it can be tested in the physical world. In his later writing Wittgenstein came to look for the meaning of a statement in the way in which it can be used: the contexts and the intentions into which it fits. That is, his early view of truth was positivist, and his later view was analytical. Wittgenstein's followers have now enthroned his later analysis of usage into a philosophical method which often seems remote from any universal test, but their aim remains, as it was his, to make our understanding of the world tally with the way in which it works in fact.

There are other philosophers who are impatient with these fine preoccupations, and for whom philosophy is more robustly a branch of natural science or even a technique for social consciousness. Maurice Cornforth, for example, sees philosophy as a communal activity which is to teach people how to change the world toward the world it ought to be. Everything else to him is mere word-spinning—certainly it is mere word-spinning to ask by what test we can subscribe to the word "ought" in the last sentence.

Like Cornforth, I should like philosophy to be more helpful than the analysts have made it. I do not think, as they do, that the words "is" and "ought" belong to different worlds, so that sentences constructed with "is" usually have a verifiable meaning, but sentences constructed with "ought" never have. I do not, however, think that the difference between the two philosophies can simply be brazened out with roughshod contempt on both sides. I remember the time when Cornforth was Wittgenstein's favorite pupil, and I therefore ask myself where the real cleavage between the two philosophies, the analytical and the practical, takes its origin.

I believe that we see into the difference between the two philosophies when we ask what is the unit from which each starts. Wittgenstein's unit, Russell's unit, is one man: all British philosophies are individualist. Cornforth's unit is that of Karl Marx and Friedrich Engels: it is the community. Thus the two philosophies look at everything through two different ends of the telescope.

Now, of course, if the only criterion of true and false which we accept is one man's, then we have no base for social agreement. The question how I "ought" to behave is a social question, which always involves several people; and if I accept no evidence and no judgment except my own, then I have no tools with which to frame an answer.

And equally a purely communal philosophy leaves no room to discuss conduct. The community lays down what we must do, and the individual has no other values on which to argue whether he as a person "ought" to do it.

For these reasons, neither of these philosophies alone is a guide to right conduct. If we are to learn what we ought to do, we must follow our thought in two directions: into the duties of men, which alone hold a society together, and also into the freedom to act personally which the society must still allow its men. The concepts of value are profound and difficult exactly because they do two things at once: they join men into societies, and yet they preserve for them a freedom which makes them single men. There is no problem, and there are no values, until you want to do both.

Let me begin from one of these philosophies, say the individualist philosophy of the positivist and the analyst, and see how it can be extended toward the other. I will take as my example a question of fact, the more precise the better. Take, then, this scientific statement: "The Crab nebula is the dust of a supernova which exploded in 1054, and it glows because some of it is radioactive carbon which was made in the supernova."

This is a fairly simple speculation, as science goes. The positivist would break it into still simpler pieces, and would then propose to verify each. But it is an illusion, and a fatal illusion, to think that he could verify them himself. Even in principle, he could not verify the historical part of this statement without searching the records of others, and believing them. And in practice, he could not verify the rate of expansion of the Crab nebula, and the processes which might cause it to glow, without the help of a sequence of instrument-makers and astronomers and nuclear physicists, specialists in this and that, each of whom he must trust and believe. All this knowledge, all our knowledge, has been built up communally; there would be no astrophysics, there would be no economics, there would not even be language, if man were a solitary animal.

The fallacy which imprisons the positivist and the analyst is the assumption that he can test what is true and false unaided. This of course prevents him from making any social judgment. Suppose now that we give up this assumption, and acknowledge that, even in the verification of facts, we need the help of others. What follows?

It follows that we must be able to rely on other people; we must be able to trust their word. That is, it follows that there is a principle which binds society together, because without it the individual would be helpless to tell the true from the false. This principle is truthfulness. If we accept truth as an individual criterion, then we have also to make it the cement to hold society together.

The positivist holds that only those statements have meaning which can in principle be verified, and found to be so or not so. Statements which contain the word "is" can be of this kind;

statements which contain the word "ought" cannot. But we now see that, underlying this criterion, there is a social nexus which alone makes verification possible. This nexus is held together by the obligation to tell the truth. Thus it follows that there is a social injunction implied in the positivist and analyst method. This social axiom is that we *ought* to act in such a way that what *is* true can be verified to be so.

I differ from other scientific philosophers in two beliefs. The first is the belief which I have just stated, that the personal activity of testing what is true implies of itself a social obligation which tells us how we ought to act to one another. And second, I hold that from this single obligation to work together for the truth, all the human values can be deduced.

If truth is to be found, and if it is to be verified in action, what other conditions are necessary, and what other values grow of themselves from this?

First, of course, comes independence, in observation and thence in thought. The mark of independence is originality, and one of its expressions is dissent. Dissent in turn is the mark of freedom. That is, originality and independence are private needs of the truthful man, and dissent and freedom are public means to protect them. This is why society ought to offer the safeguard of free thought, free speech, free inquiry, and tolerance; for these are needs which follow logically when men are committed to explore the truth. They have, of course, never been granted, and none of the values which I have yet advanced have been prized, in a dogmatic society, such as that of medieval Christianity.

Dissent and tolerance at once set up a tension between independence from the views of others and respect for them. This is, as I have stressed, the heart of the ethical problem: the confrontation of private and public needs. Freedom and tolerance in a truthful society cannot be based on indifference; they must be based on respect. And respect as a personal value implies, in any society, the public acknowledgment of justice and of due honor.

These values seem remote from the humdrum business of discovering what is true in fact and of verifying it in practice. Justice, honor, the respect of man for man: What have these human values to do with scientific philosophy? Now we see that this question is a foolish survival of those nineteenth-century quarrels which somehow seemed to equate ethics with the Book of Genesis. If critics in the past had ever looked at the way in which a truth-seeking society develops, they would not have asked the question. A dogmatic society can work otherwise; but a society like ours since the Renaissance and the Scientific Revolution grows by confronting the work of one man with that of another, and grafting each on each. It cannot survive without independence and originality, dissent and freedom, tolerance, justice, honor, and respect between man and man. These are the human values in which I believe; and I believe them all to be logically implied, by the steps which I have here argued, in the single and steadfast human object, to explore the truth.

16
THE VALUES OF SCIENCE

It is standard good form nowadays in polite society to say that the civilized values are disappearing, and then to blame science for the change. People who say this are, of course, out of sympathy with modern life; but it would be foolish to ignore their sneer that science is destroying the values for which we all care, for some feeling of this kind haunts less prejudiced people too. There is a general sense that the traditional values form an a priori set of absolute judgments, which hang together in a permanent system. By contrast, it is felt, rightly, that there is nothing absolute about the concepts of natural science, which form a flexible framework that is always building and always being rebuilt; the only thing that the framework must fit, obstinately, is the facts. It is this tyranny of the facts, not as they ought to be but as they are, that distresses even intelligent people, who fear that the spread of science is robbing them of some freedom of judgment. They feel that scientists have no spiritual urges and no human scruples, because the only success that science acknowledges is success in conforming to the material facts of the world.

This latent opposition to science appears now whenever values are debated. It can be countered only by an unbiased study of values as they actually are displayed in the behavior of people. Nothing that we say in arguing about values is practical, nothing is even reasonable, if it neglects this empirical study; and I therefore propose to begin it here and now. This essay is a short but strictly empirical examination of the way in which some of the values in our society are evolved.

I shall confine myself to some human and, in a sense, social values such as inform and govern the relations between people. And I shall confine myself particularly to values that arise in the civilization in which we now live. The characteristic mark of this civilization, the special activity to which it is committed, is the practice of science. Science is the activity of finding facts and then arranging them in groups under general concepts, and these concepts are then judged and tested by the factual outcome of the further actions which we base on them. So, in all practical matters, ours is a society which judges belief by the outcome of the actions which it inspires. We believe in gravitation because we are thereby led to act in a way which works in our world. If we are to believe in values, they must lead us to act in a way that works in the society which hopes to live and to survive by them.

The concept of gravitation is, at bottom, a compact and orderly means to describe how things fall. In this sense, the concepts of science are all means to describe how things fall out. Therefore critics of science usually call it a neutral activity, because its concepts, however subtle we make them, still tell us only what happens and not what ought to happen.

This is a sad jumble of language, which confuses the activity of science with its findings. The findings of science are indeed neutral, if by this word is meant that they describe and do not exhort. It is difficult to see what else the findings could be, unless the critics still believe, as the alchemists did, that science ought to command and to overpower nature. If the criticism is that science discovers facts and not spells, then I gladly accept it.

But of course, the facts discovered must not be confused with the activity that discovers them. And the activity of science is not neutral: it is firmly directed and strictly judged. In practicing science, we accept from the outset an end which is laid down for us. The end of science is to discover what is true about the world. The activity of science is directed to seek the truth, and it is judged by the criterion of being true to the facts.

We can practice science only if we value the truth. This is the cardinal point that has never been seen clearly enough, either by critics or by scientists themselves. Because they have been preoccupied with the findings, they have overlooked that the activity of science is something different from its findings. When we practice science, we look for new facts, we find an order among the facts by grouping them under concepts, and we judge the concepts by testing whether their implications turn out to be true to other new facts. This procedure is meaningless, and indeed cannot be carried out, if we do not care what is true and what is false.

When critics say that science is neutral, they mean that the findings are neither good nor bad in themselves; and they usually go on to say that therefore the use to which the findings are put must be determined by values which are not implied by the findings. So far, the argument is faultless; the use to which the facts are put must be determined by values which are brought in from outside the facts. But now the critics turn the argument into a verbal trick. To use the findings of science, we must have values from outside the findings; but the critics blandly read this to mean that we must have values from outside science. Even if this were true, it is certainly not implied by the argument.

What the critics are anxious to say, of course, is that the scientific civilization in which we live is not taught any values by the facts that science finds, by the machines that it builds, and even by the visions that it opens. The facts, the machines, the visions still require to be directed to an agreed end. But, of course, although the facts do not supply such an injunction or end, the activity of science does. The activity of science is committed to truth as an end in itself.

Here critics can argue, with justice, that men believed that truth is a value long before they heard of science. I could argue in turn that this belief had often defined truth very oddly; that truth as I define it, truth to fact, was not valued in dogmatic societies such as that which persecuted Galileo; and that the acceptance by any society of the material fact as an arbiter of truth really makes it a scientific society. But these are all debating points, and they are beside the point. It is beside the point to argue about the history of truth as a value: who discovered it, who brought it into our civilization. The point, the only point, is that truth is central to science. A scientific civilization like ours cannot exist unless it accepts truth to fact as its cardinal value. If our civilization did not have this value, then it would have to invent it, for it could not live without it.

I have established that the activity of science presupposes that truth is an end in itself. From this fundamental proposition, it is possible to go several ways. For example, it is possible to discuss what is implied by saying that a scientific description is true if it corresponds with the facts. For it is certain that such a correspondence cannot be perfect; in the nature of things, the description can match the facts only with a certain coarseness, with what engineers call some tolerance. A scientist therefore has to decide what coarseness he accepts, if he is ever to come to conclusions. This decision is itself an act of judgment, and I suspect that it has subtle things to teach us about how we judge and how we value. Certainly it should teach us what I miss most in the accusation that science is neutral—the sense that science involves the scientist as a person. A discovery has to be made by a man, not by a machine, because every discovery hinges on a critical judgment.

However, I want to go another way from my fundamental proposition that science must value truth. I want to take the proposition beyond the individual scientist, and ask what it implies in the society made up of men like him. This is a natural extension; we are all of us concerned not merely with our personal values but with the values of our whole society. But it is also an important extension for another reason. Many of the choices in which a man's values are expressed are precisely choices between what he would like to do as an individual and what he is asked to do as a member of a community. The social values are generated by this confrontation of individual wish and communal will. There are no conflicts of values until the man has to find a posture to his society, and the society has to find its attitude to him: until each has to adjust itself to the other.

Therefore we have only begun the elucidation of modern values when we have found that science must necessarily value truth. For truth is an individual value, which dictates the conduct of a scientist when he is alone with his work. It becomes a source of social values only when a whole society accepts the assumption that no belief will survive if it conflicts with factual truth. This is the unspoken assumption which our society makes. It is equivalent to setting up truth as the overriding value for our society, and to agreeing that the discovery of the truth is an end in itself, the supreme end, not only for individuals but for our society as a whole. It follows that a whole nexus of social values should be deducible, by logical steps, from the single injunction that society has a duty to seek the truth.

I have said that our scientific society takes it for granted that it should seek the truth: and this description is characteristic of it. For the description implies that the truth is still being sought, and will go on being sought always; the truth has not already been found. A society that believes that the truth has been finally found, for example in politics or in religion, simply imposes it; it is an authoritarian society. And what goes deeper, a society that believes that the truth has been found or revealed, that the truth is known, resists all change; for what is there to change for? When we say that our society seeks the truth, we imply that it acknowledges that it must itself change and evolve with the truth. The social values which I shall derive are, at bottom, a mechanism by which a society arranges that it shall evolve. They grow from the search for the truth in a scientific society, because the search demands that the society shall evolve.

A man who looks for the truth must be independent, and a society which values the truth must safeguard his independence. An age of reason may be anxious to persuade the unreasonable—and independent minds are always unreasonable—but it must be more anxious to ensure that they are not browbeaten. So Voltaire in his life was as belligerent for the independence of those who did not share his beliefs as for his own. A scientific society must set a high value on independence of mind, however angular and troublesome those who have it are to the rest of us.

We value independence of mind because it safeguards originality, and originality is the tool with which new discoveries are made. But although originality is only a tool, it has become a value in our society, because it is necessary to its evolution. So high is the value which a scientific society places on originality that it has ousted the value which the arts used to place on tradition. The strange and, to me, admirable result has been that the arts have become more and more imaginative, more eccentric and personal, in the last hundred years; and this has certainly been caused by the pressure for originality from what the critics still blindly call the impersonal field of science.

I do not claim that originality is always a virtue, any more than I claim that independence or even truth itself is always so. What I am showing is that originality has become a value in our society, as independence has, because both are means to foster its overriding value, the unending search for truth. There are occasions when originality, like the other values, becomes a bore. Whenever I go to an exhibition of children's paintings, I see several hundred examples of studied and uniform originality, and I sometimes suspect that originality is being taught as a classroom subject. I find this dull, but no more so than I should have found the studied and uniform conformity of children's paintings a hundred years ago, when tradition was taught as a classroom subject. The fact is that a child's painting is no more like art than a child's essay is like literature; what is dull in it today, what was dull a hundred years ago, is not the originality or the tradition, but the childishness. The child's painting has no more merit than an intelligence test; that is, it gives a hint of what the child's mind may do later; and as a scientist, I would rather be bored by the hint that it will dissent than by the conviction that it will conform.

Independence and originality are qualities of mind, and when a society elevates them to values, as ours has done, it must protect them by giving a special value to their expression. This is why we place a value on dissent. The high moments of dissent are monuments in our literature: the writings of Milton, the Declaration of Independence, the sermons of John Wesley, and the poetry of Shelley. True, we find it more comfortable if dissent takes place somewhere else: in the past or in another country. In the West, we like best to read about the dissent which Russian intellectuals have been expressing since the death of Stalin; and no doubt Russians prefer to praise the dissenting voices in the West. But when we have smiled at these human foibles, we recognize behind them that dissent is accepted as a value in the intellectual structure of our civilization. And it is a value which derives from the practice of science: from the experience that progress comes only when the accepted concepts are openly challenged, whether by Copernicus, by Charles Darwin, or by Albert Einstein, and when the challenger insists that the facts be looked at afresh because they have outgrown the old concepts. Dissent is an instrument of intellectual evolution.

A society which values dissent must provide safeguards for those who express it. These safeguards are the most familiar values in the repertory of the political orator: freedom of thought, freedom of speech and writing, and freedom of movement and assembly. But we must not take them for granted simply because lip service to them has become hackneyed, and we must not suppose that they are self-evident and natural values in any society. Plato did not offer freedom of speech and writing in his republic. Freedom is valued in a society only when the society wants to encourage dissent and to stimulate originality and independence. Freedom is therefore essential to a scientific society, a society in evolution. It is merely a nuisance, and is discouraged, in a static society. Yet freedom is the basic acknowledgment that the individual is more important than his society: and we see once again that science, in despite of its critics, prizes the individual as other systems do not.

So far, I have only deduced, from the conditions for the practice of science, those values which make for change. But a society must also have values which resist change; it must, in engineering terms, have a certain inertia, by which it resists the overthrow of what it holds to be true now, and makes the truth of tomorrow fight for life. These inertial values are, of course, more common in other, static societies; but they are also present and important in a scientific society. Respect, honor, and dignity are necessary to the stability of science as of any other social activity, and their value can therefore be demonstrated from the conditions for the practice of science, in the same way that I have demonstrated the evolutionary values. But because the inertial values hold in other societies, because they are necessary to the existence of any society at all, I shall not discuss them further here. Instead, I shall make only one point about them, which is this: in a scientific society, the inertial values are reached by a different path from that which leads to them in other societies.

In a scientific society such values as respect, honor, and dignity are approached across the value of tolerance, which forms as it were a bridge from the evolutionary values. Tolerance is a modern value, because it is is a necessary condition for the coherence of a society in which different men have different opinions. Thus tolerance is essential to make a scientific society possible, and to link the work of the past with that of the future. Moreover, tolerance in this sense is not a negative value; it must grow out of an active respect for others. It is not enough in science to agree that other men are entitled to their opinions; we must believe that the opinions of others are interesting in themselves, and deserve our attention and respect even when we think them wrong. And in science, we often think that other men are wrong, but we never think that they are therefore wicked. By contrast, all absolute doctrines think (as the Inquisition did) that those who are wrong are deliberately and wickedly wrong, and may be subjected to any suffering to correct them. The tragedy of the political division of the world today is that it has this doctrinal intolerance: the statesmen of the West believe that those of the East are not merely wrong but wicked, and the statesmen of the East believe the same of us.

This is a good point at which to stop this exposition of some of the values of science. I have made no attempt to derive all the values which I believe a scientific society generates by the nature of its activity. And even if I had found logically all the values in science, I still would not claim that they exhaust all the human values, and that the practice of science gives man and society all the values that they need. This has not been my purpose.

My purpose has been to meet head-on the current mutiny against science that runs through so many discussions of values. This current always sets off with some harmless claim that science is neutral. But the harm is done by the confusion which is hidden in this innocent sentence. The findings of science are neutral, as every fact and every grouping of facts is neutral. But the activity of science which finds the facts and which orders them is not neutral. The activity of science is directed to one overriding end, which is to find the material truth. In our scientific society, this end is accepted as the supreme value.

From this cardinal value, some other values flow of necessity; and my purpose has been to show how this happens. It happens because a society which seeks the truth must provide means for its own evolution, and these means become values for it.

In deriving some of these values, by way of examples, I have shown that there is indeed an empirical procedure for studying the values of a society. What I have been doing is to make, in outline, a short empirical study of a few values. All values are subtle, and the values of science are as subtle as any others. A value is not a mechanical rule of conduct, nor is it a blueprint of virtue. A value is a concept which groups together some modes of behavior in our society. In this sense, when I say that originality is a value for our society, I am just as empirical and as descriptive as when I say that gravitation is a phenomenon of our planetary system. And when I seek the ground or reason for the value given to originality by tracing it back to the demand for truth, I am doing exactly what I should do if I were looking for the cause of gravitation in some more fundamental structure of matter.

This does not mean that values are mere descriptions of our behavior: and that for two reasons. First, the interplay of values is more complex than any mechanical compounding of forces: it creates a tension which is the stuff of our lives. Second, and more simply, values are concepts which describe our behavior only when we understand what directs that behavior overall. Science is directed by the search for truth, and all societies are directed by the search for stability. The values of our scientific society describe our behavior as it is directed to make an evolving society which shall also be stable.

It is almost three hundred years since scientists first banded together in the Royal Society of England and the Academie

Royale of France. What scientists thought to be true then seems very primitive to us now; Isaac Newton was still a youth then, and gravitation had barely been thought of. Every scientific theory has changed profoundly, and several times, in these three hundred years. Yet the society of scientists has remained stable, and binds together Englishmen and Frenchmen, and Americans and Chinese and Russians, in a unity of spirit, a community of principles, more profound than any other body of men. Does this impressive history really lend color to the myth that science is inhuman and impersonal? Does it really suggest that the activity of science generates no values to unite those who practice it?

The point of my analysis has not been to defend science from its critics. My point has been to attack what I believe to be a fundamental error of method in the critics: the error of looking for values outside our activity. If values are to be discussed in a useful way, then they must be discussed empirically, in the realistic setting of the world in which they operate. Values take their richness from the tension between each man and his society, and we should not be human if this tension disappeared: we should be a mechanical insect society. For this very reason, it is useless to accept or even to discuss values merely as absolute norms or as universal social injunctions; and equally it is useless to go to the opposite extreme and to discuss values as personal acts of faith while we disregard the society which must give them currency. If we take either of these one-sided courses, we shall always end by importing the values of some past tradition, and regretting that they do not fit us better. There are some traditional values alive in our scientific society today; but whether they are traditional or whether they are new, they are alive not by accident, but because they are appropriate: because they fit into, and grow from, the activity of science. It is time that those who discuss values learn the reach of that activity and the power of the values which spring from its modest search, personal and communal at the same time, for the factual truth.

17
THE PRINCIPLE OF TOLERANCE

I have been proposing the substitution of the phrase "the principle of tolerance" for "the principle of uncertainty" on two grounds. In the first place it is more accurate; and in the second place it tells us more about the relation of scientific description to the descriptions which obtain in the ordinary world of common sense and natural language. So you will not be surprised when I say that at the end I shall be concerned with the relation of science to the ordinary world, and particularly with such questions as, Does or does not science represent a moral order? Does it represent some part of the moral spectrum?

That is a bold program and you will forgive me if I confine myself to indicating the main signposts on it.

Why did we think that science would be the language that would give us a closer, and ultimately a more accurate, view of reality than common sense? I once did an experiment which many of you will have seen because it was done on one of the television programs called *The Ascent of Man*.

We took a man who had come from a concentration camp at Auschwitz (his name was Stephan Borgrajewicz) and we asked a blind woman to feel his face and to say what he looked like. And I will repeat to you absolutely verbatim what she said. She said, "I would say that he is elderly. I think obviously he is not English." (I must say that was the strangest "obviously" that I had heard.) "He has a rounder face than most English people." (Again, a reflection that would never have occurred to me. He was a Pole.) "I should say he is probably continental, if not eastern-continental. The lines in his face would be lines of possible agony—I thought at first they were scars. It is not a happy face." That is a brilliant description, truthful in every detail, and one which shows that whatever mode of exploration you use you can extract a tremendous amount from it.

I would also draw your attention to the last two sentences in the blind woman's description. "The lines in his face would be lines of possible agony—I thought at first that they were scars. It is not a happy face." I draw your attention to those because I might as well signal now what will become very clear at the end of my talk, which is that it does not matter how much you say, "Give me a description," the describer always concludes by giving you a judgment.

Now at the same time it is clear that the information given by this lady is imperfect. It is as imperfect as any description would be whether we had had that face described by Marcel Proust, or by Somerset Maugham, or by Tolstoi. We are aware that these descriptions would not so much fix the face as explore it. And we accept that as the method of the artist or writer.

But what physics has now done is to show that that is the only method to knowledge. All information is imperfect. Throughout the nineteenth century, roughly speaking between the year 1800 when William Herschel discovered infrared rays and, I suppose, 1888 when Heinrich Hertz discovered radio waves (or perhaps I should go even later to 1895 when Röntgen discovered X-rays), it seemed that the brilliant elucidation of the continuity of the electromagnetic spectrum would get us over this difficulty. It seemed that we had approached an avenue, unending, in which refinement after refinement could be built up.

In *The Ascent of Man* I continued my experiment by looking at the face across the whole spectrum of electromagnetic information in order of wavelengths. If you start with radio waves and you get down to even the practical limit of a centimeter or so, you still do not see much of the face. But by the time you get down to the millimeter range of infrared it becomes recognizably a face. And if you continue through the visible spectrum, it looks as if (with the coming first of X-rays and then in 1897 with J. J. Thomson and electrons) we are on the path to getting rays so hard—wavelengths so short—that no matter what object you presented to them you could say, "It is *there*." (And lest you should think that this is simply a scientific fantasy, I will remind you that the whole of the early philosophy of Bertrand Russell is built exactly on the assumption that the universe can be constructed out of single statements such as, and I quote verbatim, "That spot is red"—a statement which looks terribly old fashioned to us since we neither believe that you can say "spot" nor that you can say "red.")

I draw your attention particularly to J. J. Thomson's discovery of electrons that immediately followed Röntgen's discovery of X-rays. Röntgen, of course, was the last of the great, benevolent father figures of physics. It is ironic that when he made his discovery nobody was in the slightest doubt that physics was the great benefiter of humanity. And Röntgen was exactly the kind of middle-aged, bearded, minor-university professor who represented that. It was absolutely fitting that the first Nobel prize in physics in 1901 was given to Röntgen. I do not think you could have heard a single dissentient voice throughout the civilized universe. How things have changed!

But obviously the thing to bore in on is the discovery of the electron. You see, X-rays have various difficulties about them—they are so penetrating that you cannot focus them, therefore you cannot build an X-ray microscope as we ordinarily understand it. And the electron offered us an opportunity to go around that. The great turning point was Max von Laue's experiments in 1912, from which it seemed that the electron would offer us devices for seeing the smallest objects in perfect outline.

Now, the electron is a particularly nice particle to concentrate on here for the following reason. As all of you know, J. J. Thomson won the Nobel prize not very long after Röntgen for proving that the electron is a particle, which was a question much in dispute for the twenty years preceding 1897. It is one of the nicer ironies of history that his son, George Thomson, got the Nobel prize for proving that the electron is a wave. That is quite the nicest father-son relationship in the history of physics.

And that duality is a splendid warning. Because if the electron had been pure wave and if it had displayed no particle properties, then this vista would have continued to be open. But as soon as you think of the electron as a particle you realize that you are using the shadowing of whatever you are looking at—of a virus, say—by throwing electrons at it. And you are essentially in the position of a man at a fair who throws knives at a girl, and when she triumphantly steps away you are left visibly with the outline of a girl. They always use a girl at fairs but you will also remember (those of you who have seen this act done) that when she steps away there is really nothing to tell you that it might not have been a man. A difference which to most of us is obvious with visible light!

In other words, the *process* of shadowing is essentially a process in which the approximation is built in by the very activity. And it is clear that there is nothing you can do with the electron which will lead you to the ultimate analysis, that is, to a shadowing so fine that all details will be revealed. I am not now speaking only of ordinary limitations (for example, that the object must be of the order of the wavelength thrown at it), but of the fact that, as soon as the waves are so hard as to have particle properties, then their freedom of position is so limited that you cannot get a perfect picture. We have pictures of thorium atoms made by electrons, we have even finer pictures than that (and very fine they are), but nobody could pretend that you could *see* anything.

This, then, is the first part of what I have to say. Herschel's discovery of 1800 seemed to promise a marvelous prospect of ever greater refinement of observation as the single octave of visible light opened up into octave beyond octave beyond octave —the electromagnetic spectrum. But it does not, in fact, give us perfect information. We lurch after exactitude, and every time it appears within our grasp it takes another step away toward infinity.

Now I will remind you that that was not a new question in 1900. The question had first been opened by Gauss in about 1807 when the Göttingen Observatory had been built for him. And indeed earlier, when in 1795 (which seems not just another century now but another universe), as a young boy of eighteen, he came to Göttingen for his university studies.

Gauss already knew that statistical analysis had to employ some other means for estimating greater accuracy than that which ordinary vision or ordinary speech could give you. It is fairly clear that by 1795 Gauss already knew that the right way to take a series of observations and try to fix a best position for the observation which is subject to errors is to take the mean of the observations (classical—known for at least two hundred years before), but in addition to estimate an area of uncertainty by looking at the scatter around that mean. The Gaussian curve (or what I would prefer to think of as the Gaussian mountain)—round a star observation, for instance—should be a constant reminder to us that Gauss's was the brilliant mind which saw that the information from the observations that you have is not all carried by the mean. The rest of the information is carried exactly by the scatter—by what Heisenberg would call the area of uncertainty, and what I would call (approaching my subject now) the area of tolerance.

The respect in which Gauss's view in the early 1800s is different from our view today is simple. Gauss was working with the idea that a man looks at a star and takes twenty observations. He does not believe that any of these observations is correct: scintillations in the air intrude; he was more fatigued when he took some than others; he can only read the micrometer to so many places of decimals. All the mechanical aids in the world cannot make it possible for him to say of one observation as against the others, "It is correct."

But Gauss did believe that there was a correct observation to be had, if only we had a god's-eye view. He believed simply that we as human beings make mistakes—we as human beings are caught in the atmosphere, in the small flaws in the lens. The great number of observations was simply an attempt to say, "If I take enough, then one kind of mistake will cancel out the others." That gives us the mean. Moreover, the scatter of the observations (this Gaussian heap) would also tell us something about how reliable that mean is, how far away from the peak of the mountain one can expect to find it in an experiment carried out under the same conditions. But I underline for you that it is posited on the assumption that there *is* a best observation—that there is a god's-eye view, that there is a star and an observation —and, if everything were perfect, the observer would see it in that place and in no other.

Now for all I know that may be true of stars, but it is not true of objects such as those discovered and disputed by the Thomsons, father and son. It is the only thing that I want to say about statistics here. But I have stopped to make the point in order that we should not overlook the fact that when people talk about the statistics of atomic measurements, electrons, fundamental particles, they are not talking about the same thing as a Gallup poll. Because a Gallup poll is taken by asking everybody a question, and in theory you can go back and ask them again; everybody has an opinion. But the electrons do not have opinions, they do not have positions, they do not have places, they do not have momenta. They only have something which is yielded when the observer looks at them. And then one of them speaks up for the community and says "Here I am."

So as to make that point quite explicit, suppose that you are looking at an electron through a microscope. Of course, in order to see the electron you must shine some energy on it. But under that energy the electron rebounds, and so, although you can now tell where it is, you cannot tell where it would have been if you had not shone the light on it. This explanation is absolutely correct; it comes out of Heisenberg's paper of 1927. Nevertheless it gives rise to a fundamental misconception. You see, it does tend to make us think that the electron is a sort of rabbit sitting at the bottom there, that we are coming along in a kind of motorcar, a light shines on the rabbit, and the rabbit is startled and goes away. That is not right. There is no rabbit. There *is* no electron, in the sense in which you put it in the equation, until you have shone that light.

The electron under the microscope is not a fact; it is not a reality; it is not an experiment; you cannot see anything. In other words, the description that the electron is "disturbed" by the observation is perfectly accurate provided you use the word "disturbed" to mean logically disturbed, not disturbed in an engineering sense. Quantum mechanics deals only with observables. What enters into the equations as the position of the particle is observable, and it is subject to the equation that Heisenberg derived— $\Delta p \Delta q$ is of the order of Planck's constant.

Now, that is the dreadful thing that happened in Göttingen between 1807, when they built the observatory for Gauss, and 1921, when they appointed Max Born. In 1807 it was possible to think you were looking at a star or an electron or anything else —it was there, there was a god's-eye view. But by the time Born had completed his twelve years at Göttingen before Hitler turned him out, none of that survived.

It would be rash to argue now what are the limitations on the possible logics of nature. Yet I myself believe that there are limitations, but that they are negative ones: we can only offer proofs that some plausible systems of logic will *not* suffice to exhaust the description of nature. In particular, I think it can be shown that no finite system of axioms can do more than approximate to the totality of a natural law. That is, I hold that nature is totally connected; and, since human experiments are always finite, it follows (on empirical as well as logical grounds) that our formulations of natural laws necessarily miss some connections. This is an argument which I develop formally elsewhere.

It is both pertinent and instructive to remark here how much positive knowledge we can derive from asking what we cannot do. There is a set of such *laws of the impossible* which are in effect powerful statements of what is crucial in the empirical structure of the different fields of physics. (Edmund Whittaker called them "postulates of impotence.") For example, a great part of mechanics can be derived from the single assertion that perpetual motion is impossible. A great part of electromagnetism follows from the assertion that it is impossible to induce an electric field inside a hollow conductor.

Various cosmological theories can be founded on different assertions of what one cannot tell either about space or about time anywhere in the universe. In special relativity it is impossible to detect one's motion if it is steady, even by measuring the speed of light. In general relativity it is impossible to tell a gravitational field from a field set up by one's motion.

In quantum physics, there are several laws of the impossible which are not quite equivalent. One of them is the principle of uncertainty, and another is that it is impossible to identify the same electron in successive observations. But at bottom, all the quantum principles assert that there are no devices by which we can wholly control what state of a system we will observe next: my formulation is that it is impossible to ensure that we shall copy a specified object perfectly.

So we have to make up our mind now that the question of looking at the fundamental entities of science presents us with quite new conceptual principles. Since I have mentioned Max Born's name, let me say that the most striking statement of his that comes to my mind is one that he made shortly after he left Göttingen when he came to England. He said, "I am now convinced that theoretical physics is actual philosophy." By this he meant that in the years that had passed in Göttingen he had come to realize that our picture of the world had been so transformed that it was right to say that in *that* sense of philosophy we had to start thinking afresh.

I am not presuming to challenge L. M. Régis's splendid analysis of what he calls "the political frontiers of philosophy" as against "the political frontiers of science."[1] But there are times (alas, I have lived through so many of them) when political frontiers change. I was born in Russia; the place has since then been Germany and is now Poland. So I am conscious of the fact that the frontier between science and philosophy is also, alas, subject to warfare and attrition. And indeed, there is good ground for saying that the most important shifts in the frontier, the most important shifts in world view, which have taken place in the last sixty or seventy years have come from a few scientists who

[1]L. M. Régis, "Anthropogenèse versus Anthropologie," *Transactions of the Royal Society of Canada* (1974), fourth series, vol. 12, pp. 31–58.

have had this kind of quite extraordinary insight. An insight particularly relevant to Régis's thesis, because it is the first time that protagonists of the distinction that he was making, between mathematics as the language of the abstract and philosophy as the language of the concrete, are in fact making a desperate attempt to get together.

I am not going to try to discuss here all the strange properties of the electron, because they are not strange. You just have to remember that an electron is exactly like, let us say, the chief of a Bantu tribe. He is part of the real world. But everything he says to you—from incest relations to the kind of food you should or should not eat, or how you should cure a stomach ache—is simply inexplicable to you because although you recognize it as being said by a human being; it has a human connotation, but it does not belong to your world. And the whole world of subatomic particles is becoming our world, but it is simply a stranger to us. And you have to keep on saying to yourself all the time, "Now do not bore me with when the electron is a particle and when it is a wave. An electron is just an electron." You shake it by the hand and then you watch its behavior.

I think it is terribly important to say these things about subatomic particles and about atoms in general. They make us realize that we ought not to be surprised that scientific statements made at the level of the subatomic are simply not accessible to that search for accuracy which so inspired the nineteenth century. That is *not* the language that they speak. And, if I may again refer to Régis's talk on which I have drawn so much already, language is the crucial factor. What, then, is the language in which this discourse is carried on?

I want you for a moment to concentrate again on the woman talking about the face after she has touched it. If we presented her with the same man again, would she recognize him? I do not know. If we shaved off his beard, perhaps she would not. Perhaps there are other things she looks for that she would recognize. But I will give you a simpler example. I met Professor Fortier for the first time three days ago. I recognized him yesterday when I met him in the street. I recognized him this morning when he came in. But I am absolutely convinced that he is not identical with the person that I met on Saturday. I mean that there are features in his face which have changed. The change is imperceptible to me, luckily. But if I met him in ten years' time and tried to focus the face, then I would realize that I had seen the beginnings of changes which have continued.

Indeed, the human face is a very good example to take because it will make it clear to you that if things had to be identical before you could recognize them, you would never recognize anything at all. Take two quarters, accepted as good coin by anybody north and south of the forty-ninth parallel: Are they identical? Patently not, they have a different date on them. But even if they had the same dates, even if they had come from the mint today, you do not believe that they would be identical. You do not believe that if we weighed them to an accuracy which made us able to detect, let us say, 10^{10} atoms that they would turn out to be identical. And 10^{10} atoms is an awful lot more than one electron. The fact is that all our ability to work and to act in the real world depends on our accepting a *tolerance* in our recognition and in our language.

It is not merely that the endeavor of the nineteenth century that science should speak the perfect factual truth has turned out to be inaccessible. The fact is that it would be fatal. If I were given the gift of being able to tell at a glance whether two things contained exactly the same number of cells, or the same number of atoms, I would have to retire and write poetry or (what is the least popular subject here?) pornography. Because I would not be able to do any experiment at all. I would keep on saying to a colleague, "You are not doing it right. It is not the same experiment."

I actually saw such an experiment once. It happened in a biochemical laboratory in which a man was working with a white powder which seemed tasteless to him and tasteless to me. Another man working in the next laboratory came in and said, "What is this frightful, bitter substance you are working with? It is impossible to work next door." It turned out that the bitter substance was phenylthiourea, which has since become famous as a genetic test that marks the difference between tasters and nontasters and is a single Mendelian recessive. But it just happened that the two people actually working with it were both recessive nontasters, and the first person who drew our attention to it was a taster. And you could be sure that if he had had the misfortune to work with the powder, we would never have discovered this property. Because it would never have occurred to him that there were people who could not taste it.

It is one of the more fascinating aspects of the history of science that you could actually make a list of inventions which, if they had been made correctly too early, would have brought science to a standstill. Let me give you a simple example. If Mendeleev had known where to place helium—which was already a known gas by the time that he made the periodic table—the whole table would have been out of kilter. Because he would have had to ask, where are the other gases? Where is argon, krypton, and that whole line of gases?

I must not digress. I must stick to the simple point. If we were given the superhuman power to identify things only when they are identical, it would be fatal to us. What Heisenberg calls "uncertainty"—what I call "tolerance"—is the essential safeguard, the essential degree of coarseness, which makes it possible to work with abstract entities in the real world. And that is why, not merely as a matter of description, but as a matter of theory, no science will come to an end. There is no foreseeable end to discovery.

Now I want to say something final about the notion of tolerance. You will realize that what I have been calling "description" is essentially a process, not merely a comparison. It is the blind woman talking for the record, and our comparing it with someone else's description. It is a scientific paper, and an experiment that someone else repeats. Language is the essential intermediary in which all this takes place.

Indeed, the human notion that there are such things as true statements and false statements, on which all science and all our activities depends, is inconceivable without the intermediacy of statements, that is, of language. We tend to forget that the whole process (whether we are discussing it in a scientific conference or in literature) is always a process in which we make a record which is a linguistic record, even if the language is a mathematical language. And it is a process in which truth and falsity (as well as other principles, values, goods, or evils) are there not in the observation itself but in the record of it which you pass to others.

I, of course, think that the principle of tolerance would exist even if all science were carried on by one human being for himself. You would still meet these difficulties. But that is not a realistic question. Because, of course, one of the most important things about the activity of science is that it is a communal activity. It is exactly because there fans out from the single discovery the influence and the echo in the minds of others that science and other human activities are able to carry on.

That statement has a very important corollary on which I would end. This corollary came out in a dispute at this conference about whether scientific discoveries or any kind of discoveries were only made by those with an IQ of 155 or better on the graph of IQ, and whether those people therefore deserve very special attention. To both of which questions the answer is yes. But, like so many answers, it is one of those grand jury answers about which you say afterwards when somebody taxes you with it, "You did not ask me anything else." Because, of course, the next question is, "How does knowledge spread?" And the answer is, "It spreads because fortunately the human race is largely populated by people whose IQ lies between 90 and 155 to whom the discoveries become instant community property."

Look at the whole of prehistory and ask yourself, Were there really 75,000 people scattered all up and down the coast of Asia Minor who invented how to tie a knot? Of course not. I do not know how many times the tying of a knot was discovered, but I would bet that it was only three or four times. But what is so marvelous about a knot is that everybody at once sees what it is for. I like talking about knots because one of the most exciting things that ever happened to me was when my oldest daughter at the age of two and a half was so thrilled by the fact that she could tie a knot.

That is a human discovery. It is that little girl tying a knot in her shoelace; it is the single man of genius whose idea instantly reawakens his discovery in the head of everyone else. And to me that is an essential part of what I have been calling the principle of tolerance. Because it reminds us all the time that people with high IQs are not always very nice people. I have, if you will forgive the expression, known several bastards with very high IQs.

Science seen as a communal activity is, in the end, an interplay between the discovery itself and those to whom it also becomes property—those who elaborate it, work it out, take the next step, lead on to other things. And this interplay can be exciting even to those who have nothing to do with the discovery except the actual pleasure of comprehending it. When I was a young undergraduate in Cambridge, all of us were excited about polytopes. To tell you the truth, nowadays polytopes bore me rigid. But then they were a marvelous new idea; they wakened the mind the way Newton's mind was wakened by the problems of his day. They made us all conscious of the fact that this was a discovery which the moment it was made involved us all.

And we were all involved in the processes of science, in the discoveries being made, by our own good fortune in living in this age. If I had to say a single thing about my lifetime, I would say it quite simply: that I have lived in the twentieth century in the most prodigious time of discovery that the human race could imagine. It has been wonderful for someone like me actually to have heard Dirac give undergraduate classes (I am not talking about J. J. Thomson and Rutherford because they only lectured to me on elementary subjects, but Dirac gave hard lectures); wonderful for someone like me to have worked in the presence of Jacques Monod and Francis Crick, or to have come into this building at the bottom of which there is a tablet about Banting and Macleod. I would not exchange this for all the tea in China.

It has been a marvelous age, and it is a marvelous age. But it is not anybody's age. Even the transformation of science in the time that I myself remember it, between when we all left atomic physics in 1945 and went into biology in the years that followed, has been an opening up. I shall be sorry not to be here twenty years from now to see how it goes on. But it depends on an understanding that the best scientific result in the world is not *right*, that the best experiment in the world is surrounded by an area of tolerance. The best exchange of opinion in the world becomes simply a confrontation of dogma if you do not understand that you can be no more accurate about the speed of light than you can be about whether communism is better than capitalism or vice versa. And I am not joking. We do not even know whether the speed of light was the same two hundred years ago, and we do not have any way of finding out. And we do not mean to give up. Unlike Brezhnev, unlike Mr. Schmidt, we do not know the answer.

When I make these statements, people say to me, "That was a farfetched analogy between atomic physics and public opinion." I just do not believe it. On the contrary, I believe that the greatest contribution which science has made in my lifetime is exactly to teach to thousands of people like us—who came out of ghettos, whose fathers could never have sat here, whose grandfathers were shoemakers—that you have to tell the truth the way you see it. And yet you have to be tolerant of the fact that neither you nor the man you are arguing with is going to get it *right*.

18
THE DISESTABLISHMENT OF SCIENCE

On February 2, 1939, my late friend and colleague Leo Szilard sent a letter to J. F. Joliot-Curie in France in which he proposed that atomic physicists should make a voluntary agreement not to publish any new findings on the fission of uranium. It was a crucial time in history. The date was shortly after Munich; Hitler was riding high, and was clearly determined to make war. And just at this threatening moment, results were published which left no doubt that the atom of uranium could be split.[1] Szilard concluded that a chain reaction could be produced and warned Joliot-Curie, "In certain circumstances this might then lead to the construction of bombs which would be extremely dangerous in general and particularly in the hands of certain governments."

Farsighted as Leo Szilard was, it is hard to believe that the events he feared could have been stopped even if other scientists had accepted his invitation to silence. The embargo on publication that he tried to improvise was too crude to be realistic, in a field in which discoveries were being made so fast and their implications were so clear and so grave. At best Szilard's scheme could have been a stopgap with which he might hope to buy a little time.

Yet it is important that a scientist with the standing of Leo Szilard should have put into words the favorite daydream of the bewildered citizen: to call a moratorium on science. It reminds us that scientists also feel helpless in the rush of events, which unseen hands seem constantly to direct toward more and more massive and unpleasant forms of death. We all want to buy time: a time to reflect, without next year's weapons program already grinning behind our backs.

A proposal to call a moratorium on science, in a strict and literal sense, would be as unrealistic today as it was thirty years ago. It could be imposed on scientists (who have a living to earn and a career to make) only by taking away their government grants. And no government would agree to do that in the middle of an arms race, when it is hidebound in the concept of negotiating

[1]The paper by Lise Meitner and O. R. Frisch on "Disintegration of Uranium by Neutrons" was published in *Nature* on February 11, 1939.

from strength—which means, by threat and counterthreat. How nice, how idyllic it would be if governments could agree to suspend weapons research and counterresearch, development and counterdevelopment: because if the conditions for such an international agreement existed, peace and the millennium would already be here.

In fact no scientist, and I hope no one who cares for the growth of knowledge, would accept a moratorium even if it were practicable. The tradition of free inquiry and publication has been essential in setting the standard of truth in science: it is already eroded by secrecy in government and industry, and we need to resist any extension of that. On this ground certainly any idea of a literal standstill in science is wrongheaded, and I do not take it seriously.

But it would be shallow to find in the popular dream of a moratorium nothing more than this literal idea. There is something there that goes deeper, and that is the idea of a voluntary agreement among scientists themselves.[2] The layman sees that he will never put an end to misuse by telling scientists what to do: that leads only to the exploitation of science by those who know how to manipulate power. He sighs for a moratorium because he wants science used for good and is convinced that this can come about only by the action of scientists themselves.

If science is to express a conscience, it must come spontaneously out of the community of scientists. But of course this hope poses the crucial questions on which in the end the whole argument hinges. Is science as a discipline capable of inspiring in those who practice it a sense of communal responsibility? Can scientists be moved, as a body, to accept the moral decisions which their key position in this civilization has thrust upon them?

These questions cut deep, and I do not think that any scientist now can sleep in peace by pushing them to the back of his mind.

[2]This was the finding of the first survey by *Mass Observation* after the atomic bombs were dropped in 1945, and has been repeatedly confirmed since then.

There are two distinct kinds of questions here, which engage different parts of his activity and personality. Both are questions of moral conscience; but I will distinguish the first kind by calling them questions of *humanity*, and the second by calling them questions of *integrity*.

The questions of humanity concern the stand that a man should take in the perpetual struggle of each nation to outwit the others, chiefly in the ability to make war. Although the scientist is more often drawn into this (as a technician) than his fellow citizens, his moral dilemma is just the same as theirs: he must weigh his patriotism against his sense of a universal humanity. If there is anything special about his being a scientist, it can only be that he is more conscious than others that he belongs to an international community.

The second kind of moral questions, those of integrity, derive from the conditions of work which science imposes on those who pursue it. Science is an endless search for truth, and those who devote their lives to it must accept a stringent discipline. For example, they must not be a party to hiding the truth, for any end whatever. There is no distinction between means and ends for them. Science admits no other end than the truth, and therefore it rejects all those devices of expediency by which men who seek power excuse their use of bad means for what they call good ends.

I begin with the questions of humanity. Since so much scientific and technical talent goes into advice and research on war, it is natural that the moral problem that stands largest in our minds (as it did in Szilard's) is still the disavowal of war. I shall be saying later that this is by no means enough; yet it is certainly the first issue before us, and has rightly troubled the public sense of decency for the last twenty-five years.

No man who is able to see himself as others do can approve making war on civilians with atomic bombs, with napalm and orbiting missiles. Yet he also knows that every government that ordered the development of these weapons, anywhere it the world, did so as a duty to its own nation. This is why the man in the street wants scientists to keep these dreadful secrets to themselves when they discover them. He knows that the heads of state have no choice: each of them has been elected to protect the interests of his nation, and to be deaf and stonyhearted to the interests of humanity at large. In a world in which diplomacy still consists of national bargaining, no statesman has a mandate for humanity, and therefore the man in the street turns to scientists in the desperate hope that they will act as keepers of an international conscience.

Some scientists will answer that they have a national duty too, which is to disclose what they know to the head of state who has been elected to put it to whatever use he judges best. At a time of world war, when the survival of a nation may be at stake, most scientists will act like this; and they will have a better conscience than Klaus Fuchs, who thought himself entitled to do as he chose with scientific secrets. Even in time of peace, there will be some who will put national loyalty first. I think this is a matter of private conscience, and that scientists who feel that their ultimate loyalty is to their nation should follow their conscience by working *directly* for their government.

But what I think is no longer tenable, in the times as they are, is the stance that Robert Oppenheimer tried to maintain, namely to be a technical adviser on weapons on some days and an international conscience on others. The rivalry of nations has now become too bitter, and the choices that it poses for the scientist too appalling, to make it possible to be involved in weapons and war policy and still to claim the right of personal judgment. And that is not merely a matter of professional independence: it comes from a deeper conflict with the morality of nationalism, government, and diplomacy.

Nationalism has now distorted the use of science so that it outrages the aspirations of the user. All over the world, from Jordan to Rhodesia, and from Northern Ireland to South America, men carry in their hands the most precise and expensive products of technology: automatic rifles, radar, infrared glasses, homing rockets, and all the refined machinery of combat and terrorism. Yet the combatants on whom these gifts are heaped have them only to kill. Nothing like this has been given them at home to live with: they may have no toilet there and no bath, not a stick of decent furniture and no tools, no medicines and no schooling to speak of. It is bad enough that the world is full of people who live in such misery; and it is an affront to humanity that there should then be pressed upon them as the blessings of technical civilization the beautiful instruments of murder.

It seems plain, therefore, that unless a scientist believes as a matter of conscience that he owes it to his nation to work directly on war research, he should not accept any indirect part in it. If he chooses war research, he should work in a government department or establishment. But if he abhors the consequences of national war, he should also reject any grant or project that comes to him from a military department, in any country.

This is not an easy counsel in those countries (chiefly the United States and Russia) where most research in the physical sciences, and much outside them, is financed by service departments. For it does not apply only to work on weapons and strategy, but by historical momentum extends over a large area of fundamental and theoretical research.[3]

The support of science from military funds has come about in a haphazard way. In the main, it grew after 1945 out of the crash methods to finance research which had been improvised during

[3]Although I begin with the physical sciences, my theme is the dependence of all science now on government support, and I ought to give the reader some measure of that. To avoid an excess of detail, I will confine myself to two statistics: Where is basic research done, and who pays the piper there? In Soviet Russia, of course, the monopoly by government is absolute. In the United States between 1965 and 1970, 62 percent of the annual cost of basic research (which rose from 2.9 to 3.5 billion dollars in these years) was paid by the federal government, and 58 percent of it was done in the universities. When research done outside the universities is stripped from the total cost, the balance sheet becomes: 75 percent of the basic research done in the universities is paid by federal grants and contracts, and only 25 percent by other funds. This is for basic research in all sciences together. The disparity is even greater for the physical sciences alone, and for nonbasic and development work. See *National Science Policies of the USA* (Unesco, 1968) and the *National Science Foundation Annual Report* for 1969.

the war. At that time, government money in most countries was channeled through the armed services, and it was convenient to go on having the service departments farm out research directly. Since they were not short of money, they often gave grants even to theoretical scientists working in fundamental fields (such as mathematics and psychology) that had no foreseeable bearing on any practical service need.

This pattern of quasi-military support still persists, both in general research grants and in specific project costs, in much of the work done in physics and chemistry, for example.[4] There is a similar pattern in the research financed by the space program in the United States; again the theoretical and fundamental scientist finds himself at the end of a long pipeline which is not strictly military, and yet whose command of funds derives from a belief by government that the department is a useful outpost of nationalism.

Because of these arrangements, it is convenient for a worker in the physical sciences to draw the money for his research, whatever it is, from one of these quasi-military pipelines. And since his university usually cannot pay for his research, and often (in the United States, for example) cannot survive without grants, he is compelled to go for help where the money is. So it comes about that physical scientists in different countries, who would not willingly work in war research, nevertheless get their funds from government departments whose main business is related to war.

It seems timely to decide now that this is a bad practice, and that grants for nonmilitary research should not come from quasi-military sources. A scientist who accepts money from such a source cannot be blind to the subtle conformity that it imposes on his own conduct and on those who work with him, including his students. The obligations that he silently incurs are dormant,

[4]Since this mode of support is most common in the United States, I draw my examples from there. But the same pattern is widespread in other Western nations, for example in the financing of computer research by NATO, and of research on atomic energy by the French government.

but they are there, and he will be in a quandary whenever a government in trouble decides to make them explicit.

I have already said that most physicists who take money from government departments have nowhere else to go; so that if they were to refuse these grants, they would have to give up their research. This would be a hardship, but it is unlikely that it could last long. For the technical society that we live in cannot afford to let research languish, and will be forced to create new channels for support if the old channels are stopped up by the receivers themselves.

I shall return later to the problem of creating a new organization of support for nonmilitary research. For the problem applies to all sciences, far beyond physics, and before I discuss it I must establish a case for detaching them also from government departments. To do so, I must move on from the inhumanity of war to the moral standing of government influence in general.

The traditional issue of conscience for scientists has been the use of their work to make war more terrible. But the problem that confronts us now is more fundamental and is all-embracing. Scientists can no longer confine their qualms to the uses and abuses to which their discoveries are put—to the development of weapons, or even to the larger implications of an irresponsible technology which distorts our civilization. Instead they are face to face with a choice of conscience between two moralities: the morality of science, and the morality of national and government power.

My view is that these two moralities are not compatible. In world affairs, science has always been an enterprise without frontiers, and scientists as a body make up the most successful international community in the world. And I have already shown in my earlier analysis that, in a world of un-United Nations, the public is searching for someone to act for the human race as a whole, and hopes that scientists will do that.

In domestic affairs also, the morality of power was laid down centuries ago by Machiavelli for *The Prince*, and is incompatible with the integrity of science. This is a more subtle and recent issue, which has grown up with the extension of government patronage to cover all branches of science.

A pervasive moral distortion, a readiness to use any means for its own ends, warps the machinery of modern government. The scientist who joins a committee becomes a prisoner of the procedures by which governments everywhere are told only what they want to hear, and tell the public only what they want to have it believe. The machine is enveloped in secrecy, which is called "security" and is used as freely to hoodwink the nation as to protect it. A great apparatus of evasion is constructed, a sort of plastic language without content, which goes by the euphemism of "the credibility gap."[5]

The scientist who goes into this jungle of twentieth-century government, anywhere in the world, puts himself at a double disadvantage. In the first place, he does not make policy; he does not even help to make it, and most of the time he has no idea what shifts of policy his advice is meant to serve. And in the second and, oddly, the more serious place (for him), he has no control over the way in which what he says in council will be presented to the public. I call this more serious for him because public respect for science is built on its intellectual integrity, and the second-hand statements and the garbled extracts that are attributed to him bring that into disrepute.

Government is an apparatus which exercises power and which is bent on retaining it, and in the twentieth century more than ever before it spends its time in trying to perpetuate itself by justifying itself. This cast of mind and of method is flatly at odds

[5]Two specific forms of evasion and obscuration are at work here. One stems from the wish of government departments to protect themselves from informed criticism, which is done most simply by hiding information: see, for example, the editorial "In Place of Information" in *Nature*, 28 June 1969. The other is more aggressive, and in the United States (as in Russia) makes constant propaganda on behalf of party and departmental policies as if they were expressions of the national will. There are good accounts of this public relations activity by several Washington observers, of which the most intimate is J. W. Fulbright's *The Pentagon Propaganda Machine* (New York, 1970).

with the integrity of science, which consists of two parts. One is the free and total dissemination of knowledge: but since knowledge leads to power, no government is happy with that. The other is that science makes no distinction between means and ends: but since all governments believe that power is good in itself, they will use any means to that end.

An example from Russia shows how damaging the dependence on government favor is for the integrity of science. There the science of biology in general, and genetics in particular, was dominated for thirty years by a second-rate scientist and charlatan, T. D. Lysenko, whose only skill was in exploiting the favors of two successive heads of state. So he was able to falsify biology on a grand scale, to bring up his students in ignorance and deceit, and, incidentally, to do lasting damage to Russian agriculture. These are the consequences of the manipulation of science for the sake of political conformity and power. Yet to my mind Lysenko did a greater harm than all these: by being able to silence those who tried to argue with him, he destroyed the trust of other Russian intellectuals in their scientists.[6]

We live in a civilization in which science is no longer a profession like any other. For now the hidden spring of power is knowledge; and more than this, power over our environment grows from discovery. Therefore those whose profession is knowledge and discovery hold a place which is crucial in our societies: crucial in importance and therefore in responsibility. This is true for everyone who follows an intellectual profession; in the sense that I have just described it, ours is an intellectual civilization, and the responsibility of the scientist is a particular case of the moral responsibility which every intellectual must accept. Nevertheless, it is fair to pin the responsibility most squarely on scientists, because their pursuits have for some time

[6]I choose this familiar example because it has been well documented recently by Zhores A. Medvedev, in *The Rise and Fall of T. D. Lysenko* (New York, 1969), and because the continued persecution of Medvedev after the publication of his book shows what energy and spite bureaucratic officials are willing to expend to hide errors by the ruling establishment, past as well as present.

had the largest practical influence on our lives, and as a result have made them favored children in the register of social importance—some would say, spoiled children. So other intellectuals have a right to ask of them, as favored children, that they accept the moral leadership which their singular status demands. This calls for both a sensitive humanity and a selfless integrity, and it is the second of these that I am now stressing.

The Russian example is a warning that scientists have to renounce the creeping patronage of governments if they want to preserve the integrity of knowledge as a means and an end which thoughtful citizens (including their own students) prize in them. In my view, there is now a duty laid on scientists to set an incorruptible standard for public morality.[7] The public has begun to understand that the constant march from one discovery to the next is kept going not by luck and not even by cleverness, but by something in the method of science: an unrelenting independence in the search for truth that pays no attention to received opinion or expediency or political advantage. We have to foster that public understanding, because in time it will work an intellectual revolution even in affairs of state. And meanwhile we as scientists have to act as guardians and as models for the public hope that somewhere there is a moral authority in man which can overcome all obstacles.

These considerations apply as much to those sciences, for example, the biological sciences, whose support comes from branches of government which have no military connections. For the moral issues that face the community of scientists now are no longer to be measured by the simple scale of war or peace. We see the growing involvement year by year of government in

[7]A special tribute is therefore due to those Russian scientists who have continued to speak out against a passive conformity: among them Igor Tamm, Pyotr Kapitza, and Andrei Sakharov. I quote from Sakharov's essay to celebrate Tamm's seventieth birthday in 1965: "A tremendous role was played by the struggle of principle that Tamm waged for decades against the primitive dogmatism that refused to accept, first the theory of relativity, and then quantum mechanics. With the same passion he came out against the arbitrary high-handedness in biology."

science and science in government; and unless we cut that entanglement, we endanger the integrity of all science, and undermine the public trust in it by which I set such store. The silent pressure for conformity exists whenever grants and contracts for research are under the direct control of governments; and then (as the Russian example shows) no science is immune to the infection of politics and the corruption of power.

The time has come to consider how we might bring about a separation, as complete as possible, between science and government in all countries. I call this *the disestablishment of science*, in the same sense in which the churches have been disestablished and have become independent of the state. It may be that disestablishment can be brought about only by the example of some outstanding scientists—as Pyotr Kapitza refused the directions of Stalin in Russia, and Max von Laue refused to work for Hitler in Germany. But the immediate need is more practical. It is to have all scientists consider the form that disestablishment should take, and for which they would be willing to make common cause.

Evidently the choice of priorities in research should not be left in the hands of governments. This is a view that government departments will not like, so that scientists who hold it will need to be single-minded if they are to make it heard. They may have to refuse to apply for grants and contracts that are allocated directly by departments. Again, this would be a hardship for many scientists, who now have nowhere else to go for money and who would be forced to suspend their research. But they must be willing to face the hardship for a time if they are serious and united in the will to put science into the hands of scientists.

In the long run, the aim should be to get a single and overall fund or grant for research, to be divided by all the scientists in a country. This would be an effective form of disestablishment, and no doubt governments would accept it rather than watch research become moribund. The alternative would be to let the scientific community build its own fund, and derive an income for itself, by pooling its discoveries and selling the rights to use them.

Once there is a single grant for all research together, its division becomes the business of scientists themselves. They have plenty of practice now in sitting on panels that grade the applicants for the money assigned to each small section of a scientific topic. But in future they will have to undertake to weigh section against section, topic against topic, field against field, and (at the top of this pyramid) each branch of science against the rest.

The disestablishment of science will compel the scientific community to assign its own priorities and divide the overall grant at its disposal accordingly. On the small scale, this is a familiar task and does not seem onerous. The consideration of the work and the promise of other scientists, the criticism of new work and new plans, is an informal part of every scientist's education. At present, it is formalized in the many small review committees which advise on grants in specialized fields. But there is no reason in principle why the procedure should not change its scale, and grow into an overall review of the whole field of scientific research. In most nations, the senior scientific bodies (for example, the Royal Society and the Medical Research Council in England, and the National Academy of Sciences in the United States) make such surveys in piecemeal fashion from time to time. That is only a faint shadow, so far, of a science policy directed in each nation by its scientists. But it is a shadow that points the way to go: it shows that the method is practical, and can be developed from known procedures.

So far, I have proposed two steps in the disestablishment of science: first, refusal to accept grants or projects directly from government agencies, and second, demand for a single national grant which is then to be allocated by the scientific community itself. There remains a third step in the more distant future, and yet it is the crucial step: the allocation of research as a single *international* undertaking.

The public in every nation in the world is looking for an international conscience—that is the point from which I began this essay, and on which it hinges. For it knows that nationalism is an anachronism, and a dying form of civilization. So the public everywhere looks to scientists to find a practical way to express the sense of international duty and decency which is so plainly waiting over the horizon. The reason for this trust is precisely that science is recognized as an international fellowship: international in its principles, and international as a body of men.

In the end, then, the disestablishment of science must mean a change from national to international policies. Evidently, these policies will have to be debated, formed, and put into practice by scientists themselves—our experience of so-called international organizations makes that plain.[8] Alas, we shall not take this third step very soon. True, it has been possible to run international committees on special fields in science already. But on the total scale of science it is an immense responsibility. The body of scientists as a whole will have to develop a system of representation to make its policy, in which the young, the bold, the idealistic, and the unorthodox have a better chance to be heard than they do in politics. There is good evidence that this happens in science, and it is the best reason of all for giving scientists their head.

So the scientific community, through its own representatives, will have to judge and balance the importance of the different branches of science at any time, and of the new lines of research in each. It will have to guess the time and the chance of success in each line. And then it will have to combine the judgments of importance with the guesses at success, in order to arrive at a scale of priorities—a scale of claims, as it were—in accordance with which it must divide its overall grant.

It would be nice to believe that the computation of priorities in this way requires nothing more than scientific competence. But alas, even the disestablishment of science cannot make life so simple. There is no judgment of the importance of a field or a line of research that can be confined to its scientific potential. Every

[8]The shortcomings of present international organizations are trenchantly described by one of their most distinguished servants, Gunnar Myrdal, in his Clark Memorial Lecture given at Toronto in 1969. Myrdal calls them inter*governmental* organizations because, he says, they are only "an agreed matrix for the multilateral pursuit of national policies." His account of the national pressures on the secretariat is a sad but salutary catalogue of intrigue, deceit, spying, and open threats.

judgment in life contains a silent estimate of human and social values too, and the representatives of science will not be able to shirk that. There is no guarantee that scientists will make a better job of fitting science to humanity than has been done so far, but it is time that they faced their moral obligations and tried.

19
THE FULFILLMENT OF MAN

The title of this essay is very general; but you will see that my aim is quite specific. I propose to spend some time in asking why rationalism today no longer seems so exciting a movement as it did one hundred and fifty years ago. What has happened to make antirational and even irrational beliefs once more attractive to many intelligent people? What is wrong with the form in which rationalism has settled down for rather a long time now? Having asked these questions, I propose also to answer them, and to say how I think rationalist and humanist thoughts must be formulated afresh in order to retain their strong meaning today. My purpose is to find the modern basis for rationalism.

The tradition of rationalism, to which we go back, has been a tradition of challenge. It began when the geologists challenged the story of the Creation, early in the last century. The British Association for the Advancement of Science traces its beginning back, indirectly, to this quarrel. For the quarrel about the age of the earth, a hundred and fifty years ago, was a major and pioneer issue. It has been forgotten since only because a much more violent quarrel followed on its heels: the quarrel about the descent of man.

More than a hundred years have passed since Charles Darwin in 1859, reluctantly, and after twenty years of labor, published *The Origin of Species*. The storm which Darwin had foreseen and feared broke punctually. Bishop Samuel Wilberforce made the most famous of all attacks at the meeting of the British Association in Oxford next year, in 1860. Ten years later the Metaphysical Society tried to mark out at least the common ground for a truce by bringing the two sides together, religious men and freethinkers: William Gladstone and John Morley, Cardinal Manning and William Clifford, Alfred Tennyson and the Archbishop of York and Leslie Stephen and Thomas Huxley. It was to define his position in the Metaphysical Society that Huxley coined the word "agnostic."

Yet today these distant heroics hardly raise a yawn. In a hundred years this has become a flat and theatrical piece of history too tedious to fire a child; and the battle of Oxford is more remote than the battle of the Boyne. Why? Because Darwin and Huxley routed those who tried to challenge them on their own ground with such finality that, alas, we can no longer muster an interest in their historic victory. Here is the irony and the price of total victory.

This would be a matter for no regret if in fact the battle of rationalism had been won. If the pioneer work of the last century had established, once for all, that rational thought is welcome to examine all human origins and institutions and human conduct, I should not ask you to be alarmed at the neglect of the pioneers. But of course nothing of the kind has occurred. What happened in the first place, in 1859 and for ten or twenty years afterwards, was that the established religions tried to fight the findings of science when they touched the place of man in the world. The established religions failed. The theory of evolution made literal church dogmas look as flimsy as four hundred years ago Copernicus had done. But at both times, against Darwin as well as against Copernicus, the established religions did not linger in defeat. They simply abandoned the ground on which they had once stood pat. The church which had humiliated Galileo found, with a great show of tolerance, that a belief that the earth is the center of the universe is not really cardinal to its doctrine. The bishops who had thundered at Charles Darwin and John Tyndall were suddenly content to abandon the literal truth of the story of the Creation and to endow it instead with a more shining splendor as some mystic parable of the evolutionary process.

For this reason you will find no respectable church authorities today who are still willing to challenge the proposition for which Buffon was once threatened with excommunication, that the crust of the earth carries the marks of its past history. No sermons are preached by educated clerics against geology, the fossil record, and evolution. Indeed, no defense of church doctrine, outside Spain, the Republic of Eire, and some states of America, takes as its ground the factual truth of these doctrines. The issue of fact has been yielded to the experimental scientist. Whatever issue is now paraded, whatever kind of truth is now claimed for ancient dogmas, truth which is accessible to rational inquiry has been abandoned.

It is of course annoying of the churches to shift their ground like this. For 1800 years and more, the dogmas laid down by the Christian churches, their predecessors, and their rivals were advanced as matters of literal truth. To fly in the face of Genesis was throughout those centuries held to be as outrageous as to fly in the face of gravity; and was in fact a great deal more dangerous. Now the great dignitaries tell us, with beatific charm, and with a smile of tolerance at our foolish materialist obtuseness, that all this meant nothing. The churches have changed their mind. They no longer believe the biblical stories—indeed, some of them plainly find the existence of the Bible an embarrassment. And anyone who went to the stake for sharing this disbelief prematurely, as so many men did, may now in retrospect bask in their regrets.

It is, I have said, annoying of the traditional faiths to shift their ground like this. But once they have done so, it is useless for us to behave as if they had not. It is useless for us to go on stamping our feet in the place where they once stood, and to offer battle to what now are only ghosts there. Religion as it existed up to and in the nineteenth century is dead. Nineteenth-century rationalism killed it, yes, but no one will be persuaded in this century if we grow indignant with that corpse, or remorselessly pursue its ghost. And just this is the compulsion, just this is the crisis, of rationalist and humanist movements today. They know themselves the victors of a historic battle, and they are still proud and fond of the weapons which won that victory. My business here is to persuade them that history is not enough.

For the doctrinaire, the obscurantist, the exploiter of traditional fears and sanctions still exists. He has new disguises, but he remains my enemy and yours as he was Darwin's and Huxley's and William Kingdom Clifford's. Our reason for detesting him, and for taking issue with what he preaches, has never been confined to the specific doctrines with which he has hobbled otherwise thinking men. The doctrinaire has shifted his ground. He has learned to avoid any ground which is free to rational inquiry. It is all the more important to pursue not the ghost but the man, not the doctrine but the doctrinaire; and to pursue him into our own century.

Today the religious faiths take as their ground man's hunger for certainty. Do you want to satisfy this hunger? they say. Look about you: you will find no certainty except in the submission to some doctrine which is not accessible to reason. Where there is reason, there grows doubt, they say; nothing is certain except the irrational.

Our forerunners would have been astonished at this odd reversal. They would have thought it patent that no belief which did not submit itself to the test of rational inquiry could claim any assurance. And they would have thought that certainty comes only by such inquiry: by the accumulation of small pieces of evidence, one by one, into a pyramid whose pieces lock and hold. The pyramid, always building and always unfinished, is experience rationally organized. The pyramid is science. Our forerunners would have said that science as a meaningful arrangement of human experience never gives final certainty, of course, but always approaches it, and that there is no other way to approach it.

But the modern acts of faith, religious or political, do not think so far as this. They content themselves simply with saying that science cannot give final certainty. Beyond each explanation of science lies another, beyond each new piece of understanding there opens up only a new question. The scientist questions the solidity of matter, and finds that it is indeed nothing but molecules and holes. Very well; but is a molecule solid? No, the molecule is made of atoms and holes. And is the atom solid? No, the atom is mostly empty too; only at its center is there a compact nucleus. And is that really compact? Evidently not: the neutrons and the protons in it have a good deal of elbow room to arrange and rearrange themselves. And the neutrons and protons are certainly not the end of the matter either. But the man in search of a faith has long thrown up his hands and decided that there is no refuge for him here. Each step opens a new step; each answer poses a new question. To the man in search of a faith, complete, compact, and safe from further questioning, science is an endless avenue of regress. And this is true of every form of reasoning which takes nothing for granted outside human experience: all reasoning is an endless regress.

So the modern faiths assert that there is only one way to close this avenue of mirrors. At some place we must simply decide, they say, arbitrarily, to go no further. This is where we stop, we are to say. Inquiry does not go beyond this. This is the absolute. This is final. This frontier, which is closed, has been fixed by God or by authority or (as Hitler used to say) by blood and soil.

To set up such absolutes is to close the door to all further inquiry: this indeed is their purpose. Of course it is only a very small door, say the faithful: it is only meant to close inquiry in one direction—on the nature of the soul, say, or the intelligence of negroes, or the inheritance of acquired characters. Alas, the infection of absolutism turns out always to be more virulent than this. Ancient and modern history alike have shown that once inquiry is forbidden in one field, it is discouraged in all. In no society, Eastern or Western, Chinese, Roman, medieval, or contemporary, have science and rational speculation long survived the imposition of absolute dogma—religious or social. If today we want to find relief from the uncertainties of a changing world in some cosy arbitrary doctrine, then we had better face the likelihood that tomorrow the Dark Ages will return.

I have glanced at this threat that all inquiry will be submerged because in fact inquiry is all of a piece. Once the nature of one science is misunderstood, all science is misunderstood. The seekers after certainty say that science is an endless process of analysis. What they say is wrong, not of one science, but of all sciences, and indeed of all reasoning.

When the inquiring man analyzes the facts as he finds them, he has indeed made the beginning for a rational view of the world: but he has made only a beginning. Science analyzes experience, yes, but the analysis does not yet make a picture of the world. The analysis provides only the materials for the picture. The purpose of science, and of all rational thought, is to make a more ample and more coherent picture of the world, in which each experience holds together better and is more of a piece. This is a task of synthesis, not of analysis.

The analysis, then, is not an end in itself; it is not an end at all. It has to be made only in order to extract the common features in what seem to be different experiences; what science is trying to do is to make a unity of these. Why did anyone ever trouble to invent atoms? Why did anyone trouble to take matter to pieces? Because they wanted to make a unity of what seemed different, of snow and ice and water and cloud and steam. You cannot make a coherent picture of the melting of ice to water, and the changing of water to steam many times its volume, until you make for yourself a picture of the same water molecules spread out or pressed together with different spacings. And the picture, because it is a unity, is an enrichment; it gives to the snowflake and the raindrop and the cloud a new because a common meaning.

The mind, then, analyzes when it reasons or when it experiments only to get the raw materials for a new synthesis.

The common content that the mind finds, the synthesis that it makes, is always a concept. And a set of concepts coheres and is consistent at its own level. It does not provide certainty for a cruder level, and it does not have to seek certainty in a more refined level. When I take your hand into mine, we are using our hands and not assemblies of atoms: it is simply nonsense to swoon at the thought that so many holes somehow get entangled in a handshake. What we are doing is orderly at its own human level.

If I go on now to discuss the orderliness of crystals, I move to another level which cannot be confused and is complete in its own right. At this level, it makes sense to say that the snowflake is beautiful because it is cold—that is, its atoms have a crystal pattern because they do not make violent random movements. This remark requires no sanction at all either from a cruder or from a more refined level of conceptual abstraction. The synthesis at this atomic level is complete in itself, and sufficient to itself. We do not need to move on to the next level of fineness, the level of electrons and nuclei, until we want to talk about some other kind of experience: about electricity and chemistry.

Consider now a very abstract concept: the concept of gravity. Newton invented it, in the form of a universal law of inverse squares, in order to organize a body of findings each of which was itself already abstract. For example, they included the laws found by Kepler, that each planet moves in an ellipse with the sun at one focus, and how fast each planet moves in its ellipse. These laws, in turn, depended on the ingenuity of Copernicus in seeing that the paths of the planets and of the earth make a simple pattern, a unity which is meaningful, if they are all looked at from the sun. And Copernicus, we must remember, was heir to centuries of astronomical speculation which, though we now think it out of date, did establish the profound idea that the paths of the stars are evidence of some deeper organized mechanism in nature.

The concept of gravity therefore holds together general laws, and they in turn summarize a network of individual observations and applications which could not be listed one by one. This is a matter of great importance. For the most common misunderstanding of science is to think of it as a fat looseleaf book of facts, into which new facts are clipped one by one as they are discovered. This picture of science is quite wrong. There is no such dictionary of science, and there could not be. The picture is mistaken, because it insists on thinking of science simply as a collection of somewhat out of the way facts, a sort of cookery book of special recipes for making atomic bombs. But science is not a collection of facts; it is the organization of the facts under general laws, and the laws in turn are held together by such concepts, such creations of the human mind, as gravitation. The facts are endless chaos; science is the activity of finding in them some order. And this order is not merely a shorthand for the facts; it is what gives them meaning, it is their meaning. Science is the human activity of finding an order in nature by organizing the scattered meaningless facts under universal concepts.

People who think of science merely as an enumeration of facts make the same mistake about human conduct. They think of ethics as a kind of book of etiquette; a set of recipes each telling you how to do one thing. "Don't talk to Mrs. A. about string; her husband was hanged." But of course ethics does not consist of a book of specific injunctions, to tell you what not to say on every tactful occasion. And ethics does not even consist of those more general rules which tell you how to avoid giving offence by the wider exercise of taste and foresight. Ethics is the organization of our conduct by concepts which hold it together as a whole: concepts such as neighborliness and loyalty and human dignity, which underlie the textbook courtesies and the Sunday-school precepts, precisely as the concepts of science underlie the facts and the laws.

And the concepts of science were not given to us by God. They were created, they were synthesized from an analysis of human experience. The concepts of ethics are reached precisely in the same way. We first analyze our experience of social life, or we accept the analysis which has been begun by our parents and teachers—as a scientist accepts much of his analysis from his forerunners. When in this way we have unraveled the strands of conduct, in a thousand situations, we wind together again a strand taken from here and a strand from there, to make new created concepts of what we find common to all. Honor, truth, loyalty are not concepts that come to us, ready-made, on the day of our birth or of our puberty; and neither are they mere conveniences which have been imposed on us by teachers or policemen who want no trouble. They are concepts in which we organize our growing experience of men and society, for ourselves. We share them with others as we share the concepts of science, as we share gravity and evolution, because they are built from experiences which are open to all of us.

I therefore hold that there is no difference in kind between the concept of loyalty and the concept of gravity. Each serves to hold together a body of experience, the one social and the other physical. Neither is a mere shorthand for some list of isolated examples of the conduct which it describes. Rather, more deeply, each gives order and meaning to the whole body of that conduct, social or physical. We reach each by the same process of human inquiry. Loyalty is a concept in which each of us elucidates, usually unconsciously, his own experience of man in society, as gravity consciously elucidates the grave gyrations of the heavenly bodies. Neither requires any higher sanction; and neither calls for an absolute end to further inquiry.

Thus I regard ethics as the study of man in society, in the same sense in which cosmology is the study of the heavenly bodies. You will notice that I say the study of man in society, and not merely the study of society. One of the errors which have been made in putting forward views of this kind has been to speak of man as if he existed only in and for society. Man and society are members each of the other, just as the physical world exists in each atom and in the whole stellar system together. The strength of modern cosmology has been that it has brought the knowledge of the atom into the study of the starry system. So we must bring the knowledge of man into the study of society, to make one study: the study of man in society.

All views of this kind are commonly attacked on the ground that science deals only with what is, and that ethics should deal with what ought to be. This criticism has some force when science is presented as a collection of facts, and ethics as a collection of injunctions. Its force weakens when we go up one step to the level of laws, of nature, and of society: it is after all not an accident that the word "law" has always been used of both. John Locke was so impressed by the work of Isaac Newton that he held that the function of government is merely to discover and to apply the laws of society.

But Locke did not go deep enough. We have to take one more step: we have to move from the laws to something more profound and more imaginative, to concepts which the human mind creates beyond the laws. In the concept of gravity, we express not a specific law of physical behavior, but a unitary picture of how nature works: what holds the world together and yet allows it to move and evolve. In just this way, such concepts as loyalty, justice, respect, and dignity transcend this community or that, and this or that application. Each gives a more embracing picture of the relation of man to society: of how our human world holds together and yet grows and evolves.

This is why I have been at such pains to present science to you as the activity of making concepts. For at the level of the concept, there is no distinction between what is and what ought to be. The concept is a more general picture, not of the specific relation between one thing and another, or one law and another, but of the general form of the relation. The concept of gravity says that only so can the world be both stable and capable of change. The concept of loyalty says that only so can any human society be both stable and capable of change.

And no concept is final: concepts are made and remade. Gravitation does not become a lie when Einstein substitutes something else for it; it becomes part of the wider concept of relativity. There will in time be unifying concepts wider than loyalty and independence and dissent. They will not make these concepts false; they will make them part of a new and wider understanding.

If we grant that what we think of man and society may change, then we must be free to inquire and speculate about both. Ethics is not a final system; it is an activity. In just the same sense, science is not a final system but an activity. This is what William Clifford said:

> Remember, then, that scientific thought is the guide of action; that the truth at which it arrives is not that which we can ideally contemplate without error, but that which we may act upon without fear; and you cannot fail to see that scientific thought is not an accompaniment or condition of human progress, but human progress itself.

And if we think in this way, constantly, about the relations which engage men in society, we shall make a stronger ethic than any preached from pulpits.

Free inquiry has given us, since the Renaissance, an unbelievable command of physical nature. It has done so because it has sought a constantly widening and yet constantly true understanding of nature. There was no science, except in secrecy, in the Dark Ages before the Renaissance.

Meanwhile our command of the resources within human society has not grown in a comparable way. We have larger states than the Renaissance had, and we share the wealth and the running of these states rather more freely. But the progress we have made toward building coherent and happy unions of men has been very small. The churches say that this is because we have abandoned the religious doctrines of the Middle Ages. This is the sort of reasoning which characterizes pulpit oratory and episcopal letters to *The Times*. By contrast, I hold the modest empirical view that the religious beliefs of the Dark Ages demonstrated, for the best part of 1,000 years, just what kind of a world they could make: and that we do not require to repeat the experiment in order to know that it would be a disaster to all men. No; it is the continued absence after the Renaissance of free inquiry in the field of ethics which has continued to make us backward there. We shall increase our understanding of ethics only in the same way as we increase our understanding of nature, by the free inquiry of the human mind.

There is indeed, I hold, no human gift which does not derive from this central urge of inquiry. Authority does not need human subjects; you can exact obedience from cows or peacocks: but you cannot stimulate them to sustained inquiry. This small but critical difference is responsible for the observable and empirical fact that we milk cows, but cows do not milk us. It is responsible for the fact that we keep peacocks because we think them beautiful, but they give no evidence of doing the same for us. And lighthearted as these examples are, they make to my mind a fundamental point: that to dictate to man by authority is to take from him what is most characteristically human, and to treat him at bottom as something less than human. To browbeat a man with absolute instructions does not merely cage the animal in him, as some churches aver; on the contrary, by caging him it makes him an animal. At least, it makes him inhuman.

If rationalism is to be a positive system today, this must be at the heart of what it has to say. It must insist that there is one thing above all else which makes man human, and that is his gift for free inquiry. It is not science, it is not rationalism which makes the world inhuman and colorless. On the contrary, what is inhuman is the surrender to authority. What robs nature of her beauty is the refusal to look at it ourselves; and you do not put the beauty back, as a personal experience, by looking at it through the mist of religious tears. Rationalism is the exploration of the world as human adventure, and it is not less human because it is an intellectual adventure—it is more human. Why do those who belittle science always behave as if the mind were the least human of our gifts? The inquiring mind is the godhead of man.

That mind, in looking at man and society, does not treat them as dead. Science does not treat any part of the universe as dead; it treats it as something which changes and evolves and, more important, our understanding of which is a constant creative change. So we as rationalists do not need to talk about man and society as if they were two stuffed museum pieces. On the contrary, what we want to understand is not only man as he is but as he can be, and the societies which the changing man can make. It is the potential of man that we must explore; it is the fulfillment of man that we must seek. By contrast, it is precisely the doctrines of the Dark Ages which treat man as fixed and dead, a sinful exhibit who can seek virtue only in self-denial. These ascetic virtues are equally the marks of the dead societies of the Middle Ages which we still perpetuate—societies constantly on the brink of famine, in which the greatest virtue of man was to achieve the heroics of an insect in a colony, and sacrifice himself for the hive. We are somewhat past those famine days, and we should be past those famine virtues. The poet William Blake put this in his downright way:

Peace and Plenty and Domestic Happiness is the Source of Sublime Art, and prove to the Abstract Philosophers that Enjoyment and not Abstinence is the food of Intellect.

Blake was himself a man of exemplary frugality, and his example makes it plain that we can rebel against the ethics of abstinence without inviting a permanent saturnalia. Let me quote Blake again on his own life:

Some People and not a few Artists have asserted that the Painter of this Picture would not have done so well if he had been properly Encourag'd. Let those who think so, reflect on the State of Nations under Poverty and their incapability of Art; tho' Art is Above Either, the Argument is better for Affluence than Poverty; and tho' he would not have been a greater Artist yet he would have produc'd Greater works of Art in proportion to his means. A Last Judgment is not for the purpose of making Bad Men better, but for the purpose of hindering them from oppressing the Good with Poverty and Pain by means of Such Vile Arguments and Insinuations.

This, written 150 years ago, is I think also the foundation of any modern rationalism. We plead to exercise our human gifts. We ask for an understanding of them more profound than the ethics of the etiquette book and the Sunday school. The understanding for which we strive is in fact contained in no book of rules, because it is not in its nature to be codified: it is an understanding and not a set of recipes. Such an understanding is essentially a rational, scientific way of looking at things. For science is not a book, either of facts or of rules; it is the creation of concepts which give unity and meaning to nature. Such concepts exist in our understanding of man and of society: truth, loyalty, justice, freedom, respect, and human dignity are concepts of this kind. But they are concepts, created by the human mind for the human mind; they are not God-given ordinances. A rational and coherent system of ethics must grow out of their exploration. It will not be a permanent system; it will not teach us what ought to be forever, any more than science teaches us what is forever. Both science and ethics are activities in which we explore relations which, though permanent in the larger sense, are also in constant evolution. This is the nature of the relations of man and society, that they must rest on what is permanently human, and yet even this slowly changes and evolves. It is not man and society as they are now that we study, but all the potential which they carry within them by virtue of being human. The studies of a new rationalism are the potential of man in society, and society in man: most deeply, the fulfillment of man.

REFERENCES

THE CREATIVE PROCESS

Bronowski, J. 1958. *Science and Human Values.* New York.

Butterfield, H. 1949. *The Origins of Modern Science, 1300–1800.* London.

Lennbursky, S. 1956. *The Physical World of the Greeks.* London.

THE REACH OF IMAGINATION

Buytendijk, F. J. J. 1921. Considérations de psychologie comparée à propos d'expériences faites avec le singe Cercopithecus. *Archives Néerlandaises de Physiologie de l'Homme et des Animaux,* vol. 5, pp. 42–88.

Einstein, Albert. 1949. Autobiographical notes. In *Albert Einstein: Philosopher-Scientist,* edited by P. A. Schilpp. Evanston, Illinois.

Galilei, Galileo. 1638. *Discorsi e Dimostrazioni Matematiche, Intorno a Due Nuove Scienze.* Leyden.

Hunter, Walter S. 1913. The delayed reaction in animals and children. *Behavior Monographs,* vol. 2, no. 1, pp. 1–86.

Jacobsen, Carlyle F. 1935. Functions of the frontal association area in primates. *Archives of Neurology and Psychiatry,* vol. 33, pp. 558–569.

Kepler, Johannes. 1967. *Somnium: The Dream, or Posthumous Work on Lunar Astronomy.* Translated by Edward Rosen. Madison, Wisconsin.

Nicolson, Marjorie H. 1948. *Voyages to the Moon.* New York.

Peirce, Charles S. 1932. Speculative grammar. In *Collected Papers,* vol. 2. Cambridge, Massachusetts.

Yates, Frances A. 1966. *The Art of Memory.* London.

THE LOGIC OF THE MIND

Braithwaite, R. B. 1953. *Scientific Explanation.* Cambridge, England.

Bronowski, J. 1951. *The Common Sense of Science.* London.

Bronowski, J. 1965. *The Identity of Man.* New York.

Carnap, Rudolf. 1937. *The Logical Syntax of Language.* New York.

Church, Alonzo. 1936. A note on the *Entscheidungsproblem. Journal of Symbolic Logic,* vol. 1, pp. 40–41, 101–102.

Church, Alonzo. 1936. An unsolvable problem of elementary number theory. *American Journal of Mathematics,* vol. 58, pp. 345–363.

Gödel, Kurt. 1931. Über formal unentscheidbare Sätze der *Principia Mathematica* und verwandter Systeme, I. *Monatshefte für Mathematik und Physik,* vol. 38, pp. 173–198.

Hilbert, David, and P. Bernays. 1934–1939. *Grundlagen der Mathematik.* Berlin.

Kleene, S. C. 1936. General recursive functions of natural numbers. *Mathematische Annalen,* vol. 112, pp. 727–742.

Kleene, S. C. 1943. Recursive predicates and quantifiers. *Transactions of the American Mathematical Society,* vol. 53, pp. 41–73.

Lucas, J. R. 1961. Minds, machines and Gödel. *Philosophy,* vol. 36, pp. 112–127.

Myhill, John. 1952. Some philosophical implications of mathematical logic. *Review of Metaphysics,* vol. 6, pp. 165–198.

Nagel, Ernest, and James R. Newman. 1958. *Gödel's Proof.* New York.

Poincaré, Henri. 1912. *Calcul des Probabilités.* Paris.

Popper, Karl R. 1963. *Conjectures and Refutations: The Growth of Scientific Knowledge.* London.

Ramsey, F. P. 1931. *The Foundations of Mathematics.* London.

Richard, Jules. 1905. Les principes des mathématiques et le problème des ensembles. *Revue Générale des Sciences Pures et Appliquées,* vol. 16, pp. 541–543.

Riesz, Frédéric. 1944/45. Sur la théorie ergodique. *Commentarii Mathematici Helvetici,* vol. 17, pp. 221–239.

Tarski, Alfred. 1936. Der Wahrheitsbegriff in den formalisierten Sprachen. *Studia Philosophica,* vol. 1, pp. 261–405.

Turing, A. M. 1936/37. On computable numbers with an application to the *Entscheidungsproblem. Proceedings of the London Mathematical Society,* series 2, vol. 42, pp. 230–265, and vol. 43, pp. 544–546.

Whitehead, A. N., and Bertrand Russell. 1910–1913. *Principia Mathematica.* Cambridge, England.

Wittgenstein, Ludwig. 1958. *The Blue and Brown Books.* Oxford.

HUMANISM AND THE GROWTH OF KNOWLEDGE

Ayer, A. J. 1936. *Language, Truth, and Logic.* London.

Bernal, J. D. 1939. *The Social Function of Science.* London.

Bronowski, J. 1965. *The Identity of Man.* New York.

Bronowski, J. 1966. The logic of the mind. *American Scientist,* vol. 54, no. 1, pp. 1–14.

Carnap, Rudolf. 1950. *Logical Foundations of Probability*. Chicago.

Clark, G. N. 1937. *Science and Social Welfare in the Age of Newton*. London.

Cornforth, Maurice. 1946. *Science versus Idealism*. London.

Gödel, Kurt. 1931. Über formal unentscheidbare Sätze der *Principia Mathematica* und verwandter Systeme, I. *Monatshefte für Mathematik und Physik*, vol. 38, pp. 173–198.

Hessen, B. 1931. The social and economic roots of Newton's *Principia*. Paper delivered at the International Congress of the History of Science, London, 1931. Reprinted in *Science at the Crossroads* (London, 1932).

Kepler, Johannes. 1609. *Astronomia Nova*. Heidelberg.

Keynes, J. M. 1921. *A Treatise on Probability*. London.

Laplace, P. S. de. 1814. Essai philosophique sur les probabilités. Introduction to the second edition of his *Théorie Analytique des Probabilités*. Paris.

Neyman, J., and E. S. Pearson. 1928. On the use and interpretation of certain test criteria. *Biometrika*, vol. 20A.

Popper, K. R. 1959. *The Logic of Scientific Discovery*. London.

Popper, K. R. 1963. *Conjectures and Refutations: The Growth of Scientific Knowledge*. London.

Ramsey, F. P. 1931. *The Foundations of Mathematics*. London.

Spinoza, Baruch. 1670. *Tractatus Theologico-Politicus*. Hamburg.

Tarski, Alfred. 1936. Der Warheitsbegriff in den formalisierten Sprachen. *Studia Philosophica*, vol. 1, pp. 261–405.

Turing, A. M. 1936/37. On computable numbers with an application to the *Entscheidungsproblem*. *Proceedings of the London Mathematical Society*, series 2, vol. 42, pp. 230–265, and vol. 43, pp. 544–546.

Whitehead, A. N., and Bertrand Russell. 1910–1913. *Principia Mathematica*. Cambridge, England.

Wittgenstein, Ludwig. 1922. *Tractatus Logico-Philosophicus*. London.

HUMAN AND ANIMAL LANGUAGES

Alexander, R. D. 1960. Sound communication in Orthoptera and Cicadidae. In *Animal Sounds and Communication*, edited by W. E. Lanyon and W. N. Tavolga, pp. 38–92. Washington.

Altmann, S. A. 1962. Social behavior of anthropoid primates: Analysis of recent concepts. In *Roots of Behavior,* edited by E. L. Bliss, pp. 277–285. New York.

Andrew, R. J. 1963. The origin and evolution of the calls and facial expressions of the primates. *Behaviour,* vol. 20, pp. 1–109.

Bally, G. 1945. *Vom Ursprung und von den Grenzen der Freiheit.* Basel.

Blest, A. D. 1961. The concept of "ritualisation." In *Current Problems in Animal Behaviour,* edited by W. H. Thorpe and O. L. Zangwill. Cambridge, England.

Bronowski, J. 1952. The logic of experiment. *Advancement of Science,* vol. 9, pp. 289–296.

Bronowski, J. 1966. The logic of the mind. *American Scientist,* vol. 54, pp. 1–14.

Bronowski, J., and W. M. Long. 1952. Statistics of discrimination in anthropology. *American Journal of Physical Anthropology,* vol. 10, pp. 385–394.

Bronowski, J., and W. M. Long. 1953. The australopithecine milk canines. *Nature,* vol. 172, p. 251

Bruner, J. S. 1962. Introduction to *Thought and Language* by L. S. Vygotsky. Cambridge, Massachusetts.

Butler, S. 1890. Thought and language. In *Collected Essays.* London.

Buytendijk, F. J. J. 1921. Considérations de psychologie comparée à propos d'expériences faites avec le singe Cercopithecus. *Archives Néerlandaises de Physiologie de l'Homme et des Animaux,* vol. 5, pp. 42–88.

Campbell, B. 1963. Quantitative taxonomy and human evolution. In *Classification and Human Evolution,* edited by S. L. Washburn, pp. 50–74. Chicago.

Carthy, J. D. 1961. Do animals see polarized light? *New Scientist,* vol. 10, pp. 660–662.

Chomsky, N. 1966. *Cartesian Linguistics.* New York.

Dart, R. A. 1955. The first australopithecine fragment from the Makapansgat pebble culture stratum. *Nature,* vol. 176, pp. 170–171.

Descartes, R. 1637. *Discours de la Méthode,* part 5. Leyden.

Einstein, A. 1905. Elektrodynamik bewegter Körper. *Annalen der Physik,* vol. 17, pp. 891–921.

Esch, H. 1961. Über die Schallerzeugung beim Werbetanz der Honigbiene. *Zeitschrift Vergleichender Physiologie,* vol. 45, pp. 1–11.

Esch, H. 1965. Private communication.

Faber, A. 1953. *Laut- und Gebärdensprache bei Insekten Orthoptera.* Stuttgart.

Frisch, K. von. 1950. *Bees: Their Vision, Chemical Senses, and Language.* Ithaca, New York.

Goodall, J. 1963. Feeding behaviour of wild chimpanzees. In *The Primates,* edited by J. Napier (Zoological Society of London Symposium, vol. 10), pp. 39–47.

Hebb, D. O., and W. R. Thompson. 1954. The social significance of animal studies. In *Handbook of Social Psychology,* edited by G. Lindsey, vol. 1, pp. 532–561. Cambridge, Massachusetts.

Hinde, R. A., and T. E. Rowell. 1962. Communication by postures and facial expressions in the rhesus monkey (Macaca mulatta). *Proceedings of the Zoological Society of London,* vol. 138, pp. 1–21.

Hockett, C. F. 1959. Animal "languages" and human language. In *The Evolution of Man's Capacity for Culture,* arranged by J. N. Spuhler, pp. 32–39. Detroit.

Hockett, C. F. 1960. Logical considerations in the study of animal communication. In *Animal Sounds and Communication,* edited by W. E. Lanyon and W. N. Tavolga, pp. 392–430. Washington.

Hockett, C. F. 1963. The problem of universals in language. In *Universals of Language,* edited by J. H. Greenberg, pp. 1–29. Cambridge, Massachusetts.

Hockett, C. F., and R. Ascher. 1964. The human revolution. *Current Anthropology,* vol. 5, pp. 135–147.

Hunter, W. S. 1913. The delayed reaction in animals and children. *Behavior Monographs,* vol. 2, pp. 1–86.

Huxley, J. 1963. Lorenzian ethology. *Zeitschrift für Tierpsychologie,* vol. 20, pp. 402–409.

Jakobson, R. 1962. Phonology and phonetics. In *Selected Writings,* vol. 1, pp. 464–504. Retrospect. Ibid., pp. 631–658. The Hague.

Jakobson, R. 1964. Towards a linguistic typology of aphasic impairments. In *Disorders of Language,* edited by A. V. S. de Reuck and M. O'Connor, pp. 21–42. London.

Jakobson, R. 1966. Private communication.

Kainz, F. 1961. *Die 'Sprache' der Tiere.* Stuttgart.

Keats, J. 1820. Ode on a Grecian urn. In *Lamia, Isabella, The Eve of St. Agnes, and Other Poems,* pp. 113–116. London.

Koehler, O. 1949. Vorsprachliches Denken und "Zählen" der Vögel. In *Ornithologie als biologische Wissenschaft,* pp. 125–146. Heidelberg.

Koenig, O. 1951. Das Aktionssystem der Bartmeise. *Österreichische Zooligische Zeitschrift,* vol. 3, pp. 247 ff.

Köhler, W. 1921. *Intelligenzprüfungen an Menschenaffen.* Berlin.

Kroeber, A. L. 1952. Sign and symbol in bee communications. *Proceedings of the National Academy of Sciences,* vol. 38, pp. 753–757.

Lack, D. 1939. The behaviour of the robin. *Proceedings of the Zoological Society of London,* vol. 109A, pp. 169–178.

Lanyon, W. E. 1960. The ontogeny of vocalizations in birds. In *Animal Sounds and Communication,* edited by W. E. Lanyon and W. N. Tavolga, pp. 321–347. Washington.

Leakey, L. S. B. 1959. A new fossil skull from Olduvai. *Nature,* vol. 184, pp. 491–493.

Leakey, L. S. B. 1961. New finds at Olduvai Gorge. *Nature,* vol. 189, pp. 649–650.

Lindauer, M. 1961. *Communication among Social Bees.* Cambridge, Massachusetts.

Marler, P. 1961. The logical analysis of animal communication. *Journal of Theoretical Biology,* vol. 1, pp. 295–317.

Müller, M. 1872. *Lectures on the Science of Language.* New York.

Oakley, K. 1957. "Tools makyth man. *Antiquity,* vol. 31, pp. 199–209.

Orowan, E. 1955. The origin of man. *Nature,* vol. 175, pp. 683–684.

Peirce, C. S. 1932. Speculative grammar. In *Collected Papers,* vol. 2, pp. 129ff. Cambridge, Massachusetts.

Pumphrey, R. J. 1953. The origin of language. *Acta Psychologica,* vol. 9, pp. 219–237.

Pumphrey, R. J. 1964. Private communication.

Robinson, J. T. 1962. The australopithecines and their bearing on the origin of man and of stone tool-making. In *Ideas on Human Evolution,* edited by W. Howells, pp. 279–294. Cambridge, Massachusetts.

Robinson, J. T., and R. J. Mason. 1957. Occurrence of stone artifacts with australopithecus at Sterkfontein. *Nature,* vol. 180, pp. 521–524.

Tarski, A. 1944. The semantic conception of truth. *Philosophy and Phenomenological Research,* vol. 4, pp. 13–47.

Thorpe, W. H. 1961. *Bird-Song.* Cambridge, England.

Tinbergen, N. 1951. *The Study of Instinct.* Oxford.

Tinbergen, N., and M. Cullen. 1965. Ritualization among blackheaded gulls. In *Royal Society Conference on Ritualization of Behaviour in Animals and Man.* London.

Tobias, P. V., L. S. B. Leakey, J. T. Robinson, and others. 1965. *Current Anthropology,* vol. 6, pp. 343–431.

Vygotsky, L. S. 1962. *Thought and Language.* Cambridge, Massachusetts.

Washburn, S. L. 1959. Speculations on the interrelations of the history of tools and biological evolution. In *The Evolution of Man's Capacity for Culture,* arranged by J. N. Spuhler, pp. 21–31. Detroit.

Washburn, S. L. 1960. Tools and human evolution. *Scientific American,* vol. 203, pp. 62–75.

Waterman, T. H. 1966. Systems analysis and the visual orientation of animals. *American Scientist,* vol. 54, pp. 15–45.

Wenner, A. M. 1962. Sound production during the waggle dance of the honey bee. *Animal Behaviour,* vol. 10, pp. 79–95.

Wenner, A. M. 1965. Private communication.

Wordsworth, W. 1800. Preface to the second edition of *Lyrical Ballads.* Bristol.

Zhinkin, N. I. 1963. An application of the theory of algorithms to the study of animal speech. In *Acoustic Behaviour of Animals,* edited by R. G. Busnel, pp. 132–180. Amsterdam.

LANGUAGE IN A BIOLOGICAL FRAME

Aristotle. 1912. *De Motu Animalium. De Incessu Animalium.* In *Works,* edited by J. A. Smith and W. D. Ross, vol. 5, 698a–714b. Oxford.

Bellugi, U. 1970. Learning the language. *Psychology Today,* vol. 4, no. 7, pp. 32ff.

Bellugi, U. 1971. Private communication.

Berlin, B., and P. Kay. 1969. *Basic Color Terms.* Berkeley.

Bernal, J. D. 1965. Molecular structure, biochemical function, and evolution. In *Theoretical and Mathematical Biology,* edited by T. H. Waterman and H. J. Morowitz, pp. 96–135. New York.

Bethe, H. A. 1939. Energy production in stars. *Physical Review,* vol. 55, p. 434.

Broca, P. 1861. Remarques sur le siège de la faculté du langage articulé, suivie d'une observation d'aphémie (perte de la parole). *Bulletin de la Societé Anatomique de Paris,* vol. 36, pp. 330–357.

Bronowski, J. 1965. *The Identity of Man.* New York.

Bronowski, J. 1966. The logic of the mind. *American Scientist,* vol. 54, no. 1, pp. 1–14.

Bronowski, J. 1967. Human and animal languages. In *To Honor Roman Jakobson, I.* pp. 374–394. The Hague.

Bronowski, J. 1969a. *Nature and Knowledge. The Philosophy of Contemporary Science.* Eugene, Oregon.

Bronowski, J. 1969b. On the uniqueness of man. Review of *Biology and Man* by G. G. Simpson. *Science,* vol. 165, no. 3894, pp. 680–681.

Bronowski, J., and U. Bellugi. 1970. Language, name and concept. *Science,* vol. 168, no. 3932, pp. 669–673.

Bryan, A. L. 1963. The essential morphological basis for human culture. *Current Anthropology,* vol. 4, no. 3, pp. 297–306.

Campbell, B. G. 1966. *Human Evolution: An Introduction to Man's Adaptations.* Chicago.

Chomsky, N. 1965. *Aspects of the Theory of Syntax.* Cambridge, Massachusetts.

Chomsky, N. 1966. *Cartesian Linguistics.* New York.

Chomsky, N. 1968. *Language and Mind.* New York.

Clark, E. V. 1971. How children describe time and order. In *The Structure and Psychology of Language,* vol. 2, edited by T. G. Bever and W. Weksel. New York.

Conrad, R. 1963. Acoustic confusions and memory span for words. *Nature,* vol. 197, no 4871, pp. 1029–1030.

Davenport, R. K., and C. M. Rogers. 1970. Intermodal equivalence of stimuli in apes. *Science,* vol. 168, pp. 279–280.

Descartes, R. 1662. *De Homine Figuris et Latinate Donatus a Florentio Schuyl.* Leyden.

Gardner, A. R., and B. T. Gardner. 1969. Teaching sign language to a chimpanzee. *Science,* vol. 165, pp. 664–672.

Geiger, L. 1880. *Contributions to the History of the Development of the Human Race.* London.

Geschwind, N. 1964. The development of the brain and the evolution of language. Georgetown University Press. Monograph series on languages and linguistics, no. 17, pp. 155–169. Washington, D.C.

Geschwind, N. 1965. Disconnexion syndromes in animals and man. *Brain,* vol. 88, pp. 237–294, 585–644.

Geschwind, N., F. A. Quadfasel, and J. M. Segarra. 1968. Isolation of the speech area. *Neuropsychologia,* vol. 6, no. 4, pp. 327–340.

Geschwind, N. 1970. The organization of language and the brain. *Science,* vol. 170, pp. 940–944.

Gladstone, W. E. 1858. *Studies on Homer and the Homeric Age.* Oxford.

Goldstein, K. 1915. Transkortikale Aphasien. *Ergebnisse der Neurologie und Psychiatrie,* p. 422.

Gray, T. 1747. An ode on a distant prospect of Eton College.

Gregory, R. 1970. *The Intelligent Eye.* London.

Harlow, H. F. 1962. The heterosexual affectional system in monkeys. *American Psychologist,* vol. 17, pp. 1–9.

Hockett, C. F. 1963. Comments on "The essential morphological basis for human culture" by Alan Lyle Bryan. *Current Anthropology,* vol. 4, no. 3, pp. 303–304.

Hockett, C. F., and R. Ascher. 1964. The human revolution. *Current Anthropology,* vol. 5, no. 3, pp. 135–167.

Hunter, W. S. 1913. The delayed reaction in animals and children. *Behavior Monographs,* vol. 2, pp. 1–86.

Jacobsen, C. F. 1936. Studies of cerebral functions in primates. I. The function of the frontal areas in monkeys. *Comparative Psychology Monographs,* vol. 13, no. 63, pp. 3–60.

Jakobson, R. 1964. Towards a linguistic typology of aphasic impairments. In *Disorders of Language,* edited by A. V. S. de Reuck and M. O'Connor, pp. 21–42. London.

Jakobson, R. 1966. Linguistic types of aphasia. In *Brain Function,* vol. 3: *Speech, Language, and Communication,* edited by E. C. Carterette, pp. 67–91. Berkeley.

Jakobson, R. 1970. The Kazan School of Polish Linguistics and its place in the international development of phonology. In *Selected Writings*, vol. 2, p. 395. The Hague.

Lamarck, J. B. 1809. *Philosophie Zoologique*. Paris.

Lancaster, J. B. 1968. Primate communication systems and the emergence of human language. In *Primates*, edited by P. C. Jay, pp. 439–457. New York.

Lashley, K. S. 1951. The problem of serial order in behavior. In *Cerebral Mechanisms in Behavior*, edited by L. A. Jeffress, pp. 112–146. New York.

Lenneberg, E. H. 1967. *Biological Foundations of Language*. New York.

Levy, J. 1969. Possible basis for the evolution of lateral specialization of the human brain. *Nature*, vol. 224, pp. 614–615.

Lieberman, P. H. 1968a. Primate vocalizations and human linguistic ability. *Journal of the Acoustical Society of America*, vol. 44, pp. 1574–1584.

Lieberman, P. H., K. S. Harris, and P. Wolff. 1968b. Newborn infant cry in relation to nonhuman primate vocalizations. *Journal of the Acoustical Society of America*, vol. 44, p. 365(a).

Lieberman, P. H., D. L. Klatt, and W. A. Wilson. 1969. Vocal tract limitations on the vowel repertoires of the rhesus monkey and other nonhuman primates. *Science*, vol. 164, pp. 1185–1187.

Lieberman, P. H., and E. S. Crelin. 1971. On the speech of Neanderthal man. *Linguistic Inquiry*, vol. 2, no. 2, pp. 203–222.

Luria, A. R. 1970. *Traumatic Aphasia. Its Syndromes, Psychology and Treatment*. The Hague.

Myers, R. E. 1961. Corpus callosum and visual gnosis. In *Brain Mechanisms and Learning*, edited by J. F. Delafresnaye. Oxford.

Oakley, K. P. 1957. Tools makyth man. *Antiquity*, vol. 31, pp. 199–209.

Pandya, D. N., and H. G. J. M. Kuypers. 1969. Cortico-cortical connections in the rhesus monkey. *Brain Research*, vol. 13, no. 1, pp. 13–36.

Penfield, W., and L. Roberts. 1959. *Speech and Brain-Mechanisms*. Princeton, New Jersey.

Premack, D. 1970. The education of S-A-R-A-H. *Psychology Today*, vol. 4, no. 4.

Russell, B. 1918. *"Mysticism and Logic" and Other Essays*. London.

Sapir, E. 1921. *Language: An Introduction to the Study of Speech*. New York.

Simpson, G. G. 1969. *Biology and Man.* New York.

Skinner, B. F. 1957. *Verbal Behavior.* New York.

Sperry, R. W. 1964. The great cerebral commisure. *Scientific American,* vol. 210, pp. 42–52.

Sperry, R. W. 1965. Hemispheric interaction and the mind-brain problem. In *Brain and Conscious Experience,* edited by J. C. Eccles. Heidelberg.

Tarski, A. 1936. Der Warheitsbegriff in den formalisierten Sprachen. *Studia Philosophica,* vol. 1, p. 261.

Thomson, G. P. 1929. On the waves associated with β-rays, and the relation between free electrons and their waves. *Philosophical Magazine,* vol. 7, p. 405.

Thomson, J. J. 1897. Cathode rays. *Philosophical Magazine,* vol. 44, p. 293.

Thorpe, W. H. 1956. *Learning and Instinct in Animals.* London.

Thorpe, W. H. 1961. *Bird-Song: The Biology of Vocal Communication and Expression in Birds.* Cambridge, England.

Tinbergen, N. 1951. *The Study of Instinct.* Oxford.

Tinbergen, N. 1953. *The Herring Gull's World: A Study of the Social Behaviour of Birds.* London.

Vygotsky, L. S. 1962. *Thought and Language,* edited and translated by E. Hanfmann and G. Vakar. Cambridge, Massachusetts.

Washburn, S. L. 1960. Tools and Human Evolution. *Scientific American,* vol. 203, pp. 62–75.

Washburn, S. L. 1968. *The Study of Human Evolution.* Eugene, Oregon.

Weir, R. H. 1962. *Language in the Crib.* The Hague.

Wernicke, C. 1874. *Der aphasische Symptomencomplex.* Breslau.

Wiesel, T. N., and D. H. Hubel. 1965. Comparison of the effects of unilateral and bilateral eye closure on cortical unit responses in kittens. *Journal of Neurophysiology,* vol. 28, pp. 1029–1040.

Wilks, Y. 1969. Review of *Language and Mind* by Noam Chomsky. *The Listener,* vol. 82, pp. 44–46.

Zhinkin, N. I. 1963. An application of the theory of algorithms to the study of animal speech. In *Acoustic Behaviour of Animals,* edited by R.-G. Busnel, pp. 132–180. Amsterdam.

NEW CONCEPTS IN THE EVOLUTION OF COMPLEXITY

Bernal, J. D. 1964. Molecular structure, biochemical function, and evolution. In *Theoretical and Mathematical Biology,* edited by T. H. Waterman and H. J. Morowitz, pp. 96–135. Waltham, Massachusetts.

Bethe, H. A. 1939. Energy production in stars. *Physical Review,* vol. 55, p. 434.

Bohm, D. 1969. Some remarks on the notion of order. In *Towards a Theoretical Biology,* edited by C. H. Waddington, pp. 18–40. Edinburgh, Scotland.

Bronowski, J. 1965. *The Identity of Man.* New York.

Bronowski, J. 1969. *Nature and Knowledge.* Eugene, Oregon.

Delbrück, M. 1949. A physicist looks at biology. *Transactions of the Connecticut Academy of Arts and Sciences,* vol. 38. Reprinted in *Phage and the Origins of Molecular Biology,* edited by J. Cairns, G. S. Stent, and J. D. Watson (Cold Spring Harbor, 1966), pp. 9–22.

Elsasser, W. M. 1958. *The Physical Foundation of Biology.* New York.

Fisher, R. A. 1930. *The Genetical Theory of Natural Selection.* Oxford.

Harrison, B. J., and R. Holliday. 1967. Senescence and the fidelity of protein synthesis in Drosophila. *Nature,* vol. 213, p. 990.

Holliday, R. 1969. Errors in protein synthesis and clonal senescence in fungi. *Nature,* vol. 221, pp. 1224–1228.

Hayflick, L. 1966. Cell culture and the aging phenomenon. In *Topics in the Biology of Aging,* edited by P. L. Krohn, pp. 83–100. New York.

von Neumann, J. 1932. *Mathematische Grundlagen der Quantenmechanik.* Berlin.

Orgel, L. E. 1963. The maintenance of the accuracy of protein synthesis and its relevance to ageing. *Proceedings of the National Academy of Sciences,* vol. 49, pp. 517–521.

Paley, W. 1794. *Evidences of Christianity.* London.

Polanyi, M. 1967. Life transcending physics and chemistry. *Chemical and Engineering News,* vol. 45, no. 35, pp. 54–66.

Polanyi, M. 1968. Life's irreducible structure. *Science,* vol. 160, pp. 1308–1312.

Schrödinger, E. 1944. *What is Life?* Cambridge, England.

Watson, J. D., and F. H. C. Crick. 1953. A structure for deoxyribose nucleic acid. *Nature,* vol. 171, pp. 737–738.

Wigner, E. P. 1961. The probability of the existence of a self-reproducing unit. In *The Logic of Personal Knowledge: Essays Presented to Michael Polanyi on his Seventieth Birthday*. London.

PUBLICATION RECORD

A SENSE OF THE FUTURE

The Listener, vol. 39, no. 1010 (3 June 1948), pp. 883–884. Broadcast on the BBC Home-Service.

THE CREATIVE PROCESS

Scientific American, vol. 199, no. 3 (September 1958), pp. 59–65.

ON ART AND SCIENCE

First produced as a radio interview in 1956 by WGBH, Boston, and recorded for subsequent distribution by the National Association of Educational Broadcasters, Urbana, Illinois. Published in *The Creative Mind and Method*, edited by Jack D. Summerfield and Lorlyn Thatcher (Austin, The University of Texas Press, 1960), pp. 99–104.

THE REACH OF IMAGINATION

The Blashfield Address, delivered to the American Academy of Arts and Letters and the National Institute of Arts and Letters on 25 May 1966. Published in the *Proceedings of the American Academy of Arts and Letters and the National Institute of Arts and Letters* (1967), second series, no. 17, pp. 31–42. Also published in *The American Scholar*, vol. 36, no. 2 (Spring 1967), pp. 193–201.

THE LOGIC OF NATURE

Political Quarterly, vol. 26, no. 3 (1955), pp. 258–266.

THE LOGIC OF EXPERIMENT

Paper delivered to the Annual Meeting of the British Association for the Advancement of Science, Section A (Mathematics and Physics), Belfast, 5 September 1952. Published in *The Advancement of Science*, vol. 9, no. 35 (December 1952), pp. 289–296.

THE LOGIC OF THE MIND

The Phi Beta Kappa–Sigma Xi Lecture, delivered to the American Association for the Advancement of Science, Berkeley, California, 29 December 1965. Published in *The American Scholar*, vol. 35, no. 2 (spring 1966), pp. 233–242. Also published in *The American Scientist*, vol. 54, no. 1 (March 1966), pp. 1–14.

HUMANISM AND THE GROWTH OF KNOWLEDGE

The Philosophy of Karl R. Popper, edited by Paul A. Schilpp (Carbondale,

Illinois, The Library of Living Philosophers, 1974), vol. 14-1, pp. 606–631.

HUMAN AND ANIMAL LANGUAGES

To Honor Roman Jakobson, vol. 1 (The Hague, Mouton & Co., 1967), pp. 374–395.

LANGUAGE IN A BIOLOGICAL FRAME

Current Trends in Linguistics, vol. 12: *Linguistics and Adjacent Arts and Sciences,* edited by Thomas A. Sebeok (The Hague, Mouton & Co., 1974), pp. 2539–2559.

WHERE DO WE GO FROM HERE?

New York Review of Books, vol. 4, no. 2, 25 February 1965, pp. 10–11.

TOWARD A PHILOSOPHY OF BIOLOGY

The sixteenth annual Alfred Korzybski Memorial Lecture, New York, 7 April 1967. Published in *General Semantics Bulletin,* June 1968, pp. 17–22.

NEW CONCEPTS IN THE EVOLUTION OF COMPLEXITY

Philosophical Foundations of Science, edited by R. J. Seeger and R. S. Cohen (Dordrecht, The Netherlands, D. Reidel Publishing Co., 1974), pp. 133–151.

A MORAL FOR AN AGE OF PLENTY

The Saturday Evening Post, vol. 233, no. 20 (12 November 1960), pp. 24–25 and 70–72.

THE HUMAN VALUES

Literary Guide, vol. 70, no. 11 (November 1955), pp. 19–21.

THE VALUES OF SCIENCE

The Rationalist Annual, March 1960.

THE PRINCIPLE OF TOLERANCE

Transactions of the Royal Society of Canada (1974), fourth series, vol. 12, pp. 69–80.

THE DISESTABLISHMENT OF SCIENCE

Encounter, vol. 37, no. 1, July 1971, pp. 8–16.

THE FULFILLMENT OF MAN

The forty-fifth Conway Memorial Lecture, delivered at Conway Hall, London, England, 23 March 1954. Published in *The Monthly Record,* vol. 59, no. 5, May 1954, pp. 5–13.

INDEX